Creating Spiritual
and Psychological Resilience

Creating Spiritual and Psychological Resilience

Integrating Care in Disaster Relief Work

Grant H. Brenner, Daniel H. Bush, Joshua Moses

EDITORS

Routledge
Taylor & Francis Group
New York London

Routledge
Taylor & Francis Group
711 Third Avenue
New York, NY 10017

Routledge
Taylor & Francis Group
27 Church Road
Hove, East Sussex BN3 2FA

International Standard Book Number: 978-0-7890-3455-7 (Paperback)

Library of Congress Cataloging-in-Publication Data

Creating spiritual and psychological resilience : integrating care in disaster relief
    work / edited by Grant H. Brenner, Daniel H. Bush, Joshua Moses.
        p. cm.
    Includes bibliographical references and index.
    ISBN 978-0-7890-3454-0 (hardback : alk. paper) -- ISBN 978-0-7890-3455-7
    (pbk. : alk. paper)
    1. Disaster relief. 2. Disaster relief--Psychological aspects. 3. Community
mental health services. 4. Church work with disaster victims. 5. Social
service--Religious aspects. I. Brenner, Grant H. II. Bush, Daniel H. III. Moses,
Joshua.

HV553.C74 2009
362.2'042--dc22   2009014785

Visit the Taylor & Francis Web site at
http://www.taylorandfrancis.com

and the Routledge Web site at
http://www.routledgementalhealth.com

Contents

Contents

SECTION III   Collaboratively Nurturing Resilience After Catastrophic Trauma

Preface

Disaster defies definition, but not practical understanding. On my 35-year watch in the field of disaster human services, formal practices for reducing disaster's anguish have grown dramatically, including the fields of disaster spiritual care and disaster mental health. The essence of this work is presence, compassion and technique. The first two are constant. It is technique that evolves. The key to future success will be growing our ability to work in dynamic partnership, not only between the disciplines of spiritual care and mental health but among all the pillars of the house called disaster human services.

The mind and spirit are inseparable. And health, nutrition, family, domicile, work, and community are essential. That is why this book is for all disaster human services practitioners—not only spiritual caregivers and mental health professionals. None is fully ready to serve without a strong understanding of *all* other sources of disaster help.

There is no disaster without loss, suffering, confusion, and distress. Disaster disrupts person, family, home, and neighborhood. Disaster damages community. Never in their lives do people need skilled comforting and guidance more than after a disaster.

You who deliver spiritual care and mental health services succeed by bringing emotional and spiritual support and then by removing measures of pain from each person's disaster experience. You do this not only with courage and commitment but also with a surprisingly complex and growing array of learned skills and knowledge.

Kai T. Erikson, a sociologist, put disaster mental health into the national discourse with his landmark 1976 book, *Everything in Its Path: Destruction of Community in the Buffalo Creek Flood.* The searing emotional and spiritual anguish he related, largely through the words of the victims, launched a broad-based search for more effective response. We are still on that quest, and this book brings us forward.

In 1972, I got a job going to fires at night for the American Red Cross. New York City was burning in those years. Four fires per 8-hour shift, 12 per day, over 4,000 incidents a year, each of which left at least one family homeless. I drove mostly impoverished families to Red Cross hotels and explained how and where to get more help the next day. Those who emerged from fires with nothing to wear benefited from the 24-hour clothing-and-spiritual care of Adventist Community Services' "retired" Pastor Adam Layman and his disaster boutique on wheels.

For me, the disasters just got bigger and farther away: a major airplane crash near JFK airport; a social club fire that killed 87 immigrants; floods in southern states; refugee camps at the Thai–Cambodian border; earthquakes in Italy, India, El Salvador, and Colombia; famines in Sudan, Ethiopia, and Somalia; war in Angola; genocide in Rwanda; and then back to tornados, hurricanes, wildfires, and terrorism in the United States.

For all their superficial diversity, what made each event a disaster was extreme disruption of body, mind, spirit, family, home, livelihood, and community. Those of us privileged to be the ones who personally bring the comforting resources of the larger community to disaster victims must and do struggle to find ways to be as effective as possible. We are obliged to be as good as we can be.

Our challenge is to know how to comfort the sufferer and to bring him to someone who can provide for his needs. Bishop Stephen P. Bouman, in his book *Grace All Around Us: Embracing God's Promise in Tragedy and Loss,* lists first steps in his outline of disaster response. Show up. Attend first to the ripples on the surface. Accompany the pain on the road. Respond, rescue, reach out, call, pray, touch, embrace, feed, shelter, touch, cry, reassure.

He relates the tender guidance of a South African bishop in New York after 9/11:

> In our culture when tragedy happens, we don't all visit at once. We come a few at a time, so that each time the person in sorrow has to answer the door and tell the story again of what happened and shed the tears. As the story is told again and again, healing can begin.

Bouman tells of Kathleen O'Connor's reflection on Lamentations:

> To honor pain means to see it, acknowledge its power, and to enter it as fully and squarely as we can, perhaps in a long spiritual process. To do so is ultimately empowering and enables *genuine love, action for others,* and *true worshipfulness.*

This is hard and necessary, but we have to do this and much more.

When the World Trade Center was attacked on 9/11, psychiatrist Anthony Ng was Medical Director for Disaster Psychiatry Outreach and Chair of New York City's Voluntary Organizations Active in Disaster (VOAD). A year or so later, I asked him about his foremost lessons from this event.

His response was singularly clear. Tony said this: "Do NOT consider yourself a *disaster* mental health professional until you can come to the arena with a comprehensive understanding of all available disaster human services, and the ability to effectively connect people to them." This is our challenge: To be fully equipped to comfort and assist.

There are numerous solutions to most of the causes of suffering and distress in most disaster victims. While death, trauma, and total destruction cannot be undone, most needs are temporal and can be addressed. We must have the training and real-time information necessary to connect people to shelters, temporary housing, home repair, legal services, family reunification, health services, child care, disaster unemployment compensation, occupational equipment replacement, eviction prevention, funeral assistance, consumer fraud protection, home debris removal, pet care, mold prevention, and insurance guidance, to name but a few essential services in disaster relief and recovery.

To succeed, to be fully equipped, disaster mental health and spiritual care practitioners will have to prepare to ensure that they will respond in a coordinated context. Who will provide shelter information to chaplains? Who will give government assistance information to clergy? How will mental health professionals know how to connect their clientele with disaster legal services?

Unfortunately, there are no consistent answers. There are admirable examples of very effective coordinative umbrellas that have come into being after certain recent disasters but no guarantee of the presence of interagency information exchange mechanisms in the future. It is simply no organization's funded mandate.

So, we are challenged to not only develop and refine the practices and protocols of our respective disciplines, but, in order for each of our own sectors to fully succeed, we must invent ways that we can become mutually aware and accessible across the many disciplines of disaster human services. To be able to bring our best to future disaster victims, we must become a functional interservice community.

Ken Curtin
U.S. Federal Emergency Management Agency (FEMA), Volunteer Liaison

Introduction

Integrated Care: An Urgent Purpose

The purpose of this book is to advance collaboration between spiritual care and mental health disaster responders so that disaster victims are better advocated for and served. In a world where catastrophic disasters are common, the urgency of this task is increasingly clear. Partnerships between professionals of divergent disciplines are crucial to overcoming the ruptures wrought by disasters. Such partnerships are central to creating and nurturing communal healing. In short, these partnerships have the potential to help societies harness the transformational capacity disasters hold for resilience—for how we might redress chronic, long-simmering ills in new ways, comfort the bereaved, rebuild with the survivors, and perhaps even help people to better situations than they were in prior to disasters.

While tragic, disasters also have the potential to help us to reimagine our relationships with one another and who and what we are as a society. When mental health professionals and clergy work together during and after a disaster, there is a great opportunity for them to fully claim their role as advocates for community healing. In envisioning this book, we have embodied the principles of collaboration, which we seek to advance in disaster relief operations. *Creating Spiritual and Psychological Resilience* represents the collaborative effort of three coeditors with very different professional backgrounds: a chaplain, a psychiatrist, and an anthropologist.

In the process of conceptualizing and completing this book, we have taken what we each started with individually and, as is always the case with disaster work, have learned and grown through the experience of trial and error, gleaning knowledge and wisdom from the hard work of others. We look at collaboration between spiritual care and mental health caregivers in terms of avenues that exist for further exploration as well as development of disaster relief work between spiritual care providers and mental health professionals.

We believe that collaboration among different actors, particularly in a crisis, is necessary for the care of affected individuals. This is the basic common goal of spiritual care and mental health coworkers, to serve populations and individuals in need. Challenges to providing services are shaped by the presence of interpersonal, interorganizational, and interdisciplinary differences and competition over resources. The purpose of this book is to provide tools for both study and for field use, to assist practitioners in developing and expanding approaches to collaboration in their work.

An ancillary purpose of this book is to augment the applied study of spiritual care and mental health collaboration as a subject of inquiry. Religious and spiritual approaches have existed since time immemorial, while mental health is a relative newcomer to the scene. Mental health practice has developed in a way that addresses voids that religious caregivers tend not to address, which at times overlaps in significant ways with religion and spirituality. Presently, both are involved in assisting individuals and communities with personal problems including disasters, and both fields therefore compete in seeking to be utilized by overlapping groups of people and for limited sources of funding.

In terms of relations between the two groups, the tone has ranged from overt hostility to grudging coexistence to greater and lesser degrees of collaboration characterized by friendly as well as standoffish attitudes; from tolerant to accepting to welcoming.

Collaboration: Major Themes in the Aftermath of Disasters

In *Creating Spiritual and Psychological Resilience*, the two themes of understanding collaboration and examining the relationship between spiritual care and mental health providers come together. Individuals, communities, governments, and organizations turn to both groups for support during all phases of disaster.

We should seize any opportunity we have to effectively work together; every opportunity not seized may result in a failure to provide care to people in need. We may learn how and seek to collaborate despite many years of historical friction between mental health and spiritual care workers. This book will help those seeking to enter and heal this breach.

We have invited an anthropological perspective within our coeditorship in order to provide perspective and enhance the reflective aspect of this work. We have learned from experience and study that collaboration requires all players to possess self-reflective processes. Without self-awareness, collaboration can easily become mired in paranoia, competition, misperception, or misunderstanding, contributing to fragmentation, anxiety, and breakdown among relationships. Breakdowns of this nature are harmful to ourselves and, even more so, to those we collectively seek to help. A third participant–observing agent, like a third surveyor triangulating the position of a valued destination, offers added depth of field—both on individual and systemic levels—in addressing the various forces that cause individual and systemic breakdowns, impeding the useful delivery of services to those in need.

This book arises out of our own intimate experiences with distress, trauma, disruption, groundlessness, fear, annihilation, terror, love, community, and healing. The creation of these chapters is deeply significant on personal levels, and within the circle of our friendship, serving as a marker of our professional development. We hope that contributing to this book has also been a meaningful journey for the authors who generously donated their time, experience, and energy with exceptional patience. We are grateful and indebted to them. We hope the book will be a meaningful experience for the reader with significance for his or her own personal history and past, present, and future disaster work.

In the pursuit of these goals, whenever possible (though not always as successfully as we wished), we have asked authors to balance didactics with experiential learning and illustrative vignettes. We ardently hope that the reader will use this book for reference, concrete application, and directions for further study. While we have incorporated examples of collaboration between mental health and spiritual care providers, we have also used examples of collaboration between other groups for their great instructive and illustrative value in application to the question at hand.

We hold with those who paint crisis and adversity as opportunities for growth and the creation of wisdom. The consequences of distressing experience are largely normal and are only pathological in some cases. Therefore, while recovery (meaning a return to a predisaster-like state) is often identified as the goal of interventions, we have come to understand that this is not possible, or necessarily desirable, though it may represent, among other things, a wish or yearning for a return to innocence as if the terrible event never happened.

People are indelibly changed by traumatic experiences. We must somehow come to terms with what has happened and with what is possible in changed circumstances. We must seize on opportunities for creative transformation, addressing previously overlooked problems, seeking wherever possible to improve conditions. Prevention of adverse events and downward-spiraling consequences, for individuals and for society, is most desirable and effective. Yet tragically, often people, and the systems in which we live (workplace, governmental bodies, religious institutions, healthcare institutions, communities, families), are only willing to expend energy and resources when disaster looms and a sense of immediacy creates a heightened sense of necessity. In short, intervention happens only at the point when it is too late for prevention and mitigation.

Origins: Healers Partnering to Seek Resilience

The origins of this undertaking are from a January 2004 meeting between Dr. Craig Katz and Anastasia Holmes of Disaster Psychiatry Outreach (DPO) and Daniel H. Bush and Peter Gudaitis of New York Disaster Interfaith Services (NYDIS). In that meeting, DPO was asked if they would be willing to form a partnership with chaplains and other clergy members engaged in 9/11 relief and recovery operations. Though slightly reluctant, they signaled their willingness to explore what such a partnership might look like. They assigned Dr. Grant Brenner as the contact person for the as-yet-to-be-defined project. Other meetings were taking place and had previously happened without sparking ongoing work, but few concrete ongoing collaborative partnerships emerged, partially because funding streams for integrated mental health services and spiritual care services are almost always separated. Mental health programs often appeal to faith-based institutions for funding but rarely with the idea of actively collaborating with clergy in providing services.

The overture from the faith-based organization, NYDIS, to mental health-based, DPO, was made intentionally, with the knowledge that getting psychiatrists to work with clergy would be an unprecedented coup in the field of disaster relief work, with the awareness that there are often substantial differences between mental health providers and clergy in terms of religious belief.

The experience of serving in New York hospitals and the federal prison in Lower Manhattan taught Chaplain Bush that some of the most strained professional relationships were those between chaplains and psychiatrists. Each discipline viewed the other warily, often as a competitor, even if a lack of interdisciplinary partnering ill-served those most in need of both mental health and pastoral care services. Disaster victims are in an even more precarious position, as they are dependent on government services that often have rigid eligibility requirements. While offering a variety of relief services, organizations are often competing with one another over limited sources of funding. In the jockeying that takes place for position, individuals slip through the cracks and whole communities are often underserved or ignored.

Yet, if both mental health professionals and chaplains could agree to work collaboratively, there would be increased space for deepening relationships across the full range of mental health practitioners and spiritual care providers. By pooling experience, particularly the data gathered of needs served and those unmet, each healing profession could work more closely together to advocate for those they were serving or who they ought to be serving, to identify gaps and to strategize on how to reach those left out.

In short, an opportunity exists in the growing field of disaster relief services to define the relationship between mental health and spiritual care providers differently than has been typical in the past. Doing so better serves those in need and offers a model of high-level professional interdisciplinary functioning that others can replicate in other established venues, such as hospitals, prisons, and the military.

In the partnership established between Dr. Brenner and Chaplain Bush, along with many others (some of whom are represented in the following chapters), the goal was to provide a framework for healing alienations between mental health providers and spiritual care providers, so that together we could more effectively provide healing to individuals and communities injured and fragmented by 9/11. We are working toward fostering a deeper, shared resilience. We believe that practitioners in each field can draw strength from each other's expertise and examine different approaches, diverse tools, and distinct languages for addressing the monumental sense of shared loss and rupture.

Because the 9/11 terrorist attacks were an order of magnitude different from any disaster to previously strike an urban center in the United States, the situation was already forcing professionals to work together in new and different ways, to acknowledge limits more readily, and to forge new ways of responding to the specific challenges at hand. In a real sense, we understood our work was not so much creating something entirely new as much as attempting to harness existing dynamics, directing them with greater intentionality, intensity, and effectiveness to achieve the public good.

The need for such collaborative partnerships has only become more clear and intensified with the tsunami in South Asia and Hurricane Katrina in the southern United States, among the myriad disasters to recently strike different countries of the world. That large-scale disasters, such as the South Asian tsunami and Hurricane Katrina occur—along with the recently coalescing sense of urgency about global warming, a steadily growing disaster—has only intensified, if not overwhelmed, our original sense of purpose. The complex, contradictory, sometimes destructive responses of our political leaders to the above disasters have made this work harder, and perhaps even more necessary.

Great obstacles and challenges remain for mental health and spiritual care professionals hoping to help heal the great ruptures of our age, at least in some measure, by providing integrated care for disaster victims. This task is further complicated by macropolitical issues that are beyond the scope of this volume to address directly. Fragmentation is not easily transformed into integrated resilience, not in individuals and not in communal structures or among parallel professions. Tensions between historically rival disciplines remain embedded. Organizational structures and funding bodies reinforce these separations by sustaining a real or perceived competition over resources. Cross-disciplinary partnerships tend to be ad hoc and informal rather than sustained and institutionalized. Because each disaster is unique and novel, although we believe the principles articulated in this book are broadly applicable; we encourage the reader to explore actively the evolving landscape of collaboration between mental health and spiritual caregivers as it is relevant for you locally, generating your own ideas, writing and researching, and discussing the subject frequently with your colleagues.

Overview: Foundations, Collaboration, Trauma, and Resilience

This book is organized in three broad sections. Whenever possible, we have invited authors from multiple perspectives to write together, with the writing itself an example of interdisciplinary disaster collaboration. The end result represents a spectrum of outcomes of these collaborations, with various degrees of fragmentation and integration in different chapters.

Section I comprises an overview of foundations relevant to disaster work, with a focus on issues relevant to parties involved in interdisciplinary collaboration between spiritual care- and mental health-based disaster workers. This section includes anthropological and ethnographic perspectives, an overview of concrete and pragmatic approaches to collaboration, a discussion of emotional theory in disaster work as a common touchstone for spiritual care and mental health alike, a comprehensive treatment of effective communication strategies during crisis, a brief look at ethical and legal considerations relevant to interdisciplinary collaboration, and a full discussion of the psychosocial impact of disasters.

Section II of the book looks at collaboration-in-action, providing concrete vignettes of collaborative work from several different contexts of disaster work, encompassing multiple perspectives from different authors. Section II includes organizational and individual work in post-Katrina Louisiana, South Asia, New York, and other areas and includes discussion of collaborative relationships between government, mental health organizations, and faith-based organizations around financial and psychosocial strains in disaster. There also is a discussion of collaboration in the setting of schools, using relationships between mental health and staff in the service of providing care for children, to illustrate principles of collaboration that are exportable to other settings.

The third and final section highlights the conjoint elements of disaster interdisciplinary collaboration pertaining to resilience and trauma (we refer the reader to other resources for more in-depth discussion as required because this book is not primarily intended to be a comprehensive manual of trauma or disasters in general). Section III addresses the role of routines and rituals, discusses resilience from various perspectives, examines retraumatization and the important role it plays in disaster work for both spiritual care and mental health responders, looks at the role of faith in collaborative settings, and examines the important issue of pathological versus normal reactions and how this pertains to collaborative work when groups and individuals with different approaches come together to address the needs of others.

Grant H. Brenner M.D.
Daniel H. Bush, M.Div.
Joshua Moses, M.A.

Contributors

Patricia M. Berliner, Ph.D., is a New York State licensed psychologist with private practice in Ozone Park, NY, and a member of Sisters of St. Joseph of Brentwood, Long Island. She is a published author and has been a member of New York State Psychological Association (NYSPA) Disaster Response Team since 1993 and of the Red Cross Disaster Mental Health Team since 1996. Dr. Berliner is a member of the Red Cross of Greater NY Disaster Mental Health Leadership Team and a member of the advisory board to the *Dr. Phil* TV program. She is the author of the book *Touching Your Lifethread and Revaluing the Feminine* and many articles related to mental health, spirituality, women's issues, and disaster response.

Grant H. Brenner, M.D., is an adjunct clinical professor at Albert Einstein College of Medicine and clinical instructor at the Mount Sinai School of Medicine (New York City). He works in educational and supervisory capacities at Beth Israel Medical Center, St. Vincent's Catholic Medical Center, and the Mount Sinai School of Medicine. He is director of the Trauma Service and chief psychiatric consultant at the William Alanson White Institute of Psychiatry, Psychology, and Psychoanalysis and national volunteer lead for Disaster Psychiatry Outreach. Dr. Brenner completed 2 years of general surgery residency at Long Island Jewish Medical Center and psychiatry residency at Mount Sinai School of Medicine, where he received the Richard L. Scharf, M.D., Memorial Award for Teaching Excellence in Psychiatry. He is a graduate of both the psychoanalytic and organizational programs at William Alanson White Institute in New York City.

Dr. Brenner is a Fellow of the New York Academy of Medicine, a Fellow of the American Academy of Dynamic Psychiatry and Psychoanalysis, and a member of the International Society for the Study of Trauma and Dissociation. He received the 2004 Gold Level President's Volunteer Service Award from the President's Council on Service and Civic Participation for disaster work in New York. He lectures and teaches regularly about disaster and trauma and has authored publications in areas related to trauma, disaster, and torture/human rights. He has volunteered in different capacities in several disasters including 9/11, Hurricane Katrina, the 2004 South Asian tsunami, and the 2008 Sichuan earthquake and has furthered the cause of interdisciplinary collaboration by co-organizing several conferences.

Sandra Buechler, Ph.D., is a training analyst at the William Alanson White Institute, supervisor of Psychiatric Institute internship and postdoctoral programs, and supervisor at the Institute for Contemporary Psychotherapy. A graduate of the William Alanson White Institute, Dr. Buechler has written extensively on emotions in psychoanalysis, including papers on hope, joy, loneliness, and mourning in the analyst and patient. In her book, *Clinical Values: Emotions That Guide Psychoanalytic Treatment* (Analytic Press, 2004), Dr. Buechler examines the role of hope, courage, the capacity to bear loss, the ability to achieve emotional balance, and other factors in treatment. Her most recent book, *Making a Difference in Patients' Lives: Emotional Experience in the Therapeutic Setting* (Analytic Press, 2008), is a personal description of the process of therapeutic change.

Daniel H. Bush, M.Div., lives in Jerusalem and serves as an educator at several programs: Yakar, Kivunim, the Conservative Yeshiva, Nesiya, and Pardes. He also works for Encounter, a Jewish organization that arranges meetings between rabbis, Jewish teachers, and Palestinians in Bethlehem and Hebron, and trains facilitators for these programs. Prior to coming to Israel on a Dorot Fellowship in the autumn of 2005, he served for 2 years as director of 9/11 Long-Term Recovery and Victim Advocacy for New York Disaster Interfaith Services. In 2003, he completed his chaplaincy residency at New York Methodist Hospital in Brooklyn. On 9/11, he was serving as a chaplain in the federal prison in Lower Manhattan while completing his Master of Divinity degree at Union Theological Seminary. His studies focused on psychology, pastoral care, biblical scholarship, theology, and the interconnections between Judaism and Christianity. An affiliated member of the National Association of Jewish Chaplains, he is also certified by New York State and St. Luke's–Roosevelt Hospital Crime Victims Treatment Center as a rape crisis advocate. He is presently working on a book of short stories about New York.

Vincent T. Covello, Ph.D., is the founder and director of the Center for Risk Communication in New York City. He is a nationally and internationally recognized researcher, consultant, and expert in risk, crisis, and high stress communications. He serves as a senior communications advisor to several hundred private and public sector organizations, including the U.S. Centers for Disease Control and Prevention, the U.S. Environmental Protection Agency, and various agencies within the United Nations. Dr. Covello's most recent assignments include trainings, workshops, and consultations related to communications concerning food safety, biotechnology, pesticide use, bioterrorism, nuclear power, and pandemic influenza.

Over the past 30 years, Dr. Covello has held positions in academia and government. Prior to establishing the Center for Risk Communication, he was associate professor of Environmental Sciences and Clinical Medicine on the faculty of Medicine at Columbia University in New York City. He received his doctorate from Columbia University and his B.A. with honors and M.A. from Cambridge University in the United Kingdom. He has authored or edited more than 25 books and over 100 published articles on risk and crisis communication in scientific and medical journals. Dr. Covello's most recent book, published in 2007 by the United Nations, is titled *Effective Media Communication during Public Health Emergencies: A World Health Organization Handbook.*

Yael Danieli, Ph.D. is clinical psychologist and traumatologist in private practice; and cofounder (1975) and director, Group Project for Holocaust Survivors and their Children, with extensive psychotherapeutic work with massively traumatized individuals, families, groups, and communities. Having studied lifelong and multigenerational impact on victim/survivors and societal and professional responses/attitudes, she has lectured/supervised/studied/trained worldwide and published extensively (translated into over 17 languages), including on victims' rights, optimal care and specialized training, and protection for related professionals. Founding director, past president, and senior representative to the United Nations of the International society for Traumatic Stress Studies (formerly, of the World Federation for Mental Health); Dr. Danieli has participated in all UN work on victims' right, consulted numerous governments and organizations, and advised the UN Secretary-General on victims (of terrorism). She is also copresident of the International Network of Holocaust and Genocide Survivors and Their Friends. Her books are *International Responses to Traumatic Stress; The Universal Declaration of Human Rights: Fifty Years and Beyond; Sharing the Front Line and the Back Hills,* published for and on behalf of the United Nations; *International Handbook of Multigenerational Legacies of Trauma; The Trauma of Terrorism*; and *On the Ground After September 11.*

Rick Daniels, Ph.D., is an independent management consultant in the area of organizational change assisting institutions in building social and technical systems that support knowledge creation and sharing. He previously worked for Philip Morris USA in IT strategic planning, with a focus on establishing the Knowledge Management discipline within the corporation. He started his professional life in the mental health field as a counseling clinician and administrator.

Dr. Daniels has a multidisciplinary education in psychology and technology, holding four graduate degrees. Two master's degrees are from New York University, one is in Rehabilitation Counseling and the second one in Interactive Telecommunications. His third master's degree as well as his Ph.D. is from Fielding Graduate University (Santa Barbara, California) in Human and Organizational Systems. Most recently he worked as a pro bono consultant assisting Delgado Community College in New Orleans post-Katrina, helping to establish a strategic plan for a distance-learning educational delivery system, given the impact to the physical infrastructure post-Katrina. He facilitated a participatory action research environment, marshalling Fielding Graduate University resources to assist in a whole-systems approach.

Koshin Paley Ellison, M.F.A., L.M.S.W., is a cofounder and coexecutive director of the New York Zen Center for Contemplative Care (www.zencare.org). He serves as the director of training for the center's Buddhist Chaplaincy Programs. Ellison is an adjunct professor at the Institute of Buddhist Studies and a cofounder of the Buddhist Psychotherapy Collective. He is currently a Jungian Analyst Candidate at the Jungian Psychoanalytic Association. He has served as a chaplain at Cabrini Medical Center and Hospice and Beth Israel Medical Center. He is the chaplain supervisor of the Integrative Medicine Department at Beth Israel Medical Center in New York. Ellison began Zen practice over 20 years ago, and he is now a senior student and Soto Zen Buddhist Priest at the Village Zendo. He teaches workshops on meditation, stress reduction, and contemplative care in a variety of settings from classrooms to corporations.

Brian Engdahl, Ph.D., earned his B.A. in 1975 and his Ph.D. in 1980 from the University of Minnesota. He has been a counseling psychologist at the Minneapolis VA Medical Center, Minnesota for nearly 30 years and is a clinical associate professor in the Department of Psychology at the University of Minnesota. He provides rehabilitation counseling to combat veterans of all wars and to active duty soldiers of the Iraq war. He is currently the principle investigator in a project using magnetoencephalography (MEG) to examine brain function alterations in people suffering from posttraumatic stress disorder (PTSD). His other research examines the health and adjustment of former prisoners of war (POWs) and other combat veterans. He has published and presented his findings to national and international audiences of trauma survivors, their families, and professionals who work with them.

Daniel Gensler, Ph.D., is a licensed clinical psychologist in private practice doing psychotherapy, supervision, and psychoeducational evaluations testing in Manhattan and Great Neck, working with adults, families, couples, adolescents, and children. He has worked in hospital, school, corporate, and clinic settings and has made many professional presentations over the years. Currently, he is director of training, Child Adolescent Psychotherapy Training Program, William Alanson White Institute, New York; supervising analyst and instructor at White; and supervisor and instructor at Adelphi University. He is coauthor of *Relational Child Psychotherapy* (Other Press, 2002) and has also published several articles and chapters in the professional literature. Dr. Gensler received his doctorate degree in psychology from Ferkauf Graduate School of Yeshiva University in 1980 and his certificate in psychoanalysis from the William Alanson White Institute in 1987.

J. Irene Harris, Ph.D., has been a counseling psychologist at the Department of Veterans Affairs Medical Center for 5 years, practicing primarily in psychiatric rehabilitation. She maintains a research program on spirituality and trauma and is presently testing the effectiveness of prayer skills training for survivors of trauma. Dr. Harris has a record of publications as well as presentations to national audiences on spirituality and mental health.

Anastasia Holmes, M.P.A., is a specialist in the management of not-for-profit organizations based in New York City. She has played leadership roles at the local and national level in integrating psychiatry into the development of mental health disaster responses. She served as the executive director of Disaster Psychiatry Outreach from 2001 through 2007 and was the architect of numerous deployments of volunteer psychiatrists to disasters, as well as acting as executive director and cofounder of the World Trade Center Worker and Volunteer Mental Health Intervention Program. She received her MPA from Columbia in 2007.

Maggie Jarry, M.S., worked in the 9/11 recovery effort for 6 years through World Vision (October 2001 to February 2002), Lutheran Social Services/ Lutheran Disaster Response of New York (February 2002 to July 2005), and New York Disaster Interfaith Services (July 2005 to 2007). As chair of the New York City 9/11 Unmet Needs Roundtable at its inception in April 2002, Jarry viewed the 9/11 Roundtable as a tool for helping individuals and as a vehicle for social justice. Later, as director of recovery and advocacy for New York Disaster Interfaith Services, Jarry managed the transition of the Unmet Needs Roundtable into a vehicle for the newly emerging needs of World Trade Center (WTC) recovery workers and the long-term needs of people with 9/11-related mental health difficulties. While attaining a master's of science in Nonprofit Management at The New School (New York City), Jarry conducted qualitative research from 2004 to 2006 (using taped interviews and questionnaires) that allowed her to reflectively engage her colleagues in discourse regarding the early stages of 9/11 recovery. Her chapter in this book is a synthesis of insight she gained from of her experience and the wisdom of the leaders she interviewed. Currently, Jarry serves as a mental health consultant in the Adult Mental Health Division of the Minnesota Department of Human Services.

Craig Katz, M.D., is a clinical assistant professor of psychiatry at the Mount Sinai School of Medicine (New York City), where he has served in various roles since 2000. Dr. Katz served as the director of the World Trade Center Worker/Volunteer Mental Health Monitoring and Treatment Program, which meets the mental health needs of people who worked or volunteered at Ground Zero after 9/11 from 2002 through July 2006, and now is the supervising psychiatrist within that program. He also serves as the director of the Fellowship in Global Mental Health at Mount Sinai. Dr. Katz has previously served as the director of Psychiatry Emergency Services and then director of Acute Care Psychiatry Services at Mount Sinai. He received separate teaching awards from medical students and residents in 2001 and was nominated as a faculty member of the Mount Sinai chapter of the AOA (alpha omega alpha) medical honor society in 2003.

Dr. Katz cofounded Disaster Psychiatry Outreach (DPO) in 1998 as a charitable organization devoted to the provision of voluntary psychiatric care to people affected by disasters and has served in various roles in the organization, currently serving as its president. His work in disasters has extended as far as El Salvador and Sri Lanka. He also serves as cochair of the American Psychiatric Association's (APA) New York County District Branch Committee on Disaster and as principal author of a number of citywide and statewide training programs in disaster mental health. He lectures, writes, and conducts scholarly work on various aspects of disasters as they relate to psychiatry, including two edited books. Dr. Katz received the APA's 2001 Bruno Lima Award in Disaster Psychiatry. He has been a Fellow of the New York Academy of Medicine since 2007. Dr. Katz graduated from Harvard College and obtained his medical degree from Columbia University. He went on to complete his residency in psychiatry at Columbia University in 1999 and a subsequent fellowship in forensic psychiatry at New York University in 2000. Dr. Katz has a private practice in general and forensic psychiatry in Manhattan.

Gregory Luke Larkin, M.D., M.S., M.S.P.H., M.A., F.A.C.E.P., is professor of surgery and associate chief for Emergency Medicine at Yale University School of Medicine. He is principal author of the *Code of Ethics* for the American College of Emergency Physicians (ACEP) and was the first to espouse cardinal virtues in the practice of emergency and disaster medicine. Dr. Larkin is ABEM (American Board of Emergency Medicine) certified in emergency medicine and provides counsel to health ministries in the United Kingdom, Iraq, and elsewhere. He serves an advisor to the Centers for Disease Control's National Center for Injury Control and Prevention as well as NIMH and SAMHSA. Dr. Larkin penned the Society for Academic Emergency Medicine's *"Code of Conduct for Academic Emergency Medicine."* He served as Atlantic Fellow in Public Policy at Guy's and St. Thomas' NHS Trust, Guy's, St. Thomas', Kings' School of Medicine, British Council, Whitehall, London. He is past chair for the ACEP subcommittee on Youth Violence and is founding chair of ACEP's Section on Trauma and Injury Prevention. Dr. Larkin's research interests are in empiric bioethics, biostatistics, injury control and prevention with a focus on the mental health causes and consequences of trauma.

Amy Manierre holds a Master of Divinity degree from New York Theological Seminary. She is an ordained American Baptist minister, certified by the Association of Professional Chaplains as a hospital chaplain, holds a master's degree from the University of Houston Graduate School of Social Work, and is an LCSW. Reverend Manierre's area of interest is the interface between religious belief systems and psychological processes. She conducts community outreach to educate clergy regarding mental illness to foster continuity of care between clinicians and clergy.

Glen Milstein, Ph.D., received his Ph.D. in clinical psychology from Teachers College, Columbia University. He is an assistant professor of psychology at the City College of the City University of New York (CUNY), is on the doctoral faculty of the clinical psychology subprogram of the Graduate Center of CUNY, and is an adjunct assistant professor of psychology in psychiatry at the Weill Medical College of Cornell University. The foundation of his work is the study of how beliefs are imbued in people through their cultural milieus. The focus of his bilingual research is on responses to emotional distress and mental disorders by clergy and religious congregations. He is a licensed clinical psychologist.

Joshua Moses is a PhD candidate in anthropology at the Graduate Center of the City University of New York and a National Institute of Mental Health Ruth L. Kirschstein Fellow. For the past five years he has been studying the role of religious and spiritual care in disaster response recovery. As a former research associate with the Nathan Kline Institute for Psychiatric Research, he conducted research on the role of religious leaders in the mental health system and authored policy reports for the New York City Department of Health and Mental Hygiene. Other areas of research include cross-cultural issues in mental health, mind/body medicine, end-of-life care, health and inequality, the emerging role of Buddhism in American healthcare, and religious responses to climate change.

Carol S. North, M.D., M.P.E., is a professor of Psychiatry and the Nancy and Ray L. Hunt Professor of Crisis Psychiatry at University of Texas Southwestern Medical Center in Dallas. Dr. North holds a joint appointment in surgery/emergency medicine in the Division of Homeland Security. She is also director of the program in Trauma and Disaster at the VA North Texas Health Care System in Dallas. Dr. North has been an international leader in shaping the science of disaster mental health epidemiology. Dr. North and her research team have studied nearly 3,000 survivors of major disasters, including the bombings in Oklahoma City and the U.S. Embassy in Nairobi, Capitol Hill anthrax attacks, the 9/11 terrorist attacks, and Hurricane Katrina.

Anand Pandya, M.D., is the director of inpatient psychiatry at Cedars–Sinai Medical Center, the president of the National Alliance on Mental Illness (NAMI-National) and a cofounder of Disaster Psychiatry Outreach, a charity that provides psychiatric care in the wake of disasters. He serves on the American Psychiatric Association Scientific Program Committee and is a reviewer for the National Institute of Mental Health. Dr. Pandya received his bachelor's degree from Harvard College with Honors in mathematics and philosophy. He received his medical degree at New York University School of Medicine and his psychiatric training at Columbia University/New York State Psychiatric Institute where he served as chief resident. He also is a board-certified forensic psychiatrist.

Dr. Pandya received the Kenneth Johnson Memorial Book Award for editing *Disaster Psychiatry: Intervening When Nightmares Come True*. He is also a coeditor of the *Disaster Psychiatry* issue of *Psychiatric Clinics of North America*. He taught for several years at NYU School of Medicine while working at Bellevue Hospital. He currently teaches UCLA (University of California/Los Angeles) medical students and lectures extensively on disaster psychiatry. He is a course director for the American Psychiatric Association annual meeting basic course on Disaster Psychiatry.

Diane Ryan, L.S.C.W., is the director of Disaster Mental Health for the American Red Cross in Greater New York. She is a licensed clinical social worker and has worked in trauma, critical incident response and disaster mental health since 1997, serving at local and national incidents including floods, aviation crashes and the World Trade Center attacks. She has expertise in working with the responder population and provided trauma protocols to 9/11 responders with PTSD for several years after the WTC disaster. She was part of a Red Cross team that created and facilitated a support program for Israeli Red Cross responders in Jerusalem in 2005. Ryan is a member of the International Society for Traumatic Stress Studies and the International Critical Incident Stress Foundation. She has presented on disaster, trauma, and critical incident response nationally and internationally and has published extensively.

Siddharth Ashvin Shah, M.D., M.P.H., is medical director of Greenleaf Integrative Strategies, LLC (www.greenleaf-is.com). As an international physician–consultant, he blends his skills in integrative medicine, medical hypnosis, group psychology, trauma recovery, and stress management research to offer cutting-edge techniques, such as neuropsychoeducation, laughter yoga, trauma-sensitive yoga, guided meditations, and pranayama (breathwork) to reduce vicarious trauma and bolster resilience in the face of disasters. Dr. Shah completed a B.A. with Honors in Comparative Religious Studies at Rice University and then earned his M.D. from Baylor College of Medicine. He did his psychiatry internship at the Menninger Clinic and then completed a Preventive and Behavioral Medicine residency and a master's in Public Health at Mount Sinai Hospital in New York City.

After the 9/11 attacks, Dr. Shah developed disaster preparedness protocols to mitigate backlash, such as Islamophobia, anti-Sikh scapegoating, and hate crimes. Under a Red Cross grant, he treated NYPD, FDNY, and other first responders suffering from treatment-resistant emotional trauma. Answering a call in the global South to train barefoot counselors in 2002, he founded Psychosocial Assistance Without Borders. Dr. Shah has served as a board member and now serves as a clinical fellow for Psychology Beyond Borders (www.psychologybeyondborders.com), a nonprofit dedicated to helping people manage the fear and terror that can result from natural and manmade disasters, terrorism, and armed conflict. He has authored audio albums, articles, book chapters, and organizational guidelines on the subjects of stress-related syndromes, cultural competency, cultural adaptation/translation, disaster mental health, and integrative treatments for trauma. With Greenleaf Integrative Strategies, he has traveled in Pakistan, Sri Lanka, India, Brazil, Ethiopia, and the United States to build capacity among humanitarian workers, medical professionals, and clergy.

Rebecca P. Smith, M.D., is an assistant clinical professor of psychiatry at Mount Sinai Medical Center (New York City). She has worked at the local, national, and international levels on issues related to mental health effects of terrorism, disaster, and trauma. She remains engaged in research on the mental health consequences of the exposures to 9/11 sustained by evacuees as well as workers and volunteers involved in the rescue and recovery efforts at the World Trade Center after the terrorist attacks of September 11, 2001, as well as with other populations affected by terrorism internationally, with a focus on human resilience in the face of uncontrollable stress. In 2003, she served on the National Institute of Mental Health's Roundtable on the Mental Health Effects of Mass Violence. In collaboration with New York City's Department of Health and Mental Health, she created a course in psychosocial effects of bioterrorism for the doctors and nurses at New York City hospitals. She worked with the Baton Rouge (Louisiana) Mental Health authority to assist in the development of structures for managing the mental health needs of survivors of Hurricane

Katrina. Dr. Smith continues to consult and collaborate in the analysis of data on disaster and trauma.

Julie Taylor, M.Div., CTR, is executive director of Disaster Chaplaincy Services. She is the author of the chapter "Spiritual First Aid" in *Disaster Spiritual Care: Practical Clergy Responses to Community, Regional, and National Tragedy*, the first comprehensive resource for pastoral care in the face of disaster. She also coauthored "Roles in Respite Centers: Peers, Chaplains and Mental Health," *International Journal of Emergency Mental Health*. Reverend Taylor is a certified trauma responder (CTR) through the Association of Traumatic Stress Specialists, an approved instructor by the International Critical Incident Stress Foundation, and a member of the Hudson Valley CISM Team. She received her master's of divinity from Union Theological Seminary in New York City. Reverend Taylor lives in New York City and has responded to both local and national disasters.

Susan L. Thornton, M.Div., M.A., has a Master of Divinity degree from Union Theological Seminary in New York, and a master's in counseling psychology from University of St. Thomas, St. Paul, Minnesota. She has been a United Church of Christ clergywoman for 34 years and a clinical pastoral education supervisor for 15 years. She presently leads the Clinical Pastoral Education program at the Minneapolis VA Medical Center and acts as a theological consultant in Dr. Harris' research program. She has been a first responder in several disasters.

Alfonso Wyatt, M.Div., is an associate minister and elder on the staff of The Greater Allen Cathedral of New York under the leadership of Dr. Floyd H. Flake. Reverend Wyatt ministers to the unemployed, youth, parents, and the broader community. He has designed innovative workshops for married couples and seminars for church leaders. Reverend Wyatt is a national role model and leader on issues that impact youth, health, family, and community development. He is an advisor and consultant to government, universities, public schools, community-based organizations, faith-based institutions, foundations, and civic groups. He is a frequent public speaker, bringing a message of hope around the nation and world.

Reverend Wyatt is vice president of the Fund for the City of New York, a highly regarded operating foundation and public charity started by the Ford Foundation in 1968. The mission of the Fund for the City of New York is to improve the quality of life for all New Yorkers through its strategic work with government and nonprofits. Reverend Wyatt attended Howard University (Washington, D.C.), Columbia Teacher's College, The Ackerman Institute for Family Therapy, Columbia Institute for Nonprofit Management, and New York Theological Seminary where he has served as an adjunct professor and program advisor. Reverend Wyatt serves as a board member and advisor to organizations that address progressive social policy issues. He is the chair of The 21st Century Foundation, an organization that advances philanthropy in the African American Community and chair of Black Leadership Commission on AIDS/New York City affiliate.

Section I

---

*Foundational Considerations
for Effective Collaboration*

1

Fundamentals of Collaboration

Grant H. Brenner

Introduction

Disasters are occurrences of variable time course, which are sufficiently different from the usual and expected course of events such that they significantly disrupt individual and collective function past the point of stress tolerance. The usual processes that are in place, and which people and organizations take for granted, start to show dysfunction ranging from mild to moderate to total breakdown. Furthermore, the disruption of usual individual and collective functioning itself becomes part of the disaster. This makes a difficult situation worse than it needs to be, creating "spin-off" crises from the inciting event, which reciprocally worsen response to the original event (Stacey, 2001). If poorly handled, disasters risk falling into a repetitive, self-amplifying cycle, loosely analogous to a person who keeps walking on a sprained ankle, not only keeping it from healing, but reinjuring it in the process, perhaps rippling out to other consequences as well.

This brief overview presents principles that may help to mitigate a potential avalanche of destructive aftershocks of disaster. Importantly, this chapter also addresses the issue of preparedness in between disasters, advocating the wisdom of expending scarce resources preventively, in the interest of maintaining resilient networks when there is no looming threat demanding them. It is imperative that on all levels, from the individual to the family to the workplace and other organizations to the societal and governmental levels, that we have developed effective collaboration when disaster strikes. What we learn from disaster collaboration will pay off in other unexpected areas as well. Being able to communicate, develop relationships and awareness of patterns of relatedness with others, recognize and verbalize our own needs, become aware of emotions and thoughts and their impact on decisions and behavior, and identify how we get in our own and others' way and generate better choices are all highly relevant, not only in disasters and crises, but in the everyday trauma of ordinary living we all encounter. It is important to make good collaboration practice habitual because it is difficult to remember and implement effective approaches when one is spread too thinly, other priorities are more pressing, and capacities are diminished secondary to impaired cognition from distress (Covello, McCallum, & Pavlova, 1989). Burnout, compassion fatigue, and primary, secondary, and systemic trauma impede collaboration. As in other endeavors, the most effective approach is to develop proficiency by practice and over-learning when pressure is low and other resources are replete, so that when skills are needed they are at our figurative fingertips—implicit and less effortful.

I will (a) review collaboration, (b) discuss relevant aspects of trauma and its effects on individual and systemic function, (c) describe a framework for approaching the complex interactions that arise out of the chaos of disaster, (d) discuss features of effective collaboration and suggest some concrete tools that may foster collaboration, and (e) discuss some of the less concrete aspects of collaboration that are not as easily implemented.

Developing and maintaining a collaborative stance requires sustained, long-term effort and allocation of personal and organizational resources. Understanding how the expenditure of such resources is worthwhile requires a commitment to looking at the long-term picture and seeing how collective needs over the long haul outweigh apparent short-term gains. Taking this long-range view is often in contrast to where the immediacy of our crisis emotions may compel our expectations and perspective. Effective collaboration allows for synergy of participants working together, in which the whole of the work effort is greater than the sum of the parts. Collaboration results when complementarity wins out not just some of the time, but at all times, over competition, secrecy, and paranoia. Because disasters present novel and unpredictable situations every time, it may not be possible to be fully prepared other than to expect to be caught off guard and prospectively take appropriate steps to sustain functionality knowing some of the challenges disasters pose.

Collaboration: A Basic Overview

In this section, we will outline key elements pertaining to collaboration. We will briefly look at collaboration from four points of view:

1. What is collaboration?
2. What is necessary for collaboration?
3. What facilitates collaboration?
4. What impedes collaboration?

What is collaboration? Merriam–Webster's online dictionary defines "collaborate" as (a) to work jointly with others or together especially in an intellectual endeavor, (b) to cooperate with or willingly assist an enemy of one's country and especially an occupying force, (c) to cooperate with an agency or instrumentality with which one is not immediately connected. We can see immediately that this word has positive and negative connotations, and this is reflected in the great difficulty people have in collaborating effectively and especially in the paranoia that must be addressed when attempting to collaborate with groups that may not have all of the same common interests as you or your group. Collaboration arises unexpectedly, taking on a life of its own, when people smoothly and reciprocally act together in pursuing shared goals while maintaining their own distinct sets of goals individually and organizationally. From this point of view, collaboration and competition are seen to exist in a dynamic tension in relation to one another across a continuum.

What is necessary for collaboration? At bare minimum, collaboration requires the presence of basic dynamic elements for it to "catch fire" sufficiently to sustain its own process. The individuals seeking to constitute a working group, though collaboration waxes and wanes, must mindfully attend to these elements. Required elements include trust, communication, shared purpose, sharing of resources, contingent well-being (mutual interdependence), and perceived and actual goodwill coupled with sufficient shared necessity to offset absence of goodwill.

What facilitates collaboration? Beyond the bare necessities for a marginally effective but still sufficient degree of collaboration, several factors enhance collaborative process for a more effective (and enjoyable) experience and process. As noted, while collaboration is much more probable when necessity demands it, "bare necessity" collaboration falls apart quickly when there is no urgency. However, off-again, on-again collaboration is really insufficient, as it impedes efforts to remain prepared in between crises. Since in between crises resources dwindle and the sense of urgency dissipates, more conscious intention and effort is required to sustain the collaborative potential when there is no looming disaster.

Collaboration is facilitated by the cultivation of genuine goodwill, for example, through regular meetings and networking events, working through difference, and actively seeking better understanding of oneself and the other's point of view. Effective negotiation of conflict, the cultivation of common goals and interests, the use of tact and diplomacy, and sharing and development of resources helps to bolster a healthy collaborative process. It is useful to make good collaborative practice routine, through regular meetings and the use of explicit contracting to address differences effectively, rather than by conflict and flight. It is easier to be angry than hurt. Collaboration is also facilitated by the adoption of a common system for communication and organizational structure to avoid a Tower of Babel effect. In the United States, responder organizations may all share the National Incident Management System (NIMS), or Incident Command System, in order to facilitate collaboration (FEMA, 1997).

While this may seem overly simplistic, what follows is much easier to write about in a state of relative calm than to deploy in any crisis, real or perceived. Human beings, like other animals, tend to act to relieve distressing feelings, and they act quickly, often without the capacity to reflect (Van der Kolk, Roth, Pelcovitz, Sunday, & Spinazzola, 2005). As discussed in more detail below, impulsive action may lead to destructive repetition, and this is no less true in the oft-times threatening and stressful circumstances surrounding disaster situations and efforts to work with other people who have different goals and interests; both situations contain elements of the uncertain and unknown. However, and this is key to collaboration, human beings have access to speech, formulated linguistic discourse, as a form of behavior, alternative to more destructive action. We can learn, when faced with the feeling of threat and when under distress, to act by speaking and speaking only when one is ready emotionally, spiritually, and cognitively, even though this may seem to be more anxiety-provoking than other forms of action. Developing the capacity to speak calmly and without distortion, and eschewing other more destructive and less contained forms of action and interaction is essential for sustainable collaboration.

What impedes collaboration? Generally, when seeking to understand how to make something work better, it is useful to identify and avoid common pitfalls. Therefore, in a basic sense, anything that interferes with the above helpful elements will impede collaboration. This is true, whether they are absent or present, but in an inauthentic "checking the boxes" way or other disconnected form. Actively present factors that disrupt collaboration include poor communication practice, especially inability to openly discuss, when appropriate; any unpleasant feelings and perceived or actual slights; or a negative, hostile, or oppositional stance, whether mutual or unilateral, such as characterized by prejudice, contempt, or other feelings that engender an "us–them" attitude. This includes the presence of overt deception, manipulation, and the bad-faith intention of one party to use the other parties without their consent to pursue clandestine goals. While there will inevitably be both goodwill and rancor in the normal process of relations—and, in fact, rupture and successful renegotiation around conflict leads to stronger collaborative relationships (Winnicott, 1992)—unmitigated bad will inevitably leads to irreparable breakdown in collaboration when necessity no longer moves groups together. Another factor that will disrupt collaboration is deliberate sabotage by one group or person toward another. While this is so self-evident as to almost seem not worth mentioning, it is nevertheless sadly common and noteworthy as a factor to bear in mind and try to mitigate when possible. More effort is required to restore broken trust than would have been required to prevent the breaking of trust in the first place.

A Basic Framework: Trauma, Dissociation, and Enactment

Trauma is nearly always an intimate aspect of disaster, at least for some of the involved people, organizations, and communities. It is helpful to understand some basics of trauma and dissociation theory, therefore, in order to understand the most effective ways of approaching collaboration in the presence of traumatic experience and its consequences. Trauma, a hotly debated concept, has many definitions. For our purposes, we can understand trauma as an event or experience, which passes a "tipping point" (Gladwell, 2002, pp. 7–9) of distress in which usual process becomes disrupted to the point of being overwhelmed. Exactly where this tipping point comes into play varies according to many factors: type of trauma; extent/intensity of trauma; presence of mitigating factors, such as innate hardiness and good support structures and routines; and factors relating to vulnerability, such as prior history and innate factors (Yehuda, 2004).

Traumatic experience may lead not only to functional impairment but also emotional distress and behavioral and relational consequences, any of which cannot be contained or articulated (Van der Kolk et al., 2005). In the absence of being processed and spoken of, traumatic experience instead may become displaced, avoided, and fragmented—a process known as *dissociation* (Howell, 2008)—literally a disruption of associational processes, which normally function both for the individual mind as well as for groups of individuals communicating within organizations to accomplish various tasks. When associative capacity starts to fray or break, information cannot be processed by individuals and systems, and emotions cannot be contained or adaptively expressed, leading to individuals feeling overwhelmed and group conflict and communication breakdown, impairing function and distracting from focusing on the task. This may concretely be seen as a cascading series of misunderstandings, which lead not only to poor work quality and deviation from desired outcomes, but also rancor and rupture of formerly good relationships, along with the weakening of already tenuous work arrangements via the magnification of existing conflict. Once ruptured, collaborative relationships are difficult to repair, though they may grow from the process of rupture and repair via mutual negotiation of needs, expression of feelings, and the potentially transformative experience of being understood and responded to by a caring other (Winnicott, 1992). It is important to note, however, that there is a time and a place for "processing" traumatic experience, and that attempting to do so when the circumstances are not right may lead to further trauma. In fact, not explicitly addressing troubling issues may at times be the most effective, diplomatic, and tactful approach. Lastly, there are times of heightened vulnerability in which communication is needed for systemic function, but individual participants are not ready to do so effectively.

In addition, for various reasons in the presence of dissociation and trauma, repetitive maladaptive *enactments* (Danieli, Chapter 14; Howell, 2008) may occur. An example is when an organization keeps making the same mistake, such as sending inexperienced people into a hazardous situation and their failing to learn from prior destructive repetitions, as a result of cognitive and emotional distortion, and frank dissociation, resulting in poor decision making and maladaptive behaviors. The above horror show is what happens when trauma caused by disaster is not handled well and spins out of control. Fortunately, systems and individuals generally can sustain a lot of stress, and crisis enhances the sense of community, creating the necessity to work together, which in turn leads to positive experiences and good functional outcomes that coexist with, and may offset, tragedy and loss (Walsh, 2007).

To the extent that traumatic experience for individuals and groups passes their particular tipping points, fragmentation will occur. To use a whimsical analogy, when baking certain confections, sometimes a hot liquid must be slowly and smoothly incorporated into a cold liquid. If this is done too quickly, if the proportions aren't right, if the temperature changes too fast, or if the batter is jostled too much, the batter may "break," meaning that it ends up in icky clumps surrounded by watery liquid, rather than as a smooth batter ready for baking. Then, there is no choice but to throw it out and start over (or go to the local bakery).

In an analogous way, "breaking" can occur in individuals (where it may be seen in various normal and pathological responses to stress and trauma) and in groups and organizations, where it may be seen in the kind of miscommunication and functional breakdown described above. This situation, of course, is antithetical to collaboration. The only way fragmentation is useful is when it is recognized as a signal that there is a problem and responded to differently either before it happens or while it is happening. That is to say, when we can either learn from past experience and take preventive action or reflect on experience as it is happening and respond "on the fly" in a fluid and flexibly effective manner, or at least intend to do so. This state of fluid poise has been termed *fliessgleichgewicht* ("flowing balance"; von Bertalanffy in Capra, 1997).

Level of Complexity: A Simple Framework for Understanding Complex Processes

No conceptual framework is applicable as a cookie-cutter approach for every situation. Anything presented in theory has to be viewed in context and pragmatically adapted by the user to changing situations and for his or her own needs and style. However, because disasters represent situations in which the individual and groups are strained in terms of cognitive function (Covello, Chapter 4), emotional and spiritual impact, and functional and behavioral impact, it is all the more difficult to be thoughtful about and focused toward achieving ongoing collaboration during disasters. As such, I will sketch out a useful conceptual framework for the reader as she or he considers the intricacies of disaster collaboration, as it interacts with the particular interdisciplinary issues facing spiritual care and mental health providers working together.

The basic framework I would like to propose is of a dynamic systems approach (Smith & Thelen, 1996), though it is not necessary to have a technical background to use this frame. Armed with such an approach, multiple levels of organization are considered simultaneously. By multiple levels, I mean, in order from smallest to largest, a range of scale going from biological to individual to pairs of people to small groups of people (such as families and work teams) to organizations of varying sizes (such as the ones for which we work or with which we volunteer) to societal and cultural collectives that take on a life of their own (such as governments, ethnic groups, religious groups, professional groups, and other belief systems [spiritual, scientific, literary, and so on] to which we belong), and, even more broadly, countries, and, finally, the global level. I also like to add "wildcard" areas to this framework to create a conceptual space in which to locate anything unexpected, unpredictable, unresolved, or confusing, until such a time as they might resolve or fit in better.

While in actuality these levels coexist and interact complexly with one another in a fluid and self-organizing manner, in order to combat confusion, it is conceptually helpful to simplify and organize them in our ongoing thought process in an organized manner, either from bottom-up or from top-down (or both if you can). Having such a conceptual framework in mind makes it much easier to keep track of everything going on during a crisis, when traumatic experience can be flooding our minds and interfering with our usual capacity to process information. As the complex circumstances surrounding disaster start to unfold, it is helpful to have a loose system to plug experience into. At the same time, there is room for the unexpected and for events to shape how we think about them as they unfold without overly rigidly adherence to any one framework.

Phase of Disaster and Effects on Variable Groups

Disasters overlap and vary a great deal in terms of character and time scale. Some disasters happen in an instant, such as an explosion or accident. Others are spread out in different patterns over time; the spread of an illness, the course of a storm, a series of terrorist attacks as a cluster versus a single event, or even the long, drawn out disaster of a war and the return of aggregates of traumatized veterans and the resultant impact on the family and culture. Some disasters affect the individual or a small group, such as the death of a family member; others affect a town or city; while others may affect a region, nation, or even the entire world, such as a global epidemic or massive act of nature. Disasters have different effects on different groups of people, as in racial or ethnic discrimination. Finally, though not comprehensively, the effects of disaster may be unpredictable, more widespread, or affect unexpected groups (Halpern & Tramontin, 2007).

Likewise, the aftermath of a disaster may follow different time courses, ranging from a relatively brief initial response shifting into longer-term chronicity, or a less protracted aftermath with more or less full resolution in a short time, all depending on the nature of the disaster, who is affected, and preexisting factors. To further compound matters, disasters may overlap one another, and, as described above, one event may even trigger a cascade of complex and overlapping reverberations. Disasters are not discrete events but rather are like overlapping chains of events sliding over one another, with no clear start and no clear end but a process. While individual disasters may have more discrete limits, we are always moving from prior disasters while dealing with the present disasters and preparing for future disasters. This makes collaboration very tricky.

Collaboration changes in character over time, and what it takes to collaborate also shifts, requiring not only preparation but also creativity and careful consideration to deal with situations as they arise. More concretely, collaboration is typically easier when a crisis is present, in the immediate aftermath and short-term response to disaster, because the high level of necessity creates a strong common purpose, and people both set aside differences in the face of necessity as well as make resources available with a greater generosity than at other times.

This is one beautiful thing about disasters—adverse circumstances often bring out the best in people, which is as beautiful as it is ugly when goodwill dissipates in the absence of crisis. In the period in between disasters, collaboration becomes attenuated due to a lowered sense of urgency and a related scarcity of resources. It is a special challenge between disasters to maintain networks of responders and to practice and prepare in order to remain in a state of readiness. However, what may seem like a pointless waste of time at one moment may in an instant become of paramount and pressing importance during disaster. In retrospect, it is time, energy, and money well spent if disaster strikes but, prospectively, a potential huge waste if no disaster materializes, and no way to know which is which. The inability to fully predict and the fear of wastage create a state of tension about allocating resources toward collaborating.

Pragmatic Approaches to Collaboration

I am drawing on my experience working in every phase of disaster, in many situations of disaster and crisis, to identify what works and what does not work. These experiences include, among others, working acutely in 9/11 both clinically and academically/administratively; working over 7 years on ongoing clinical problems and systemic preparedness and response since 9/11; traveling to Louisiana immediately after Hurricane Katrina in 2005 and doing direct clinical care and organizational intervention, collaboration and consulting; working with Hurricane Katrina-affected individuals and families in New York; planning and organizing several conferences on interdisciplinary collaboration training in psychoanalytic and organizational work; traveling to Sri Lanka as an advisor/consultant in multiorganization NGO (nongovernmental organization) work a year after the tsunami in 2004; conducting distance-learning trainings for Chinese mental health responders after the 2008 Sichuan earthquake; conducting trainings in Mumbai, India after the November 26, 2008 terror attacks; and, importantly, working for 2 years as a surgical resident as part of a well-functioning surgical team, the most highly efficient group collaboration I have experienced, sustained under conditions of chronic crisis and trauma. The planning processes for many of these activities, including working on this book, was at times characterized by great difficulty collaborating leading to crisis, when the self-induced crisis itself would then create the necessity to get the work moving, in a vicious and inefficient, yet seemingly inalterable, cycle. Disasters may introduce "cracks" into disaster service delivery networks, which impair function (Gillespie & Murty, 1994).

Without the factors described in the introduction to this book, i.e.,

- The will to collaborate overriding other goals (even some of your own other goals or the needs of the involved organizations).
- The desire and ability to be self-reflective.
- The ability to regulate one's own emotional states to find alternatives, such as "thoughtful-speech-as-action" to replace knee-jerk divisive reactive action out of, for instance, anger, aggression, fear, flight and avoidance leading to incorrect conclusions miscommunication.
- The open-mindedness and self-interest to see another's point of view in order to build bridges.
- A sense of putting aside short-term needs in favor of long-term ones.
- The dedication to learning to be tactful and diplomatic in addressing hot-button topics.
- Clear leadership and appropriate delegation of authority and responsibility.
- The willingness and ability to ignore perceived slights and set aside differences when they might get in the way of the primary task of working together.
- The development of a trusting relationships over time.

No applied tools will be effective as desired. With the above considerations in mind (and the understanding that these approaches be tailored to individuals and organizations, that they are a moving targets for which good enough is desirable, and perfect is the enemy of good), here are approaches and illustrative examples. The reader is encouraged to think of and develop his or her own:

Regular Meetings

During a crisis, it is helpful to meet on a regular schedule. The frequency of meetings should be determined through a careful need assessment, with ongoing reassessment as a designated task and role. When the level of distress is high and/or the situation is developing rapidly, it is useful to meet more often and for longer periods and to expect meetings to take longer than they normally would. The purposes and goals of meetings should be articulated clearly, and purposes and goals should be discussed and agreed upon by consensus or by a designated leader. This has to be as explicit as possible because what is assumed and unspoken, in fact, may be different for different participants, leading to problems that are avoidable. There may be several possible purposes to such meetings: support and debriefing, sharing information and other resources, planning and logistics, assigning and keeping track of work projects, identifying unmet needs, developing groups to address specific problems, and so on. Some of these purposes may be served during one meeting, while in other cases, if necessary, there should be separate meetings for different tasks, as required. It is important to balance task orientation and structure with enough open, unstructured time for people to bring up important, unanticipated issues, including dealing with various personal and interpersonal problems and organizational issues. It is important to maintain boundaries and tasks and have clear roles and leadership. As the situation cools down, meetings will be less charged and may be less frequent, going from daily or twice a day to once every few days, to weekly, monthly, or quarterly. Ad hoc meetings should be scheduled as needed, but, if the same need keeps arising, this is a signal that more attention may be required. It is important to keep networks active in between disasters and resist the urge to let networks decay.

Staying in Contact Outside of Formal Meetings

It is necessary to have designated personnel available to provide support and to address issues that may come up: from emotional unrest to logistical issues to furnishing key information. In addition, while people develop informal relationships, it is important not to be left alone under difficult circumstances, so it is always advisable to work at least in pairs and consider establishing formal peer support relationships and mentorships, all of which buffer tension and conflict and increase the probability of collaboration. Spontaneous debriefings are useful and often happen in hallways and over meals, for instance. Computer-based communications and information centralization save time and permit more efficient processes.

Assessment and Referral of Individuals for Specific Help

Because collaborative efforts can be impeded by a variety of normal problems that comes up in disaster work, it is important to make sure that there is ongoing monitoring of people's well-being in a nonintrusive way. This can be accomplished by informal monitoring at regular meetings, where warning signs of instability may be evident. It may be helpful to instate standard one-on-one meetings on an ongoing basis to both protect individuals and the development of collaborative relationships by nipping problems in the bud. Burnout prevention and good self-care are essential to maintain on individual and organizational levels in order to permit effective functioning, and, likewise, it is of paramount importance to screen workers so they are placed whenever possible in assignments for which they are well suited.

Training Exercises

Rather than leaving collaboration to chance, it is advisable to explicitly include training to foster collaboration, including practical exercises, such as role playing difficult circumstances (e.g., role-playing a disagreement between a chaplain and a mental health specialist over a client's management). This should be followed by subsequent group discussion and correlation with didactic material pertaining to relevant issues, such as communication skills in high-stress situations and cross-disciplinary and cultural competency education to facilitate mutual understanding. Informal and formal events mixing groups in a safe and supportive environment allow for training as well as more natural social networking, essential for developing over time the trusting relationships that underlie collaboration. It is unrealistic to expect trust and relationship to develop quickly. In some cases, due to crisis and necessity, relationships will appear to develop very rapidly; however, when the acute crisis passes, relationships will often break down in the absence of a dedicated effort to process the experience and maintain connectedness. The bottom line is to identify and prioritize functional collaboration as an explicit goal and, from the start, cement habits and integrate efforts that foster self-sustaining collaboration into routine activities. If difficulties arise, specific workshops on communication and dealing with conflict may be useful to schedule as well as individual coaching on communication and conflict resolution on a case-by-case basis.

Recording Lessons Learned in a Concrete and Accessible Format

Individuals and organizations accrue a great deal of experience over the course of doing disaster work as well as during less stressful times. While much of this experiential learning becomes intuitive, it is easy when stressed to lose track of lessons learned and revert to less effective functional states, in the absence of mitigation. It is useful to take time to identify strategies that have worked and that haven't worked and to make note of this information in a manner readily accessible to everyone (e.g., in a manual or handouts or online). Furthermore, what has worked should be actively incorporated as lessons learned into trainings and everyday work practices. A conscious distinction should be drawn between what works during crisis and what works when there is no crisis and to develop plans for all circumstances. This information then can be used to modify future training exercises in an ongoing process of progressive improvement based on explication, articulation, and integration of implicit learning.

Decisions and Work Flow

As noted, multiple factors cause work impairment and impede collaborative process, requiring additional attention and effort to maintain a reasonable level of efficiency. This is notable with regard to inability to make decisions, distorted judgment, and disrupted work process, specifically, communications distortions, inadequacy of time devoted to working out problems, a sense of urgency causing groups to reach decisions prematurely without mutual clarification, false assumptions about one another's needs, and misperceptions of meaning lead to divergent opinions about what decision was made and what are the expected next steps, and who is responsibility for what. Dysfunctions affect all levels of the organization, from leadership on down, and play out in disrupted work processes. The most effective way to deal with these problems is to (a) extensively and redundantly clarify decision making and work allocation at every stage of planning, explaining why this is necessary even if it seems annoying or pointless; (b) frame discussion of decisions clearly as such, stating needs in short, straightforward messages; (c) recheck consensus prior to moving forward; and (d) make an explicit record of what agreements were reached. When possible, it is useful to develop clear, simple work protocols to ensure consistency, which include routine error checking for quality control, and confirming consensus.

Conclusion

Collaboration takes work. It does not happen by chance. Collaboration must be approached with purpose, as a shared high-priority task, explicitly agreed upon by all parties whenever possible. It cannot be overemphasized that the absence of dissent is not consent, that silence is likewise not consent, and that initial agreement may later yield true feelings of disagreement that, if unaddressed, foster destructive resentment and broken trust, risking serious compromise to the vulnerable developing collaboration; exquisite attention must be paid to notice potentially false assumptions of tacit agreement and, as often as is necessary, additional time must be devoted to recontracting around needs and goals. Taking a moment to pause and reflect, to consider carefully how to proceed, will allow systems to be put in place that reduce individual error, relieve burden, and build organizational intelligence, freeing people to do what they do best. Leaders must make it part of their responsibility to model effective strategies in order to set the tone for others, including embodying the use of speech to resolve problems between people, rather than other forms of less useful action. While during crises, collaboration may come more easily due to necessity and an enhanced sense of community; it is inadvisable to take for granted the ongoing intentional efforts required to generate self-sustaining collaborative processes. It is important to engage difficult issues diplomatically, addressing disagreement directly and taking care to use language, gestures, and silence effectively with a thoughtful consideration of where others' needs stand in the communication process. It is important to maintain an atmosphere of empathic understanding even in the face of significant differences in belief, personality (of individuals and organizations), and goals. It is essential to be clear and direct in communications without expressing excessive anxiety, anger, or other powerful emotions, which are contagious and lead to interpersonal conflict and systemic dysfunction. In order for collaboration to happen, there has to be an ongoing process of mutual negotiation and expression of needs and concerns without excessive rancor. It is essential to have opportunities to talk through divisive issues before they reach the point of being disruptive and traumatic and find alternatives to acting vindictively or withdrawing from discourse, either of which will set back the process. It is advisable, as tolerated, to routinize discussion about and awareness of commonalities of purpose and values and to seek shared metaphors, which remedy areas of difference while acknowledging the value of difference. It is important to identify modes of engagement that are effective and intentionally employ these approaches over ones that have been proved not to work well, while always seeking to learn and incorporate new experience into the status quo. Finally, and perhaps most importantly, maintaining an attitude of mutual respect goes far toward allowing basic trust and communication to develop. Mutual respect constitutes the foundation of enduringly stable synergistic relationships. It is necessary to be watchful for early warning signs, such as resentment, withdrawl, refusal to communicate, contempt, paranoia, neglect, aggression, and complacency. Recognition allows us to respond to small problems before they spiral out of control, rather than ignoring them until they have become significant problems in and of themselves.

References

Capra, F. (1997). *The web of life: A new understanding of living systems.* New York: Random House.

Covello, V. T., McCallum, D. B., & Pavlova, M. T. (1989). Principles and guidelines for improving risk communication. In V. T. Covello, D. B. McCallum, & M. T. Pavlova (Eds.), *Effective risk communication: The role and responsibility of government and non-government organizations.* New York: Plenum.

FEMA. (1997). IS-700 national incident management system (NIMS), an introduction. Retrieved October 30, 2008, from Emergency Management Institute, FEMA Web site: http://www.training.fema.gov/EMIWeb/IS/is700.asp

Gillespie, D. F. & Murty, S. A. (1994). Cracks in a postdisaster service delivery network. *American Journal of Community Psychology, 22*(5), 639–647.

Gladwell, M. (2002). *The tipping point: How little things can make a big difference.* Boston: Back Bay Books.

Halpern, J. & Tramontin, M. (2007). *Disaster mental health: Theory and practice.* Pacific Grove, CA: Thomson Brooks/Cole.

Howell, E. (2008). *The dissociative mind.* New York: Taylor & Francis.

Merriam–Webster online. Retrieved October 11, 200 from http://www.merriam-webster.com/dictionary

Smith, L., & Thelen, E. (1996). *Dynamic systems approach to the development of cognition and action.* Cambridge, MA: MIT Press.

Stacey, R. (2001). *Complex responsive processes in organizations: Learning and knowledge creation.* New York: Taylor & Francis.

Van der Kolk, B., Roth, S., Pelcovitz, D., Sunday, S., & Spinazzola, J. (2005). Disorders of extreme stress: The empirical foundation of a complex adaptation to trauma. *Journal of Traumatic Stress, 18*(5), 389–399.

Walsh, L. (2007). Traumatic loss and major disasters: Strengthening family and community resilience. *Family Process, 46,* 207–227.

Winnicott, D. (1992). *Through paediatrics to psycho-analysis: Collected papers by Donald W. Winnicott.* New York: Routledge.

Yehuda, R. (2004). Risk and resilience in posttraumatic stress disorder. *Journal Clinical Psychiatry, 65*(Suppl. 1), 29–36.

2

An Anthropologist Among Disaster Caregivers

Joshua M. Moses

Entering the Field*

I entered anthropological fieldwork not in the usual manner associated with the discipline of anthropology—boarding a plane for the Fiji Islands or another exotic destination and living in a hut among indigenous people—but instead by stepping out of the subway on a beautiful autumn morning in New York City. Rather than me going into the field, the field sprung up around me.

In September of 2001, I embarked on my graduate school career at the Graduate Center of City University of New York. About a week after the semester began, exiting the F subway stop on Houston Street and 2nd Avenue, and still sleepy, a minivan with a whirling siren raced downtown at top speed, nearly hitting me. I stopped at the corner, cursing the driver. It was then I noticed dark smoke rising from downtown. Several people were intently gazing upward. With mild interest, I asked, "What building is that?" "The Trade Center," the man next to me said. While I watched, minutes, maybe seconds later, with a flash and ground-shaking boom the second tower burst into flame. I stood on that corner for what seemed like an hour but might have been 15 minutes, reluctant to leave the small group

* This article is adapted from the author's dissertation (Moses, 2009). The National Institute of Mental Health (NIMH) National Research Service Award (NRSA), Award Number F31, supported the research. The author would like to thank Dr. Kim Hopper and the Nathan Kline Institute for Psychiatric Research for the conception and early financial and ongoing intellectual support of this project.

of people that had formed, watching dumbfounded, until a wild-eyed man made his way toward the small group that had formed. He told us, maniacally, that he had seen people flinging themselves from burning buildings. "They were falling to the ground in flames," he said.

Thinking him a raving lunatic, I continued on to my Hindi class at New York University. Class, of course, had been cancelled. As the dutiful and zealous new graduate student—and at a loss for what else I might do—I wandered into NYU's Bobst Library, which was deserted save for some befuddled-looking staff. It was then I realized my day was not going to be completely normal, as the initial shock dissipated enough for the enormity of what was happening to sink in a little bit.

Anthropology, Culture, and Disaster

A year later, I began working for the Nathan Kline Institute on a project for the New York Department of Health and Mental Hygiene, studying the role of clergy in disaster mental health response. As an anthropologist, I have tried to understand the different interpretive frameworks employed by those with whom I have been working, and often how these different frameworks are connected to very real histories. I have also tried to understand how abstract ideas, scientific and medical discourses are employed in real-life settings. Do disaster caregivers—clergy and mental health professionals—distinguish between religious suffering and mental health suffering? Where are the lines and are they as clear as some would like us to believe? These are at once theoretical and pragmatic questions that, in the midst of disaster, demand quick action.

I offer that it is crucial to step back from the maelstrom of disaster work and understand that what we are wrestling with today is part of complex history and cultural context. By understanding the history and cultural particularity of what we are confronting, we stand a better chance of maintaining an open stance, learning from experience, and creating collaboration between spiritual care and mental health orientations. Anthropologists engage in participant observation, or what is often called "an ethnographic approach." We spend our days watching and talking to people, where over the course of time, we try to understand the way different groups perceive their "local worlds" (Kleinman & Benson, 2006). The hallmark of ethnography is the attempt to see things from the perspective of the "native." This native might be a FEMA worker, a spiritual care provider, mental health provider, or any one of a number of others commonly involved in disaster response.

When we enter people's daily lives, spending time in local churches or mental health clinics, talking with people in local communities, we stand a much better chance of understanding not only how people experience catastrophic disaster, but how they cope with more quotidian disasters. Understanding this kind of coping would help both mental health professionals and spiritual care providers support the strategies that are already working.

Early in my fieldwork, I began to take notice of the different way that arguments were framed, how people spoke about suffering, and what idioms were used to describe distress. Cultures have highly specific and very different ways of understanding the origins of distress, and the interventions that are likely to diminish stress. Within any given culture, there is a great degree of variability. But the variability is nested within cultural and historical narratives that give them meaning (Harrington, 2008). Mental health and spiritual care providers have their own cultures, which often tacitly, without recognition of the impact of these cultures, determine the options that might be used. Awareness of our own professional cultures may point to some of the obstacles to collaboration.

How can anthropologists improve collaboration between various mental health and religious care providers? Throughout my research among disaster caregivers, I have kept a keen eye on the contextual nature of distress, the culturally and historically contingent nature of both religion and mental health practice. I have tried to understand that how we describe what someone might be experiencing is not just about that person, but rather is embedded in a complex network of historical and cultural relationships. How does this perspective help a clinician struggling to provide care or a clergy person talking to a congregant? Understanding the moral meaning of suffering (Kleinman & Benson, 2006), what's at stake for the help-seeker, the spiritual care provider and the mental health professional, the overlaps and differences, helps to illuminate a common goal: the reduction of suffering.

When confronted with someone whose cultural beliefs may differ from our own, perhaps we will be less likely to make hasty conclusions. Imagine, for instance, if someone from Indonesia told a Westerner that his or her anxiety was in fact *Latah,* an Indonesian name for distress of a particular kind. Likely, the reaction would be dismissive. But, in order to respond to the needs of help-seekers, one can take into account the possibility that those he or she is treating may have radically different views of their own experience. Collaboration then takes place in the context of potentially messy intertwining of interpretive viewpoints.

Every time we stop and examine our operating assumptions, reach across disciplinary lines, or try to see things from the perspective of a minister, if you happen to be a mental health provider or the other way around, we create possibility for doing things differently. This "transient anthropological stance" loosens the grip that rigid categories of analysis have on us, providing the necessary space to rethink how we might respond. The potential space for doing things differently, even if only a narrow crevice for a tentative toe-hold, permits us the chance to find better concrete, pragmatic solutions when dealing with crisis and other situations, by understanding one another's perspectives, needs, strengths and limitations.

In order to gain traction over the conflict and ambivalence surrounding how to understand and manage distress, we need to look at history and the ways that people create their worlds. But, those histories weigh heavily on how we make decisions today by providing the idioms that give meaning to the events in our lives.

A chaplain whom I interviewed articulated the tension between clergy and mental health professionals that resulted from 9/11:

> During 9/11, psychologists came out of the woodwork to help, but were not prepared for acute psychological trauma. They were used to providing long-term care. Many burnt out. People wanted to talk to clergy. If mental health is going to be involved in acute care, they need to learn how to deal with these situations.

This statement articulates many of the tensions that can make collaboration challenging, if not impossible. I was often told in my interviews with clergy and mental health professionals that the *other* group was unqualified or misguided or even condescending and willfully obstructive. Spiritual care providers often told me, "Mental health professionals don't respect us. They bring their psychological models to us and don't think we have much to offer."

At the heart of these criticisms is a belief that the *other* professional does not have the ability to respond to real-life problems, that their interpretive frameworks are inadequate, with a sense of resentment and disrespect. However, an opportunity exists for examining the skills that might be shared among disparate professions if common goals, such as reducing suffering, can be recognized. An anthropological lens can provide the perspective for a broader view that facilitates this kind of examination.

Conclusion

Collaboration requires both rapid response coupled with creating the space to reflect by taking a step back and understanding the underlying assumptions that govern our actions. We live in a world of interconnected and, importantly, interdependent human cultures. We often fail to recognize our own possibilities for reaching across cultural divides or even to see that our own assumptions inhibit our understanding. Adopting an anthropological perspective, trying to understand how other people see their worlds, and an awareness of the historically and culturally contingent nature of our own construction of reality goes a long way in fostering collaboration between mental health and spiritual care providers moving toward shared goals in disaster work.

REFERENCES

Harrington, A. (2005). Uneasy alliances: The faith factor in medicine: The health factor in religion science. In R. Proctor (Ed.) *Religion and human experience* (pp. 287–307). Oxford: Oxford University Press.

Harrington, A. (2008). *The cure within: A history of mind–body medicine.* New York: W.W. Norton.

Kleinman, A. & Benson P. (2006). Anthropology in the clinic: The problem of cultural competency and how to fix it. *PLoS Medical, 3*(10). Retrieved October 24, 2009, from 294. doi:10.1371/journal.pmed.0030294..

Moses, J. (2009). *A new age of anxiety: Religion, spirituality and mental health in disaster expertise.* Unpublished doctoral dissertation, the Graduate Center, City University of New York.

3

Disaster Relief
Emotional Values

Sandra Buechler

Introduction

What can a psychoanalyst contribute on the subject of disaster relief? Analysts are trained to notice and question basic assumptions. In a sense, that is all we do. When we analyze "transferences," we are challenging fundamental assumptions about relationships. When we address "resistances" and "defenses," we are calling attention to how people believe they have to defend themselves. Accordingly, in this brief contribution, I first examine and question some problematic assumptions that relate to disaster relief that I believe are prevalent in our society. Then, I summarize some ideas I have drawn from theories about human emotionality, which I believe can help us when we address people that are in great pain.

Society's Problematic Assumptions

Health Means Getting Over Grief

From my point of view, all too often we assume that the healthy response is to "get past" mourning losses. We estimate how long grieving should take, as though we were timing baking a cake or cooking a turkey. A bit of unintentional humor and, more importantly, some significant assumptions underlie this quotation from the *New York Times* (Carey, 2006, p. F8):

"Another kind of therapy helps people understand, express, and resolve longstanding feelings of grief over losing a husband or loved one."

Aside from the unintended implication that a husband can't also be a loved one, the more serious, intended implication is that, in working with grief, the goal is to "get past" it. Life's profound losses are, in this view, no different from bouts of the flu. When we have sustained a loss, we are ill and not ourselves for a while, but then we recover our healthy selves. Our healthy, pristine selves are unblemished by loss. To me, this set of assumptions can be extremely damaging, especially when we are not even aware of it enough to question it.

I imagine Joan Didion's eyes flashing when, in her poignant account (2005) of her husband's death and its aftermath for her, she challenges received wisdom about the mourning process. Among many similar statements, she wonders how members of the helping professions can presume to know the meaning of her loss as well as she does. Didion quotes from an article on "re-grief therapy," a technique developed to treat pathological mourning. The psychiatrist Didion quotes is Vamik D. Volkan, M.D., who describes a point in the treatment when

> we help the patient to review the circumstances of the death—how it occurred, the patient's reaction to the news and to viewing the body, the events of the funeral, etc. Anger usually appears at this point if the therapy is going well … 'emotional reliving' may then take place and demonstrate to the patient the actuality of his repressed impulses. Using our understanding of the psychodynamics involved in the patient's need to keep the lost one alive, we can then explain and interpret the relationship that had existed between the patient and the one who died. (pp. 55–56)

Along with Didion, I see this point of view as assuming that "pathological" mourners are unable to comprehend the true meaning of their losses because they cannot come to terms with the relationships they really had with those who died. It is assumed that mourning for some specifiable period of time is normal, and beyond that it is pathological and indicative of an inability to make repressed feelings conscious. Mourning for "too long" is seen as the product of an unwillingness or inability to face our anger, resentment, or other negative feelings toward the person who died. It assumes that once we are brave enough to face these complicated feelings we will "get over" our abnormal mourning.

Didion (2005, p. 56) questions the idea that a mental health professional can understand her relationship with her husband better than she does. I would add other questions. When someone has lost his or her parents or partner or child or home or some other aspect of his or her life, just what can it mean to "get over" it? When a child dies, is there ever a time her parents stop dreaming about her or stop their painful yearning? Would recognizing that they sometimes felt angry with her cause them to "get over" her death?

To me, bearing pain, unexpected losses, tragedy, is part of the human condition. We can no more get over it than we can get over being ourselves.

So then, when a disaster strikes, what is "relief"?

Insight Helps Us Moderate the Intensity of Our Emotional Reactions to Pain

In my view, the belief that cognitive insight has the power to delimit emotions is a mistaken premise. It is held as much by the public as it is by members of various mental health professions. To my way of thinking, it is an absurdly rose-colored view. Victims of disasters, veterans who have witnessed the unspeakable, those who have known life at its most ghastly can, in this view, erase horror with some positive mantras. Just say the magic words to yourself and presto! Suffering fades like laundry stains succumbing to the latest detergent.

I believe that only other emotions have enough power to change how we feel. What can make life worth living when, as Emily Dickinson poetically asks, the "wreck has been"? To me it seems possible, for example, that a person in extreme pain may nonetheless want to live out of love for her child. The depression hasn't disappeared or been tamed by any magic words. It is, however, modified by love that is also very real. Love, alongside pain, may have the power to modify it.

The idea that one emotion has the power to change another rests on the vision of how emotions work that I have adapted from discrete or differential emotions theory (Buechler, 1993, 1995; Izard, 1977). I now spell out some of the basic tenets of that theory about human emotionality and how they might inform anyone trying to work with the intense feelings of a human being in emotional pain.

Theory as a Guide for Working With Intense Emotional Reactions

The most fundamental tenet of emotion theory is that "… the emotions constitute the primary motivational system for human beings" (Izard, 1977, p. 3). Emotions, in contrast to the older notion of drives, are more varied, do not dictate specific behaviors, and are not necessarily cyclic. Consequently, seeing the emotions as *our fundamental human motives* leaves tremendous room for individual variation. This may help us check the impulse to assume we understand why a person behaved as she did, when we may not have inquired enough about her feelings. We might be better able to continue a curious inquiry when we think in terms of each of us having a vast personal history of emotions, combinations of emotions, and emotion-cognition patterns. Thus, I have a whole history of experience of Sandra-being-angry. I bring that history to each angry moment I face.

Seeing emotions (rather than the older notions of drives) as primary means to me that sexual and aggressive impulses express only two of the many emotionally shaped motivational forces in human beings. Emotions, such as fear, shame, guilt, curiosity, and many others, can make a sexual or aggressive pull a very different experience. As is true for any other significant aspect of being a human being, our interpersonal history (along with our endowments) shapes our personal experience of these motives.

I will hear any human story differently if I hold a viewpoint that puts a wealth of interpersonal emotional experience at the helm. My hearing can then be more open-ended than if I believed in a closed system of motivating forces. Putting the emotions in center stage means that there can be an *infinite* variety of emotion–cognition patterns, shaped partially by one's interpersonal history, at play at any particular moment. Thus, for example, if I see both a patient and myself as driven, partially, by our loneliness, then for each of us our history of being lonely is salient. A particular array of feelings and feeling–cognition combinations comes more strongly into play, as we make each other lonelier in how we interact. My own memory of being a lonely seventh grader is more relevant than usual when I am hearing about the loneliness felt by someone else. Furthermore, if loneliness has a history of making one of us very anxious, that will have an impact on my ability to empathize. On the other hand, if one of us tends to get very curious about being lonely, that will have a different impact. How loneliness tends to affect each of us cognitively may be particularly salient. For each of us, has loneliness frequently evoked moments of intense, sharp concentration or a confused, blank absent-mindedness or neither of these possibilities?

Understanding the emotions as the primary motivational system in human beings gives me a very flexible, yet orienting theory. With this way of thinking, I can hold all my motivational hypotheses lightly. I don't come into an interaction without *any* theory of what motivates people. While some might argue that such a clean slate is best, I believe it is difficult to perceive anything without some ready-made constructs. Just as it would be hard to see a circle without a concept of circularity, I would have trouble seeing loneliness as a driving force in a person unless I entered the situation already understanding that gnawing loneliness can drive human beings.

How can we formulate a theory that honors the infinite variety of interpersonal emotional experience that a particular person may need in order to profoundly change? More specifically, in the present context, I want my theory to help me toward a nuanced understanding of any moment with someone I am trying to help bear great grief, pain, or other aspects of life. While I don't want to jump to a predetermined motivational schema, I also don't want to have to "reinvent the wheel." That is, I don't want to feel (or pretend to feel) that I have no beliefs about human behavior in general and about my own patterns in particular. I want a theory that helps me move toward greater understanding of the interpersonal moment, not one that starts with a predetermined explanation or one that leaves me groping in the dark.

Anyone in a helping profession needs to be able to move back and forth, between the present clinical moment and a *complex and flexible* theory of human motivation. Human beings have certain inherent fundamental emotions, but our life experience patterns them differently in each of us. You and I are both capable of shame. But, maybe very intense, early taunting has tinged your shame with rage. My shame comes with a different history, perhaps bringing more guilt than rage in its wake. Of course, these would be relative, not absolute, differences. For example, an event that leaves you bereft might remind you of early experiences, fraught with shame, where you had less than other children. These defining moments of shame might then easily recruit your rage at life's injustice. But I, with my own emotional baggage, might respond with a different set of feelings. My shame at feeling I now have very little might come, for me, at the expense of my self-esteem. Given my particular experiences, my history might predispose me to feel that, once again, I have let myself down and failed at life.

The theoretical slant I am outlining allows cognition an equal recognition along with the emotions. How we think and how we feel so mutually interconnect that sorting them out can occupy much time. I believe I am best prepared to help people with their painful life experiences if I enter every interchange with loosely held notions about how loneliness "smells," the "taste" of fear, the "texture" of intense shame. These are leads that can help me orient, but not certainties that prematurely close down my intuitive understanding. They allow me to honor the tremendous variety of individual emotional life experience, and their impact on who we each become.

The second basic belief derived from emotion theory that I find extremely useful is the idea that, fundamentally, emotions are adaptive. "Emotions have motivational functions that give them critical adaptive qualities; for example, interest gives focus and selectivity to perception; fear and anticipatory shame protect from physical and psychological harm; guilt motivates moral reasoning, empathy, and reparation of damaged relationships; and joy works as an antidote for stress and a stimulus to social interaction and creative thinking" (Izard, 2001, p. 253).

Understanding the emotions as fundamentally adaptive has broad human implications. It shapes our notions of the helper's goals, methods, and the meaning of progress. This view of emotionality affects how we define normality and pathology and affects our focus in our efforts to work with people. What we see as important, worthy of our attention, memorable, and so on, depends on our basic stance toward human emotionality. Henry Krystal (1975) has been critical of what he calls "riddance" theories that assume it is always a goal to diminish emotionality. In teaching, I have referred to the implicit "pus theory of emotions" that I believe many clinicians (and nonclinicians) hold. It was especially popular in the 1970s to believe that if we could express (rather than suppress) anger in treatment, we would be cured of our troublesome emotions. To me, this reflects an antiemotionality prejudice.

Along with the concept that the emotions are fundamentally adaptive, I also believe that every emotion has an optimal range of intensity. Too little, even of painful agitation, is as much of a problem as too much. We would probably be as concerned if an infant never cried as we would be if crying took up her whole waking life. I don't assume my aim should be to cure anyone of their intense feelings although, eventually, we may try to help someone be better able to modulate them. I begin with a relatively unformulated sense that a person's agitation is her current (perhaps often ineffective) emotional language.

The belief that emotions are fundamentally adaptive has especially important implications for how we define ideal health in human beings. For example, many behavioral and cognitive approaches would see agitation as a symptom and something to cure. This pits one aspect of a human being against another aspect. If I am working to cure a person of her agitation, I am working to cure her of a part of her. Bromberg (1998) has been especially clear about how such a position can become problematic. Referring to Freud's treatment of Emmy von N, Bromberg says:

> Even though she welcomed his trying to "cure" her, she didn't want him to "cure" her of being herself. She was "unruly" because she needed to get all of

her selves into a human relationship and was afraid Freud was going to lose
patience because she was insisting, through her symptoms, on her right to have
him accept that her "crazy" (unruly) reactions to his therapeutic efforts had to
do with him as well as her. (p. 235)

Thus, in the example of Joan Didion's efforts to bear her grief over the
loss of her husband, my understanding of emotion theory would suggest
that it *is not* my job to help Didion feel *less*. I don't want to "cure" her of her
grief but, rather, to help her feel it fully enough to find, within it, its adaptive potential. Grief can, for example, bind us more fully to each other, in
our appreciation of the universal pain of the human condition.

The third basic belief, drawn from emotion theory, is that social competence requires the ability to communicate emotions and read them sufficiently accurately when others express them.

A wealth of data support the view that very young infants are capable
of discerning different facial expressions of emotions, and no one can
argue with the notion that emotionality is our first language. But, clinically, we certainly can differ about how much the ability to read faces can
or should be taught to children and/or adults. (For a very positive view
about teaching adults to read emotional expressions, see Ekman, 2003.)
Once again, this touches on issues of "normal" and "ideal" emotional
perception and expression.

I don't think it would be useful for me to simply teach people what a
smiley face looks like. But I come to my work with the assumption that
human beings naturally learn about the interpersonal impact of our emotions as we develop, so something must have blocked this ability if someone is unable to read the feelings of others or adequately communicate his
or her own feelings to others.

Next is the fourth tenet, that "each of the fundamental emotions has
unique motivational properties of crucial importance to the individual
and the species, and each adds its own special quality to consciousness as
it mobilizes energy for physical or cognitive adventure. An intense emotion may be considered as a special state of consciousness experienced as
highly desirable or highly undesirable" (Izard, 1977, p. 83).

The viewpoint that there are fundamental emotions, which are separate or discrete, rather than merely different in intensity or some other
aspect, is derived from Charles Darwin's (1872) fascinating contribution,
The Expression of the Emotions in Man and Animals. So, for example,
rather than seeing fear as on a continuum with surprise, with fear as
a reaction to a greater degree of novelty, the fundamental or discrete
emotions perspective sees fear and surprise as *two separate emotions*,

discernible by their differing facial expressions, that create different states of mind.

I believe that the practical implications of this point of view are enormous. This means that, for example, my life long, periodic experience of "myself angry" is a building block of my identity, a crucial part of who I am to myself, and a separable self-state from my experience of "myself afraid." Additionally, this point of view envisions each fundamental emotion as having characteristic effects on consciousness itself, so that, for example, when we are angry, our focus is narrower and less free-wheeling than when we are less angry or when we are predominantly curious. Of course, this is as true for health workers as it is for everyone else. I feel it would be hard to overestimate the significance of the emotions as self-states. If each emotion is a discernibly different self-state, then (as I have already suggested above) we accumulate a history (conscious and unconscious) of how we have felt when curious, for example. We bring this memory bank to every new day, just as we also bring memories of what it is like for us to feel fear, or joy, and how we each tend to experience sadness. These (formulated and unformulated) emotional profiles are a significant aspect of who we are to ourselves.

When I start to work with someone, I want to know how their curious self-state feels to them. I assume it is somewhat like my own but not exactly the same, since it is partially shaped by a different set of life experiences. I also assume that intense curiosity and intense fear have some experiential similarities for my new patient as well as significant differences. Of course, this is all greatly over simplified because no one is ever in a pure state of any one emotion. But, as human beings, I believe we all have some experience of being curious, so we can recognize that state in others. This is a significant aspect of our capacity for empathy. However, it also accounts for some of our frequently occurring empathic failures because my curious state is somewhat different from yours. Empathic capacity is partially based on a skillful projection. Just as I can only know my own experience of the color "red" and I have to assume that is largely what you see when you say you see "red," so it is with my experience of sadness, loneliness, and other emotional self-states.

I assume I bring my history of emotional self states to work with me in the morning as well as a rich personal history of being with people who are in varying emotional self-states. How do our personal histories affect what we each can register about the other person? While I believe none of us has a definitive knowledge of what we can and can't register, ongoing self reflection may help increase our personal awareness of our strengths and limitations as witnesses to the human array of feelings.

The fifth and perhaps most crucial assumption, drawn from emotion theory, is that the emotions *form a system*, with a change in one emotion affecting the experience of all the others. This assumption has tremendous human implications. It means, for example, that when someone hopes to diminish his depression, we could just as well focus on his (relative) absence of curiosity as on the presence of intense depression. Any change in any emotion will affect the whole system of emotions. This can be very helpful because a person can become obsessively fixated on her depression. If we join her in this exclusive focus, we may both fail to notice crucial aspects of her emotional and interpersonal life. In addition, if the person brings an expectation that we will make her depression vanish instantaneously, she may be impatient with the process. We can all be tempted by the hope that emotions will operate like a thermostat, and we can learn a simple and quick way to raise or lower their intensity.

I believe that we each have a "theory" (parts of which may or may not be consciously formulated) about what emotionally fortifies us to cope with the human condition. How much do we each rely on will power to pull ourselves through crises? What do we each count on to enable us to bear the potential losses and emotional hardships of aging? Some of us look to religion, work, and/or human connections for strength and for the sense that our lives are meaningful. But, all we each have is a personal theory about what can give us the strength we will need.

Perhaps it is equally important to look at what can delimit our emotional strength to cope with life. I think certain defensive patterns cut us off from potential emotional fortification. The severely paranoid person won't fully know curiosity's delight. The profoundly obsessive person will cling to routine too much to fully enjoy life's surprises. The chronically depressed won't be lifted up by joy. The intensely schizoid person won't feel the healing warmth of love. When we cut ourselves off from significant emotional experiences, we delimit our own resources for coping with our lives.

Next is the idea that what we each feel about our own emotionality depends on the interpersonal "socialization of emotions" (Tomkins, 1970). Everyone has a history of how others have reacted to our expressions of each of the fundamental emotions, and this history is a significant aspect of our identity. Therefore, it is essential to understand, for example, a person's inwardly held "reputation" (with himself) about his expressions of anger. Was he known as a child who had violent tantrums? In first grade, was he handled like a time bomb? This has enormous impact on the person he became, in his own eyes. That "rageful" little boy is likely to grow up to be a rageful big boy, partially on the basis of inborn temperament but also because of how others have responded to him and how he has come to think of himself. "Studies have found that even in infancy, emotion expression styles have considerable stability over time, and that toddler's expression styles predict behavioral outcomes in later years." (Izard, 2001, p. 251).

As I have suggested above, I think of this emotional identity as a very significant aspect of who we each are to ourselves. This emotional profile can contribute to or detract from self-confidence, self-esteem, and expectations from interpersonal life. In a sense, we each develop a certain "reputation" with each other and with ourselves that can become an inflexible prejudice. Do I see myself as unable to change how I act when I am angry (or anxious, sad, ashamed, and so on)? Do I see my teenager or husband as hopelessly unable to maintain emotional equilibrium when provoked?

It can be particularly troublesome when we develop hardened stereotypes about the emotional capacities of those to whom we are the closest. It is so easy to fall into: "he always blows up" or "she is always too emotional." Thinking we know each other well has its advantages and disadvantages. We are probably each only aware of a portion of our assumptions about each other. When we work in the mental health field, I think it is especially important that we actively question our own assumptions about "healthy" or "normal" emotional reactions to stress. It is vital that we become conscious of any rigid stereotypes we might hold about our own typical stress reactions or how we imagine others usually respond.

The last theory-based assumption I consider here is that the relationship between emotion and cognition is not unidirectional. That is, sometimes emotions shape cognitions, and sometimes cognitions are primary. A voluminous literature passionately advocates various conceptions of the relationship between cognition and emotion. Some authors provocatively advance notions that deny importance to one or the other, but most are more balanced in their appreciation of the importance of cognition and emotion in human experience. An important tenet of Izard's differential emotions theory (1971, 1977, 2001) is that "... emotions do not always depend on knowledge or cognitive mediation, (that) emotions make independent contributions to individual and social functioning ..." (2001, p. 250). The topic of the roles of cognition and emotion in human functioning is, of course, complex, and I will not attempt to summarize it. However, I do suggest that it is consonant with discrete emotions theory to view insight as most often following, rather than creating, emotional and behavioral change, in treatment and other walks of life. Discrete emotion theorists would not be surprised by the idea that the most powerful aspect of a therapeutic engagement can be an emotional experience that is never verbalized or even formulated.

Since I believe unformulated emotions are often primary in every human interchange (that is, shaping cognition more than the reverse), I trust them to do much of my work.

Emotion theory gives us a way of understanding how unformulated interpersonal emotional experience can facilitate change by having an impact on the person's overall balance of emotions. The emotional sources of the capacity to effect change are the same for the clinician as they are for the teacher, theologian, or political leader. In thinking about this, I am guided by my own experience and my faith in the motivating power of human emotions. But, I think I do not differ from many others in my belief that to be transformed in any meaningful way, we need to be inspired by an emotional experience.

Good Mourning

I turn from general beliefs about human emotions to my more personal and specific ideas about how human beings bear great pain. Sometimes, as a clinician and as a human being, I hope to help myself and other people cut our losses. Loss is cut down to size if, firstly, it is just sad. Sadness is a perfectly appropriate response to loss. I would suggest that when human beings feel mainly sad, in response to loss, they can generally bear it. But other intense emotions, such as regret, can make sadness unbearable. Elsewhere, I have dealt at greater length with the place of regret in our lives (Buechler, 2008). Here I want to point out how frequently I think it complicates loss. So I have trained myself to question the role regret is playing, as I listen to sadness.

This viewpoint supports the need for collaboration in relief work. My training in psychology and psychoanalysis prepares me to address some of grief's complications. I can sometimes sort out what feelings are running alongside sorrow. I may be able to discern the regret in the sadness, much as a musician can discern the themes in a complicated composition. To the trained artist, the roles of color, composition, and shadow stand out in a painting. To the analyst, the roles of sadness, regret, guilt, shame, and other feelings may similarly form strands. This is not to say that naming the strands eradicates the feelings (as might Dr. Volkan, quoted earlier in this chapter). But, it can be a first step in recognizing the whole experience a person is having. Recognizing and reverberating with an experience is not the same as trying to erase or eradicate it.

For me this raises the complicated issue of the nature of human empathy, another question I address more fully elsewhere (Buechler, 2008). But, here I would say that empathy in a time of tragedy can include recognition that loneliness is intensifying someone's sadness, or that profound regret about unlived potential is making grief unbearable.

But, often, this is not enough. And even when pain is mostly "pure" of other feelings, it can still paralyze. From where can come the will to go on? Collaboration is so necessary, in my view, precisely because what I have to offer may not suffice to help people feel their lives have purpose.

Purpose

Elsewhere I have discussed the sense of having purpose, as separable from any particular goal (Buechler, 2004). I believe it is a necessary ingredient in life. I would suggest that its core is often spiritual. Thus, it seems natural to me that relief work often requires the collaborative effort of mental health workers and spiritual guides. In my better moments, I can discern the truly lonely from the prevailingly sad. But, though I may try, I may not be able to help either one feel sufficient reason to go on.

Sometimes my work with someone does help him or her connect with motivations for living. They may recognize how much they care for a partner, child, or others. But, for many, spiritual beliefs augment the will to live. Victor Frankl (1985), in his moving autobiographical story of survival in concentration camps in World War II, quotes Nietzsche, who said that if we have a "why" we can live with any "how." A strong enough sense of purpose can carry us through much that would otherwise be unbearable. Some of us go on for each other. Martha Manning, a victim of paralyzing depressions, tells us:

> At the very end, I kept going only for my daughter. Every morning, Keara stumbles semiconscious into the bathroom and turns on the shower. Within the space of thirty seconds she starts to sing. She starts out humming so softly that her voice blends with the spray as it bounces off the wall. And then she chooses her song—sometimes sweet and lyrical, sometimes loud and rocking. Each morning, when I had to face another day on two hours of sleep and absolutely no hope, I leaned against the bathroom door waiting for her to sing and let her voice invite me to try for one more day. (Casey, 2001, p. 266)

But, for others, love is not enough. What inspires life?

Although not of a Christian faith, I have always been fascinated by paintings of the annunciation. It is, to me, the moment of the most profound, divine inspiration. Inspiration is about infusing life with spirit. Paintings of the annunciation portray the moment when Mary begins to understand her purpose. The Holy Spirit enters her and, for the first time, she intuits why she lives. She receives her calling.

Whether or not we understand it in religious or spiritual terms, I think we each need to find our calling. What are we here to do? While the therapist can help us sort out the various strands of our reactions to a tragedy, more is often needed to help us find the purpose that can animate our lives.

References

Bromberg, P. M. (1998). *Standing in the spaces: Essays on clinical process, trauma, and dissociation.* Hillsdale, NJ: The Analytic Press.

Buechler, S. (1993). Clinical implications of an interpersonal view of the emotions. *Contemporary Psychoanalysis, 29*, 219–236.

Buechler, S. (1995). Emotion. In M. Lionells, J. Fiscalini, C. H. Mann, & D. B. Stern (Eds.), *Handbook of interpersonal psychoanalysis* (pp. 165–188). Hillsdale, NJ: The Analytic Press.

Buechler, S. (2001). Emotional intelligence or adaptive emotions? *Emotion, 1*, 249–257.

Buechler, S. (2004). *Clinical values: Emotions that guide psychoanalytic treatment.* Hillsdale, NJ: The Analytic Press.

Buechler, S. (2008). *Making a difference in patients' lives: Emotional experience in the therapeutic setting.* Hillsdale, NJ: The Analytic Press.

Carey, B. (2006, March 21). Major strides in fending off depression among the elderly. *New York Times*, p. F8.

Casey, N. (Ed.). (2001). *Unholy ghost: Writers on depression.* New York: Harper Collins.

Darwin, C. (1872). *The expression of emotions, in man and animals.* London: John Murray.

Didion, J. (2005). *The year of magical thinking.* New York: Alfred A. Knopf.

Ekman, P. (2003). *Emotions revealed.* New York: Holt and Company.

Frankl, V. (1985). *Man's search for meaning.* New York: Simon and Schuster.

Izard, C. E. (1971). *The face of emotion.* New York: Meredith Corp.

Izard, C. E. (1977). *Human emotions.* New York: Plenum Press.

Izard, C. E. (2001). Emotional intelligence or adaptive emotions? *Emotion, 1*, 249–257.

Krystal, H. (1975). Affect tolerance. *Annual of Psychoanalysis, 3,* 179–217.
Tomkins, S. S. (1970). Affect as the primary motivational system. In M. B. Arnold (Ed.), *Feelings and emotions* (pp. 101–110). New York: Academic Press.

4

Principles of Risk Communication

Vincent T. Covello

Introduction

Effective risk communication establishes confidence in the ability of individuals and organizations to deal with threats to that which we value. It is integral to the larger process of information exchange aimed at eliciting trust and promoting understanding.

The National Academy of Sciences has defined risk communication as

> ... an interactive process of exchange of information and opinion among individuals, groups, and institutions. It involves multiple messages about the nature of risk and other messages, not strictly about risk, that express concerns, opinions, or reactions to risk messages or to legal and institutional arrangements for risk management.

Numerous studies have highlighted the importance of risk communication in enabling people to make informed choices and participate in deciding how risks should be managed. Effective risk communication provides people with timely, accurate, and credible risk information. It is the starting point for creating a population that is

- Involved, interested, reasonable, thoughtful, solution-oriented, cooperative, and collaborative
- Appropriately concerned about the risk
- More likely to engage in appropriate risk-related behaviors

While an overarching objective of effective risk communication is to build, strengthen, or repair trust, its specific objectives vary from situation to situation. In some situations, the objective is to raise awareness of a risk or to provide people with information that allows them to better respond to a risk. In other cases, the purpose is to disseminate information on actions to take. In yet other cases, the purpose is to build consensus or engage people in a dialogue about appropriate behaviors and levels of concern.

In a crisis, disaster, or emergency, the goals of risk communication are more specific. For example, recent research (Hobfoll et al., 2007) indicates effectiveness in managing a crisis, disaster, or emergency is closely linked to effectiveness in communicating

- Safety
- Calm
- Self- and group efficacy
- Connectedness
- Hope

Risk Communication Models

Effective risk communication is based on models that describe how risk information is processed, how risk perceptions are formed, and how risk decisions are made. These models provide the intellectual and theoretical foundation for effective risk communication.

The Risk Perception Model

One of the most important paradoxes identified in the risk perception literature is that the risks that kill or harm people, and the risks that alarm and upset people, are often very different. For example, there is virtually no correlation between the ranking of hazards according to statistics on expected annual mortality and the ranking of the same hazards by how upsetting they are to people. There are many risks that make people worried and upset many people but cause little harm. At the same time, there are risks that kill or harm many people but do not make people worried or upset.

This paradox is explained in part by the major factors that affect how risks are perceived. Several of the most important are described below:

- *Trust.* Risks from activities associated with individuals, institutions, or organizations lacking in trust and credibility (e.g., organizations with poor health, safety, or environmental track records) are judged to be greater than risks from activities associated with those that are trustworthy and credible (e.g., regulatory agencies that achieve high levels of compliance among regulated groups).

- *Voluntariness.* Risks from activities considered to be involuntary or imposed (e.g., exposure to chemicals or radiation from a waste or industrial facility) are judged to be greater and, therefore, are less readily accepted than risks from activities that are seen to be voluntary (e.g., smoking, sunbathing, or mountain climbing).

- *Controllability.* Risks from activities viewed as under the control of others (e.g., releases of toxic agents by industrial facilities or bioterrorists) are judged to be greater and are less readily accepted than those from activities that appear to be under the control of the individual (e.g., driving an automobile or riding a bicycle).

- *Familiarity.* Risks from activities viewed as unfamiliar (such as from leaks of chemicals or radiation from waste disposal sites) are judged to be greater than risks from activities viewed as familiar (e.g., household work).

- *Fairness.* Risks from activities believed to be unfair or to involve unfair processes (e.g., inequities related to the siting of industrial facilities or landfills) are judged to be greater than risks from fair activities (e.g., vaccinations).

- *Benefits.* Risks from activities that seem to have unclear, questionable, or diffused personal or economic benefits (e.g., nuclear power plants and waste disposal facilities) are judged to be greater than risks from activities that have clear benefits (e.g., jobs, monetary benefits, or automobile driving).

- *Catastrophic potential.* Risks from activities viewed as having the potential to cause a significant number of deaths and injuries grouped in time and space (e.g., deaths and injuries resulting from a major industrial accident) are judged to be greater than risks from activities that cause deaths and injuries scattered or random in time and space (e.g., automobile accidents).

- *Understanding.* Poorly understood risks (such as the health effects of long-term exposure to low doses of toxic chemicals or radiation) are judged to be greater than risks that are well understood or self-explanatory (e.g., pedestrian accidents or slipping on ice).

- *Uncertainty.* Risks from activities that are relatively unknown or that pose highly uncertain risks (e.g., risks from biotechnology and genetic engineering) are judged to be greater than risks from activities that appear to be relatively well known to science (e.g., actuarial risk data related to automobile accidents).

- *Delayed effects.* Risks from activities that may have delayed effects (e.g., long latency periods between exposure and adverse health effects) are judged to be greater than risks from activities viewed as having immediate effects (e.g., poisonings).

- *Effects on children.* Risks from activities that appear to put children specifically at risk (e.g., milk contaminated with radiation or toxic chemicals, pregnant women exposed to radiation or toxic chemicals) are judged to be greater than risks from activities that do not (e.g., workplace accidents).
- *Effects on future generations.* Risks from activities that seem to pose a threat to future generations (e.g., adverse genetic effects due to exposure to toxic chemicals or radiation) are judged to be greater than risks from activities that do not (e.g., skiing accidents).
- *Victim identity.* Risks from activities that produce identifiable victims (e.g., a worker exposed to high levels of toxic chemicals or radiation, a child who falls down a well, or a miner trapped in a mine) are judged to be greater than risks from activities that produce statistical victims (e.g., statistical profiles of automobile accident victims).
- *Dread.* Risks from activities that evoke fear, terror, or anxiety (e.g., exposure to cancer-causing agents, AIDS, or exotic diseases) are judged to be greater than risks from activities that do not arouse such feelings or emotions (e.g., common colds or household accidents).
- *Media attention.* Risks from activities that receive considerable media coverage (e.g., accidents and leaks at nuclear power plants) are judged to be greater than risks from activities that receive little (e.g., on-the-job accidents).
- *Accident history.* Risks from activities with a history of major accidents or frequent minor accidents (e.g., leaks at waste disposal facilities) are judged to be greater than risks from those with little or no such history (e.g., recombinant DNA experimentation).
- *Reversibility.* Risks from activities considered to have potentially irreversible adverse effects (e.g., birth defects from exposure to a toxic substance) are judged to be greater than risks from activities considered to have reversible adverse effects (e.g., sports injuries).
- *Personal stake.* Risks from activities viewed by people to place them (or their families) personally and directly at risk (e.g., living near a waste disposal site) are judged to be greater than risks from activities that appear to pose no direct or personal threat (e.g., disposal of waste in remote areas).
- *Ethical/moral nature.* Risks from activities believed to be ethically objectionable or morally wrong (e.g., foisting pollution on an economically distressed community) are judged to be greater than risks from ethically neutral activities (e.g., side effects of medication).
- *Human versus natural origin.* Risks generated by human action, failure, or incompetence (e.g., industrial accidents caused by negligence, inadequate safeguards, or operator error) are judged to be greater than risks believed to be caused by nature or "acts of God" (e.g., exposure to geological radon or cosmic rays).

These risk perception factors determine a person's emotional response to risk information. For example, levels of fear, worry, anxiety, anger, and outrage tend to be greatest and most intense when a risk is perceived to be involuntary, unfair, not beneficial, not under one's personal control, and managed by untrustworthy individuals or organizations.

These risk perception factors are also subject to biases that affect judgments of risk. These biases include

- *Information availability.* The availability of information about an event frequently leads to overestimation of the frequency of the event. People tend to assign greater probability to events of which they are frequently reminded (e.g., in the news media, scientific literature, or discussions among friends or colleagues) or to events that are easy to recall or imagine through concrete examples or dramatic images.
- *Overconfidence.* People are often overconfident about their ability to avoid harm. A majority of people, for example, consider themselves less likely than average to get cancer, get fired from their job, or get mugged. Overconfidence is most prevalent when high levels of perceived personal control lead to reduced feelings of susceptibility. Many people fail to use seat belts, for example, because of the unfounded belief that they are better or safer than the average driver. In a similar vein, many teenagers often engage in high-risk behaviors (e.g., drinking and driving, smoking, unprotected sex) because of perceptions, supported by peers, of invulnerability and overconfidence in their ability to avoid harm.
- *Aversion to uncertainty.* People typically have a strong aversion to uncertainty concerning risks. This often translates into a marked preference and demand by the people for statements of fact over statements of probability: the language of risk assessment. Despite statements by experts that precise information is seldom available, people frequently demand absolute answers. For example, people often demand to know exactly what will happen, not what might happen.
- *Confirmatory bias.* People often seek out information that confirms their preexisting beliefs. Once a belief about a risk is formed, new evidence is made to fit, contrary information is filtered out, ambiguous data are interpreted as confirmation, and consistent information is seen as "proof."

The Mental Noise Model

The mental noise model focuses on how people process information under stress. Mental noise is caused by the stress and strong emotions associated with exposures to risks. When people are stressed and upset, their ability to process information typically becomes severely impaired. In high-stress situations, people often display a substantially reduced ability to hear, understand, and remember information.

Mental noise typically increases when people are exposed to risks associated with negative psychological attributes (e.g., risks perceived to be involuntary, not under one's control, low in benefits, unfair, or dreaded contribute greatly to mental noise). Because of mental noise, stressed and upset people often

- Attend to no more than three messages at a time.
- Process information at four or more levels below their educational level.
- Focus their attention on information they hear first and last.

The Negative Dominance Model

The negative dominance model describes the processing of both negative and positive information in high-concern and emotionally charged situations. In general, the relationship between negative and positive information is asymmetrical. In high-stress situations, negative information typically receives significantly greater attention and weight. The negative dominance model is consistent with a central theorem of modern psychology that people put greater value on losses (negative outcomes) than on gains (positive outcomes).

One practical implication of the negative dominance model is it takes several positive or solution-oriented messages to counterbalance one negative message. On average, in high-concern or emotionally charged situations, it takes three or more positive messages to counterbalance a negative message.

Another practical implication of negative dominance theory is that messages containing negatives (e.g., words such as no, not, never, nothing, and none as well as words with negative connotations) tend to receive closer attention, are remembered longer, and have greater impact than messages containing positive words. The use of unnecessary negatives in high-concern or emotionally charged situations can have the unintended effect of drowning out positive or solution-oriented information. Risk communications are often most effective when they focus on positive, constructive actions; on what is being done, rather than on what is *not* being done.

The Trust Determination Model

A central theme in the risk communication literature is the importance of trust in effective risk communications. Trust is generally recognized as the single most important factor determining perceptions of risk. Only when trust has been established can other risk communication goals, such as consensus-building and dialogue, be achieved.

Trust is typically built over long periods of time. Building trust is a long-term, cumulative process. Trust is easily lost. Once lost, it is difficult to regain.

Because of the importance of trust in effective risk communication, a significant part of the risk communication literature focuses on the determinants of trust. Research indicates that the most important trust determination factors are

- listening, caring, empathy, and compassion
- competence, expertise, and knowledge
- honesty, openness, and transparency

A host of other factors can also affect perceptions of trust. These include accountability, perseverance, dedication, commitment, responsiveness, objectivity, fairness, and consistency.

Trust can be created by a proven track record of caring, honesty, and competence. It can be enhanced substantially by endorsements from sources of information perceived as credible by the target audience. Trust determinations are often made in less than 9 to 30 seconds.

Surveys indicate that among the most trustworthy individuals in controversies involving risks include health care workers, pharmacists, firefighters, safety professionals, educators, religious leaders, and citizen advisory groups. Trust in individuals varies greatly depending on their perceived personal attributes and communication skills.

Strategies for Effective Risk Communication

These models provide the intellectual foundation for the following strategies for effective risk communication.

Strategies for the Effective Development of
Risk Communication Messages

To communicate effectively about risks, messages must be carefully framed. One of the most powerful tools available to risk communicators for developing effective risk communication messages is the "message map."

A message map is an organized means for displaying layers of information. A message map template and example are provided in Appendix A at the end of the chapter. A message map is a lens through which principles for effective risk message development can be focused into effective and powerful communication.

A message map contains detailed, hierarchically organized responses to anticipated questions or concerns. It is a visual aid that provides, at a glance, the organization's messages for high-concern issues. The message map template enables spokespersons to meet the demands of the public, the media, and other interested parties for timely, accurate, clear, concise, consistent, credible, and relevant information.

Message maps are constructed as a hierarchy of messages at increasing levels of complexity. The first layer of the map identifies the audience, or stakeholder, for the message map as well as the question or concern that the message map is intended to address.

The next layer of the message map contains the key messages, which function singularly and collectively as a response to a stakeholder question or concern. The key messages also can serve singularly or collectively as a media sound bite; sound bites are critical to successful media interviews.

The next tier of the message map contains supporting information, which is blocked in groups under the key messages. These supporting messages amplify the key messages and provide additional facts or details. Supporting messages can also take the form of visuals, analogies, personal stories, or citations to credible sources of information.

As a strategic tool, a message map affords multiple benefits. For example:

- Message maps provide a reference for leaders and spokespersons who must respond swiftly to questions on topics where timeliness and accuracy are critical.
- Message maps provide spokespersons with consistent messages that can be delivered across a wide spectrum of communication channels.
- Message maps provide a standardized, unifying framework for disseminating information about a wide range of risk issues.

When used consistently, message maps promote in multiple partners the ability to speak in harmony. Message maps also minimize chances of "speaker's regret" (regretting saying something inappropriate or regretting not saying something that should have been said).

A printed copy of a message map allows spokespeople during interviews to "check off" the message map talking points they want to make in order of their importance. This helps prevent omissions of key facts or misstatements that could provoke misunderstandings, controversy, or outrage. Message maps allow organizations to develop messages in advance for emergencies and crises. Once developed, the effectiveness of message maps can be tested through focus groups and other empirical studies.

Message maps were first developed in the early 1990s as a specialized tool for communicating effectively in high-stress, high-concern, or emotionally charged situations. Message maps were first widely adopted as a risk communication tool in the aftermath of the anthrax attacks in the autumn of 2001. For example, early in 2002, the Centers for Disease Control and Prevention conducted intensive message mapping sessions focused on the communication challenges posed by a potential smallpox attack. One product of this workshop was several hundred smallpox messages maps.

Seven steps are involved in constructing a message map:

Step 1
The first step in message mapping is to identify stakeholders—interested, affected, or influential parties—for a selected issue or topic of high concern. Stakeholders can be distinguished further by prioritizing them according to their potential to affect outcomes and their credibility with other stakeholders. For example, stakeholders in a crisis situation might include

- Victims
- Victim families
- Directly affected individuals
- Emergency response personnel
- Public health personnel (local, county, state, national)
- Law enforcement personnel
- Hospital personnel
- Families of emergency response, law enforcement, and hospital personnel
- Government agencies (all levels)
- Politicians/legislators
- Unions
- The media (all types)

- Legal professionals
- Contractors
- Consultants
- Suppliers/vendors
- Ethic/minority groups
- Groups with special needs (e.g., elderly populations, disabled populations, home bound)
- Health agency employees
- Advisory panels
- Nongovernment organizations
- Educators
- Scientific community
- Religious community
- Business community
- Professional societies
- General public

As part of this first step, stakeholders can be further distinguished according to (1) their potential to affect outcomes, (2) their credibility with other stakeholders, and (3) whether they are apathetic, neutral, supportive, nonsupportive, critical, adversarial, or ambivalent regarding issues on the table.

Step 2
The second step in message mapping is to identify a complete list of questions and concerns for each important stakeholder group. Questions and concerns typically fall into three categories: (a) overarching questions (e.g., what is the most important thing for people to know?); (b) informational questions (e.g., who, what, where, when, why, and how?); and (c) challenging questions (e.g., why should we trust what you are telling us?). Lists of questions generated for different scenarios and stakeholders are provided in the Appendices B, C, and D at the end of the chapter.

Questions and concerns for specific scenarios and stakeholders can be generated through empirical research, including media content analysis (print, radio, television); analysis of Web site material; document review, including public meeting records, public hearing records, and legislative transcripts; reviews of complaint logs, hotline logs, toll-free number logs, and media logs; focused interviews with subject matter experts; facilitated workshops or discussion sessions with individuals intimately familiar with the issues; focus groups; and surveys. Examples of potential stakeholder questions and concerns can be found in the appendices.

Step 3

The third step in message map construction is to analyze the lists of questions and concerns to identify common sets of concerns or categories of questions and concerns. These might include categories of concern, such as safety, control, economics, and accountability.

Step 4

The fourth step in message mapping is to develop key messages in response to each stakeholder question or concern. Key messages should be based on what the target audience most needs to know or most wants to know.

Key messages are typically developed through brainstorming sessions with a message mapping team. The message mapping team typically consists of a subject matter expert, a communication specialist, a policy/legal/management expert, and a facilitator. The brainstorming session produces message narratives, usually in the form of complete sentences, which are entered as abbreviated key messages onto the message map.

The brainstorming session can be used to produce keywords as a memory aid for the fully scripted key message. These keywords are then entered onto the message map. Keywords are typically more easily accessed and recalled by spokespeople than narratives and scripts. Most people have difficulty memorizing or delivering scripts; however, they can deliver agreed-upon key words using their own words to form whole sentences.

Construction of message maps is guided by the theories and principles of risk communication. For example, mental noise theory indicates that when people are upset, they often have difficulty hearing, understanding, and remembering information. Mental noise can reduce a person's ability to process information by more than 80%. The challenge of mental noise to message mapping is to (a) overcome the barriers that mental noise creates, (b) produce accurate messages for diverse audiences in diverse social and cultural contexts, and (c) achieve maximum communication effectiveness within the constraints posed by mental noise.

Risk communicators use a variety of means to overcome mental noise. For example, they limit the number of key messages offered to typically no more than three. They limit the amount of time and words used to express their three key messages to typically no more than 9 seconds and 27 words. They construct messages that are clearly understandable by the target audience. For example, message maps produced for populations in highly developed nations are typically constructed to be easily understood by an adult with a sixth- to eighth-grade education. Message comprehension can be tested in part using the readability utility contained in most word processing programs.

Studies indicate that it is crucial that key messages be concisely stated if they are offered as sound bites or quotes. Analysis of print and media coverage of emergencies and crises in the United States indicates that

- The average length of a sound bite in the national print media was 27 words.
- The average duration of a sound bite in the national broadcast media was 9 seconds.
- The average number of messages reported in both the national print and broadcast media was three.
- The quotes most likely to be used by the national news media as sound bites contained elements of compassion, conviction, and optimism.

Step 5

The fifth step in message map construction is to develop supporting facts, information, or proofs for each key message. The same principles that guide key message construction guide the development of supporting information. Supporting facts are usually developed in groups of three under the key messages. Proof points, especially when they are highly complex or technical, do not necessarily need to be included in the message map. They are often attached to the map as an appendix. In addition, proof points are often held in reserve to support a particular message if challenged.

Step 6

The sixth step in message map construction is to conduct systematic message testing using standardized message testing procedures. Message testing should begin by asking subject matter experts, who are not directly involved in the original message mapping process, to validate the accuracy of information contained in the message map. Message testing should then be done with (a) individuals or groups who have the characteristics to serve as surrogates for key internal and external target audiences and (b) partner organizations. Sharing and testing messages with partners ensures message consistency and coordination.

Step 7

The final step is to plan for the delivery of the prepared message maps through (a) trained spokespersons, (b) trusted individuals or organizations, and (c) chosen communication channels.

Once developed, message maps can be used to structure press conferences, media interviews, information forums and exchanges, public meetings, Web sites, telephone hotline scripts, and fact sheets or brochures focused on frequently asked questions.

Message maps are valuable tools for the effective communication of risk information. They ensure that risk information has the optimum chance of being heard, understood, and remembered. Message maps allow organizations to convey timely, accurate, clear, and credible information. They enable audiences to better understand issues, act constructively upon the information provided, recover more quickly from the stress of the event, and gain and/or regain trust in risk managers.

Strategies for the Effective Delivery of Risk Communication Messages

To communicate effectively about risks, messages must be carefully delivered. An example of such delivery occurred on September 11, 2001. New York Mayor Rudolf Giuliani shared the outrage that Americans felt at the terrorist attack on the World Trade Center. He delivered his messages with the perfect mixture of compassion, anger, and reassurance. He displayed virtually all the risk communication skills needed to be effective as a leader in a crisis. These include

- Listen to, acknowledge, and respect the fears, anxieties, and uncertainties of the many public and key stakeholders.
- Remain calm and in control, even in the face of public fear, anxiety, and uncertainty.
- Provide people with ways to participate, protect themselves, and gain or regain a sense of personal control.
- Focus on what is known and not known.
- Tell people what follow-up actions will be taken if a question cannot be answered immediately or tell people where to get additional information.
- Offer authentic statements and actions that communicate compassion, conviction, and optimism.
- Be honest, candid, transparent, ethical, frank, and open.
- Take ownership of the issue or problem.
- First impressions are lasting impressions.
- Avoid humor because it can be interpreted as uncaring or trivializing the issue.
- Be extremely careful in saying anything that could be interpreted as an unqualified absolute ("never" or "always"): it only takes one exception to disprove an absolute.

- Be the first to share bad or good news.
- Balance bad news with three or more positive, constructive, or solution-oriented messages.
- Avoid mixed or inconsistent verbal and nonverbal messages.
- Be visible or readily available.
- Demonstrate media skills (verbal and nonverbal), including avoidance of major traps and pitfalls; for example, speculating about extreme worst-case scenarios, saying "there are no guarantees," repeating allegations or accusations, or saying "no comment."
- Develop and offer three concise key messages in response to each major concern.
- Continually look for opportunities to repeat the prepared key messages.
- Use clear, nontechnical language free of jargon and acronyms.
- Make extensive but appropriate use of visual material, personal and human interest stories, quotes, analogies, and anecdotes.
- Find out who else is being interviewed and make appropriate adjustments.
- Monitor what is being said on the Internet as much as other media.
- Take the first day of an emergency very seriously; drop other obligations.
- Avoid guessing, check and double-check the accuracy of facts.
- Ensure that facts offered have gone through a clearance process.
- Plan risk and crisis communications programs well in advance using the APP model (anticipate/prepare/practice); conduct scenario planning, identify important stakeholders, anticipate questions and concerns, train spokespersons, prepare messages, test messages, anticipate follow-up questions, and rehearse responses.
- Provide information on a continuous and frequent basis.
- Ensure partners (internal and external) speak with one voice.
- Have a contingency plan for when partners (internal and external) disagree.
- When possible, use research to help determine responses to messages.
- Plan public meetings carefully; unless they are carefully controlled and skillfully implemented, they can backfire and result in increased public outrage and frustration.
- Encourage the use of face-to-face communication methods, including expert availability sessions, workshops, and poster-based information exchanges.
- Be able to cite other credible sources of information.
- Admit when mistakes have been made; be accountable and responsible.
- Avoid attacking the credibility of those with higher perceived credibility.
- Acknowledge uncertainty.
- Seek, engage, and make extensive use of support from credible third parties.

Mayor Giuliani particularly understood the danger in delivering unfounded or premature reassuring statements. Unfounded or premature reassuring statements are often motivated by a desire to calm the public and avoid panic and hysteria. Panic and hysteria describe an intense contagious fear among individuals. However, research indicates that most people respond cooperatively and adaptively in emergencies. Among the risk factors that cause panic and hysteria are

- The belief that there is a small chance of escape.
- Seeing oneself as being at high risk of being seriously harmed or killed.
- Available but limited resources for assistance.
- Perceptions of a "first come, first served" system.
- A perceived lack of effective management of the disaster.
- Loss of credibility of authorities.
- The lack of meaningful things for people to do (e.g., tasks that increase group interaction or increase connectedness).

One of the most important risk communication skills demonstrated by Mayor Giuliani was his ability to communicate uncertainty. He recognized the importance of the following principles related to communicating uncertainty:

- Acknowledge uncertainty in communications.
- Explain that data are often uncertain because it is hard to measure many health, safety, and environmental effects.
- Explain how the risk estimate was obtained and by whom.
- Share risk information promptly, with appropriate reservations about its certainty.
- Tell people what you believe (a) is certain, (b) is nearly certain, (c) is not known, (d) may never be known, (e) is likely, (f) is unlikely, (g) is highly improbable, and (h) will reduce the uncertainty.
- Tell people that what you believe now with certainty may turn out later to be wrong.
- Announce problems promptly.

Strategies for Effective Risk Communication With the Mass Media

The mass media includes printed newspapers and journals, television, radio, and, more recently, blogs and other Internet tools. The mass media are critical to effective risk communication. Among other functions, they typically

- Gather and spread information quickly
- Act as the public watchdog
- Set public agendas
- Attract listeners/viewers
- Reach hundreds, thousands, or millions of people
- Express viewpoints

Effective communication with the mass media can help risk communicators:

- Get information out quickly
- Reach major target audiences
- Rally support
- Calm a nervous public
- Prevent undue fear and anxiety
- Provide people with needed information
- Correct erroneous information
- Encourage appropriate behaviors

One of the challenges to effective communication with the media is that reporters typically are looking for stories that

- Attract attention
- Boost the number of readers, viewers, or listeners
- Reflect the agendas of the organization's owners or publishers
- Serve the public interest
- Advance their personal careers
- Increase viewer or reader subscriber ratings

Media stories with the following characteristics tend to attract the largest audiences:

- Disasters or other high-profile events
- Drama with personal aspects
- Controversy or conflict
- Exposure of malpractice and negligence
- Scandals
- Children adversely affected
- Situations that appear to be out of control
- Many people adversely affected
- Unexpected events
- Rapid or surprising expansion of adverse effects (the "ripple effect")

- Polarity of views
- Miracles
- Villains, victims, and heroes

Given these challenges, provided below are strategies for effective communication with the media. This list is adapted from Hyer and Covello (2007).

Accept the Media as a Legitimate Partner
Recognize that effective media communication in an emergency or crisis

- Enables the media to play a constructive role in protecting the public's health.
- Enables public health officials to reach a wide range of stakeholders.
- Enables public health officials, in cooperation with the media, to build trust, calm a nervous public, provide needed information, encourage cooperative behaviors, and save lives.
- Demonstrates respect for the media by keeping them well informed of decisions and actions.
- Establishes good working relationships with media contacts before an emergency arises.
- Includes journalists in public emergency response planning exercises.
- Is polite and courteous at all times, even if the reporter is not.
- Avoids embarrassing reporters.
- Provides information for onsite reporters on the location of electrical outlets, public telephones, restrooms, hotels, restaurants, and other amenities.
- Avoids being defensive or argumentative during interviews.
- Includes elements in interviews that make a story interesting to the media, including examples, stories, and other aspects that influence public perceptions of risk, concern, and outrage.
- Uses a wide range of media communication channels to engage and involve people.
- Adheres to the highest ethical standards—recognizes that people hold you professionally and ethically accountable.
- Strives to inform editors and reporters of agency preparedness for a public health emergency.
- Offers to follow up on questions that cannot be addressed immediately.
- Strives for "win–win" media outcomes.
- Involves the media in training exercises and preparedness drills.

Plan Thoroughly and Carefully for All Media Interactions
- Assess the cultural diversity and socioeconomic level of the target populations.

- Assess internal media-relations capabilities.
- Recognize that all communication activities and materials should reflect the diverse nature of societies in a fair, representative, and inclusive manner.
- Begin all communication planning efforts with clear and explicit goals, such as:
  - Informing and educating
  - Improving knowledge and understanding
  - Building, maintaining, or restoring trust
  - Guiding and encouraging appropriate attitudes, decisions, actions, and behaviors
  - Encouraging dialogue, collaboration, and cooperation
- Develop a written communication plan.
- Develop a partner communication strategy.
- Establish coordination in situations involving multiple agencies.
- Identify important stakeholders and subgroups within the audience as targets for your messages.
- Prepare a limited number of key messages in advance of potential public health emergencies.
- Post the key messages and supporting information on your own well-publicized Web site.
- Pretest messages before using them during an interview.
- Respect diversity and multiculturalism while developing messages.
- Train key personnel—including technical staff—in basic, intermediate, and advanced media communication skills.
- Practice media communication skills regularly.
- Never say anything "off-the-record" that you would not want to see quoted and attributed to you.
- Recruit media spokespersons who have effective presentation and personal interaction skills.
- Provide training for high-ranking government officials who play a major role in communication with the media.
- Provide well-developed talking points for those who play a leading role in communication with the media.
- Recognize and reward spokespersons who are successful in getting their key messages included in media stories.
- Anticipate questions and issues that might be raised during an interview.
- Train spokespersons in how to redirect an interview (or get it back on track) using bridging phrases such as: "What is really important to know is . ...."

- Agree with the reporter in advance on logistics and topic, for example, the length, location, and specific topic of the interview, but realize that the reporter may attempt to stray from the agreed topic.
- Make needed changes in strategy and messages based on monitoring activities, evaluation efforts, and feedback.
- Work proactively to frame stories rather than waiting until others have defined the story and then reacting.
- Carefully evaluate media communication efforts and learn from mistakes.
- Share with others what you have learned from working with the media.

Meet the Functional Needs of the Media
- Assess the needs of the media.
- Be accessible to reporters.
- Respect their deadlines.
- Accept that news reports will simplify and abbreviate your messages.
- Devise a schedule to brief the media regularly during an emergency, even if updates are not newsworthy by their standards; open and regular communication helps to build trust and fill information voids.
- Refer journalists to your Web site for further information.
- Share a limited number of key messages for media interviews.
- Repeat your key messages several times during news conferences and media interviews.
- Provide accurate, appropriate, and useful information tailored to the needs of each type of media, such as sound bites, background videotape, and other visual materials for television.
- Provide background material for reporters on basic and complex issues on your Web site and as part of media information packets and kits.
- Be careful when providing numbers to reporters; these can easily be misinterpreted or misunderstood.
- Stick to the agreed topic during the interview; do not digress.
- If you do not know the answer to a question, focus on what you do know, tell the reporter what actions you will take to get an answer, and follow up in a timely manner.
- If asked for information that is the responsibility of another individual or organization, refer the reporter to that individual or organization.
- Offer reporters the opportunity to do follow-up interviews with subject-matter experts.
- Strive for brevity, but respect the reporter's desire for information.
- Hold media-availability sessions where partners in the response effort are available for questioning in one place at one time.

- Remember that it benefits the reporter and the agency when a story is accurate.
- Before an emergency occurs, meet with editors and reporters who would cover the story.
- Work to establish durable relationships with reporters and editors.
- Promise only that which can be delivered and then follow through.

Be Candid and Open With Reporters
- Be the first to share bad news about an issue or your organization, but be sure to put it into context.
- If the answer to a question is unknown or uncertain, and if the reporter is not reporting in real time, express a willingness to get back to the reporter with a response by an agreed deadline.
- Be first and proactive in disclosing information about an emergency, emphasizing appropriate reservations about data and information reliability.
- Recognize that most journalists maintain a "healthy skepticism" of sources, and trust by the media is earned; do not ask to be trusted.
- Ask the reporter to restate a question if you do not understand it.
- Hold frequent media events to fill information voids.
- Do not minimize or exaggerate the level of risk.
- Acknowledge uncertainty.
- Be careful about comparing the risk of one event to another.
- Do not offer unreasonable reassurances (i.e., unwarranted by the available information).
- Make corrections quickly if errors are made or if the facts change.
- Discuss data and information uncertainties, strengths, and weaknesses, including those identified by other credible sources.
- Cite ranges of risk estimates when appropriate.
- Support your messages with case studies and data.
- If credible authorities disagree on the best course of action, be prepared to disclose the rationale for those disagreements and why your agency has decided to take one particular course of action over another.
- Be especially careful when asked to speculate or answer extreme or baseless "what if" questions, especially on worst-case scenarios.
- Avoid speaking in absolutes.
- Tell the truth.

Listen to the Target Audience
- Do not make assumptions about what viewers, listeners, and readers know, think, or want done about risks.
- If time and resources allow, prior to a media interview, review the available data and information on public perceptions, attitudes, opinions,

beliefs, and likely responses regarding an event or risk. Such information may have been obtained through interviews, facilitated discussion groups, information exchanges, expert availability sessions, public hearings, advisory group meetings, hotline call-in logs, and surveys.

- Monitor and analyze information about the event appearing in media outlets, including the Internet.
- Identify with the target audience of the media interview and present information in a format that aids understanding and helps people to act accordingly.
- During interviews and news conferences, acknowledge the validity of people's emotions and fears.
- Be empathetic.
- Target media channels that encourage listening, feedback, participation, and dialogue.
- Recognize that competing agendas, symbolic meanings, and broader social, cultural, economic, or political considerations often complicate the task of effective media communication.
- Recognize that although public health officials may speak in terms of controlling "morbidity and mortality" rates, more important issues for some audiences may be whether people are being treated fairly in terms of access to care and medical resources.

Coordinate, Collaborate, and Act in Partnership
With Other Credible Sources

- Develop procedures for coordinating the activities of media spokespersons from multiple agencies and organizations.
- Establish links to the Web sites of partner organizations.
- Recognize that every organization has its own culture and this culture impacts upon how and what it tries to communicate.
- To the extent possible, act in partnership with other organizations in preparing messages in advance of potential emergencies.
- Share and coordinate messages with partner organizations prior to media interviews or news conferences.
- Encourage partner organizations to repeat or echo the same key messages; such repetition and echoing by many voices helps to reinforce the key messages for target audiences.
- In situations involving multiple agencies, determine information clearance and approval procedures in advance when possible.
- Aim for consistency of key messages across agencies; if real differences in opinion do exist, be inclined to disclose the areas of disagreement and explain why your agency is choosing one course of action over another.
- Develop a contingency plan for when partners cannot engage in consistent messaging; be prepared to make an extra effort to listen to their

concerns, understand their points of view, negotiate differences, and apply pressure if required and appropriate.

- Devote effort and resources to building bridges, partnerships, and alliances with other organizations (including potential or established critics) before an emergency occurs.
- Consult with internal and external partners to determine which organization should take the lead in responding to media enquiries and document the agreements reached.
- Discuss ownership of specific topics or issues in advance to avoid one partner treading upon the perceived territory of another.
- Identify credible and authoritative sources of information that can be used to support messages in potential emergencies.
- Develop a plan for using information from other organizations in potential emergencies.
- Develop contact lists of external subject-matter experts able and willing to speak to the media on issues associated with potential emergencies.
- As part of your message, cite credible and authoritative sources that believe what you believe.
- Issue media communications together with, or through, individuals or organizations believed to be credible and trustworthy by the target audience.

Speak Clearly and With Compassion
- Be aware that people want to know that you care before they care what you know.
- Use clear, nontechnical language.
- Explain medical or technical terms in clear language when they are used.
- Use graphics or other pictorial material to clarify and strengthen messages.
- Respect the unique information needs of special and diverse audiences.
- Express genuine empathy when responding to questions about loss; acknowledge the tragedy of illness, injury, or death.
- Personalize risk data by using stories, narratives, examples, and anecdotes that make technical data easier to understand.
- Avoid distant, abstract, and unfeeling language about harm, deaths, injuries, and illnesses.
- Acknowledge and respond (in words, gestures, and actions) to the emotions people express, such as anxiety, fear, worry, anger, outrage, and helplessness.
- Acknowledge and respond to the distinctions people view as important in evaluating risks, such as perceived benefits, control, fair-

ness, dread, whether the risk is natural or manmade, and effects on children.

- Be careful to use risk comparisons only to help put risks in perspective and context, and not to suggest that one risk is like another; avoid comparisons that trivialize the problem, that attempt to minimize anxiety, or that appear to be trying to settle the question of whether a risk is acceptable.
- Give people a sense of control by identifying specific actions they can take to protect themselves.
- Identify significant misinformation, being aware that repeating it may give it unwanted attention.
- Recognize that saying "no comment" without explanation or qualification is often perceived as guilt or hiding something; consider saying instead: "I wish I could answer that. However, …"
- Be sensitive to local norms, such as those relating to speech and dress.
- Always try to include in a media interview a discussion of actions taken by organizations responding to the threat as well actions that can be taken by the public.

Conclusion

Organizations have made substantial advances in recent years in their ability to detect, respond to, and control threats to that which people value, such as their health, safety, and the environment. Many of these advances are technologically based. Mechanisms for international and global cooperation and pooling of resources and efforts have also advanced.

Despite the above, it is the communication of our knowledge of the threat and our actions that remains a significant challenge. Effective risk communication can be extremely difficult. It needs to be carefully planned and executed. Effective risk communication is essential to constructively engage and inform policy makers, experts, officials, and the public. Experiences and challenges posed by 9/11, anthrax, SARS (severe acute respiratory syndrome), and pandemic influenza underline the importance of risk communication. Communication challenges are particularly pronounced when the fear spreads faster and farther than the actual threat. One of the most effective antidotes for fear is effective risk communication.

Appendix A.

Part 1: Message Mapping Template

Risk Communication Scenario or Issue:

Stakeholders (Interest or Affected Individuals or Groups):

Question or Concern:

Key Message 1:

- *Supporting Information 1:*

- *Supporting Information 2:*

- *Supporting Information 3:*

Key Message 2:

- *Supporting Information 1:*

- *Supporting Information 2:*

- *Supporting Information 3:*

Key Message 3:

- *Supporting Information 1:*

- *Supporting Information 2:*

- *Supporting Information 3:*

Additional Supporting Information

Part 2: Sample Risk Communication Message Map

Risk Communication Scenario or Issue: **Chloramines and Drinking Water Disinfection**

Stakeholders (Interest or Affected Individuals or Groups): **Public/Media**

Question or Concern: **What Are Chloramines?**

Chloramines are disinfectants used to treat drinking water.

- Chloramines are most commonly formed when ammonia is added to chlorine to treat drinking water.
- The most typical purpose of chloramines is to protect water quality as it moves through pipes.
- Chloramines provide long-lasting protection as they do not break down quickly in water pipes.

Chloramines of greatest regulatory interest are monochloramine, dichloramine, and trichloramine.

- If chloramines are used to disinfect drinking water, monochloramine is the most common type.
- Dichloramine and trichloramine are produced when treating drinking water but at much lower levels than monochloramine.
- Trichloramines are typically associated with disinfected water used in swimming pools.

Government agencies regulate the safe use of chloramines.*

- Government agencies require water utilities to meet strict health standards when using chloramines to treat water.
- Chloramine regulations are based on the average concentrations of chloramines found in a water system over time.

---

* The drinking water standard for chloramines is 4 parts per million (ppm) measured as an annual average. More information on water utility use of chloramines is available at http://www.epa.gov/safewater/disinfection/index.html and in the 1997–1998 Information Collection Rule, a national survey of large drinking water utilities for the Stage 2 Disinfection Byproducts Rule (DBPR). Information on the Stage 2 DBPR is available at http://www.epa.gov/safewater/disinfection/stage2/.

- Government agencies regulate chemicals formed when chloramines react with natural organic matter* in water.

---

* Natural organic matter is a complex mixture of compounds formed as a result of the breakdown of animal and plant material in the environment; source: http://www.iwahq.org

Appendix B.

77 Most Frequently Asked Questions by Journalists in a Disaster or Crisis

1. What is your name and title?
2. What are you job responsibilities?
3. What are your qualifications?
4. Can you tell us what happened?
5. When did it happen?
6. Where did it happen?
7. Who was harmed?
8. How many people were harmed?
9. Are those that were harmed getting help?
10. How certain are you about this information?
11. How are those who were harmed getting help?
12. Is the situation under control?
13. How certain are you that the situation is under control?
14. Is there any immediate danger?
15. What is being done in response to what happened?
16. Who is in charge?
17. What can we expect next?
18. What are you advising people to do? What can people do to protect themselves and their families—now and in the future—from harm?
19. How long will it be before the situation returns to normal?
20. What help has been requested or offered from others?
21. What responses have you received?
22. Can you be specific about the types of harm that occurred?
23. What are the names of those that were harmed?
24. Can we talk to them?
25. How much damage occurred?
26. What other damage may have occurred?
27. How certain are you about damages?
28. How much damage do you expect?
29. What are you doing now?
30. Who else is involved in the response?
31. Why did this happen?
32. What was the cause?
33. Did you have any forewarning that this might happen?
34. Why wasn't this prevented from happening?
35. What else can go wrong?
36. If you are not sure of the cause, what is your best guess?
37. Who caused this to happen?
38. Who is to blame?
39. Could this have been avoided?
40. Do you think those involved handled the situation well enough?

41. When did your response to this begin?
42. When were you notified that something had happened?
43. Who is conducting the investigation? Will the outcome be reported to the public?
44. What are you going to do after the investigation?
45. What have you found out so far?
46. Why was more not done to prevent this from happening?
47. What is your personal opinion?
48. What are you telling your own family?
49. Are all those involved in agreement?
50. Are people over-reacting?
51. Which laws are applicable?
52. Has anyone broken the law?
53. How certain are you about whether laws have been broken?
54. Has anyone made mistakes?
55. How certain are you that mistakes have not been made?
56. Have you told us everything you know?
57. What are you not telling us?
58. What effects will this have on the people involved?
59. What precautionary measures were taken?
60. Do you accept responsibility for what happened?
61. Has this ever happened before?
62. Can this happen elsewhere?
63. What is the worst-case scenario?
64. What lessons were learned?
65. Were those lessons implemented? Are they being implemented now?
66. What can be done to prevent this from happening again?
67. What would you like to say to those that have been harmed and to their families?
68. Is there any continuing danger?
69. Are people out of danger? Are people safe? Will there be inconvenience to employees or to the public?
70. How much will all this cost?
71. Are you able and willing to pay the costs?
72. Who else will pay the costs?
73. When will we find out more?
74. What steps need to be taken to avoid a similar event?
75. Have these steps already been taken? If not, why not?
76. Why should we trust you?
77. What does this all mean?

Appendix C.

Questions Frequently Asked by Journalists During Disease Outbreaks

Listed below are questions that journalists have asked by the public and the media during disease outbreaks. These questions can be organized by grouping them according to categories or themes (e.g., clinical, epidemiological, accountability/blame, vulnerable groups, protective actions, etc.).

How contagious is the disease?

Can people be vaccinated? Will antibiotics and antiviral medicines work? How effective is vaccination, antibiotics, or antiviral medicines for those with the disease? How effective is vaccination, antibiotics, or antiviral medicines for those who do not have the disease?

What are the signs and symptoms of the disease?

Who is in charge of the disease control effort? Are all efforts being coordinated?

Is the outbreak due to terrorism? Has the disease been "weaponized"? How certain are you that it is not a deliberate release? What if the disease is a genetically altered strain that is resistant to any known medical treatment?

What makes you think that the disease control strategies of the past will work today?

What's being done to stop the spread of the disease?

What kind of medical care is available to the population at risk? Are there enough medical care facilities? What happens if these care facilities are overwhelmed by demand?

What resources are being used to respond to the disease outbreak?

Can the disease be treated? How effective is treatment? Are there strains of the disease that cannot be treated?

How does one know if the vaccination, antibiotics, or antiviral medicines are working?

Are laboratories able to quickly diagnose the disease? How long does confirmation take?

How do you know that existing vaccines, antibiotics, or antiviral medicines will work?

Is the disease airborne? Waterborne?

Can people get the disease from insects, pets, farm animals, and wild animals?

What are authorities in nonaffected areas doing to prepare for an outbreak?

How is the vaccine made? How are the antibiotics and antiviral medicines made? Is there enough vaccine, antibiotics, or antiviral medicine for everyone who wants them? Who will pay for vaccines, antibiotics, or antiviral medicines?

How will vaccines, antibiotics, and antiviral medicines be distributed? How much time will be needed? Where can people be vaccinated, get antibiotics, or get anti-viral medicines? If there is a shortage, who will get priority? Who will make these decisions?

What should people do if they think they have the disease?

Do you recommend that people get vaccinated, take antibiotics, or take antiviral medicines now? How long does protection last?

Is the vaccine, antibiotic, or antiviral medicine licensed and approved? What is the expiration date? Should people be concerned?

Is the vaccine, antibiotic, or antiviral medicine safe? Who should not get vaccinated, should not take antibiotics, or should not take antiviral medicines? What can these people do to protect themselves?

Who will tell people when to get vaccinated, take antibiotics, or take antiviral medicines?

Is there an adequate supply of medicines available to treat complications from getting the vaccine, from taking antibiotics, or from taking antiviral medicine?

What are the alternatives to vaccination, antibiotics, or antiviral medicine?

How safe are people who get vaccinated, take antibiotics, or take antiviral medicine?

Do you have a contingency plan if current control measures fail?

What does the contingency plan say? What is the worst case?

Who developed and approved the plan?

What is the risk to the population? How many could die?

How prepared were you for the disease outbreak?

How do you know whether the outbreak is real? Could it be a false alarm?

If people get sick from the vaccination, from taking antibiotics, or from taking antiviral medicine, who will care for their families, pets, homes, and property?

How common are side effects from vaccination, taking antibiotics, or taking antiviral medicine? What are the risks of each side effect occurring?

Can pets and farm animals be vaccinated, take antibiotic, or take antiviral medicine?

Can people with HIV/AIDS, transplants, cancer, and other causes of weakened immune systems be treated?

Can the elderly and children be treated?

What are you recommending for your own family?

How long does it take for the vaccination, antibiotics, or antiviral medicine to protect people against the disease?

Are there people who will not be protected even after getting vaccinated, taking antibiotics, or taking antiviral medicine? How many people are in this category? What are their options?

How can people keep the disease from spreading to others?

Will people be forced to be vaccinated, take antibiotics, or take antiviral medicine?

Will infected people be isolated or quarantined?

How long will quarantine and isolation last?

What are the legal bases for quarantine and isolation?

How effective is quarantine and isolation for preventing spread of the disease?

How will bills be paid while people are in quarantine or isolation?

How will people get healthcare, water, food, and other services while in quarantine or isolation?

Where will people in quarantine or isolation be put?

Will people in quarantine or isolation be isolated from each other?

Under what circumstances will people be put in quarantine or isolation?

What are the legal rights of a person who is quarantined or isolated?

Are there alternatives to quarantine and isolation?

How is quarantine or isolation done?

What is life like in quarantine or isolation?

Under what circumstances would a large-scale quarantine or isolation effort be started?

If someone becomes sick in quarantine or isolation, who will care for them? How good will the medical care be?

Will people in quarantine or isolation be able to communicate with family and friends?

Will a person's job be protected while in quarantine or isolation?

What happens to people who refuse to be quarantined or isolated?

Can people get sick when in quarantine or isolation?

What happens if someone dies in quarantine or isolation?

What happens to facilities after they are used for quarantine or isolation?

Can people bring their pets, family, and friends into a quarantine or isolation facility?

Can a community refuse to have a quarantine or isolation facility located nearby?

How will quarantine and isolation affect community life, including transportation?

Are there differences of opinion among experts about the need for and effectiveness of quarantine or isolation procedures?

After release from quarantine or isolation, will people be able to go back to work?

What are the personal, family, and job consequences for people in quarantine/isolation?

In quarantine or isolation, will special provisions be made for cultural, religious, and ethnic beliefs and values?

Who will pay the costs for quarantine or isolation?

Who will pay the costs for lost wages of people in quarantine or isolation?

Appendix D.

50 Most Frequently Asked Questions by Terminally Ill Patients

1. How long do I have to live?
2. Are you sure about your diagnosis?
3. How much pain and suffering will I experience?
4. Is there anything that can be done to prolong my life?
5. Are there any experimental programs I might be able to join?
6. What exactly will happen to my body?
7. Is there any hope?
8. You can't be serious?
9. What's next?
10. How did this happen?
11. If you are not sure of the cause, what is your best guess?
12. Is my condition contagious? Can I spread it to others?
13. Is my condition hereditary?
14. Is there something I did that caused this? Am I to blame?
15. When did my illness begin?
16. How much will medical treatment cost: medicines, nursing home, hospital care, doctors, tests?
17. Will my health insurance cover the costs of medical treatment?
18. Are there medicines I can take?
19. What are the side effects of the medicine?
20. Are there any experimental programs or clinical trials related to this illness?
21. How do I get enrolled in an experimental program or clinical trial?
22. How much will it cost me to join an experimental program or clinical trial?
23. Is there research currently being done in this area?
24. Is there anything good you can tell me?
25. Is there any immediate threat of dying?
26. Are there medicines I will be able to take to relieve any pain?
27. What would you advise me to do next?
28. Should I tell my family?
29. Should I tell my coworkers and boss?
30. What should I tell others?
31. When should I tell others?
32. Who else knows about this?
33. Can I get a second opinion?
34. What will happen to my body and mind? Will they waste away?
35. What will be my quality of life near the end?

36. Will I be conscious at the end?
37. Can I stay at home near the end?
38. Can I be with my family at the end?
39. Will I need to go to a hospital or nursing home? If so, when?
40. What else can go wrong?
41. Why did God do this to me?
42. How would you recommend I spend my remaining time?
43. Will you assist me if I want to end my life?
44. Is there anything you are not telling me?
45. What is the worst-case scenario?
46. What is the best-case scenario?
47. Have you treated people with similar illnesses?
48. How can I find out more about my illness?
49. Who will take care of [my family, my pet, my business] … ?
50. Why me?

References

Hobfoll, S., Watson, P., Bell, C. C., Bryant, R. A., Brymer, M. J., Friedman, M. J., et al. (2007). Five essential elements of immediate and mid-term mass trauma intervention: Empirical evidence. *Psychiatry, 70*(4), 283–315.

Hyer, R., & Covello, V. T. (2007). *Effective media communication during public health emergencies: A World Health Organization handbook.* Geneva: World Health Organization.

Bibliography

Aufder Heide, E. (2004). Common misconceptions about disasters: Panic, the "disaster syndrome," and looting. In M. O'Leary (Ed.), *The first 72 hours: A community approach to disaster preparedness* (pp. 340–380). Lincoln, NB: iUniverse Publishing.

Bennett, P., & Calman, K. (Eds.). (1999). *Risk communication and public health.* New York: Oxford University Press.

Bennett, P., Coles, D., & McDonald, A. (1999). Risk communication as a decision process. In P. Bennett & K. Calman (Eds.), *Risk communication and public health.* New York: Oxford University Press.

Blendon, R. J., Benson, J. M., DesRoches, C. M., Raleigh, E., & Taylor-Clark, K. (2004). The public's response to severe acute respiratory syndrome in Toronto and the United States. *Clinical Infectious Diseases, 38,* 925–931.

Brunk, D. (2003). Top 10 lessons learned from Toronto SARS outbreak: A model for preparedness. *Internal Medicine News, 36*(21), 4.

Cava, M., Fay, K., Beanlands, H., McCay, E., & Wignall, R. (2005). Risk perception and compliance with quarantine during the SARS outbreak (severe acute respiratory syndrome). *Journal of Nursing Scholarship, 37*(4), 343–348.

Centers for Disease Control and Prevention. (2002). *Emergency and risk communication.* Atlanta/Author.

Chess, C., Hance, B. J., & Sandman, P. M. (1986). *Planning dialogue with communities: A risk communication workbook.* New Brunswick, NJ: Rutgers University, Cook College, Environmental Media Communication Research Program.

Covello, V. T. (2003). Best practice in public health risk and crisis communication. *Journal of Health Communication, 8*(Suppl. 1), 5–8.

Covello, V. T. (2005). Risk communication. In H. Frumkin (Ed.), *Environmental health: From global to local* (pp. 988–1008). San Francisco: Jossey-Bass/Wiley.

Covello, V. T. (2006). Risk communication and message mapping: A new tool for communicating effectively in public health emergencies and disasters. *Journal of Emergency Management, 4*(3), 25–40.

Covello, V. T., & Allen, F. (1988). *Seven cardinal rules of risk communication.* Washington, DC: U.S. Environmental Protection Agency.

Covello, V. T., Clayton, K., & Minamyer, S. (2007). *Effective risk and crisis communication during water security emergencies: Summary report of EPA sponsored message mapping workshops.* (EPA Report No. EPA600/R-07/027). Cincinnati, OH: National Homeland Security Research Center, U.S. Environmental Protection Agency.

Covello, V. T., McCallum, D. B., & Pavlova, M. T. (Eds.). (1989). *Effective risk communication: The role and responsibility of government and nongovernment organizations.* New York: Plenum Press.

Covello, V. T., Peters, R., Wojtecki, J., & Hyde, R. (2001). Risk communication, the West Nile virus epidemic, and bio-terrorism: Responding to the communication challenges posed by the intentional or unintentional release of a pathogen in an urban setting. *Journal of Urban Health, 78*(2), 382–391.

Covello, V. T., & Sandman, P. (2001). Risk communication: Evolution and revolution. In A. Wolbarst (Ed.), *Solutions to an environment in peril* (pp. 164–178). Baltimore, MD: Johns Hopkins University Press.

Covello, V. T., Slovic, P., & von Winterfeldt, D. (1986). Risk communication: A review of the literature. *Risk Abstracts, 3*(4), 171–182.

Cutlip, S. M., Center, A. H., & Broom, G. M. (1985). *Effective public relations* (6th ed.). Upper Saddle River, NJ: Prentice-Hall.

Douglas, M., & Wildavsky, A. (1982). *Risk and culture: An essay on the selections of technological and environmental dangers.* Berkeley, CA: University of California Press.

Embrey, M., & Parkin, R. (2002). Risk communication. In M. Embrey, R.T. Parlain, & J.M. Balbus (Eds.), *Handbook of CCL microbes in drinking water.* Denver, CO: American Water Works Association.

Fischhoff, B. (1995). Risk perception and communication unplugged: Twenty years of progress. *Risk Analysis, 15*(2), 137–145.

Hance, B. J., Chess, C., & Sandman, P. M. (1990). *Industry risk communication manual.* Boca Raton, FL: CRC Press/Lewis Publishers.

Kahneman, D., Slovic, P., & Tversky, A. (Eds.). (1982). *Judgment under uncertainty: heuristics and biases.* New York: Cambridge University Press.

Kahneman, D., & Tversky, A. (1979). Prospect theory: An analysis of decision under risk. *Econometrica, 47*(2), 263–291.

Kasperson, R. E., Renn, O., Slovic, P., Brown, H. S., Emel, J., Goble, R., et al. (1987). The social amplification of risk: A conceptual framework. *Risk Analysis, 8,* 177–187.

Lundgren, R. & McKakin, A. (2004). *Risk communication: A handbook for communicating environmental, safety, and health risks* (3rd ed.). Columbus, OH: Batelle Press.

McKechnie, S., & Davies, S. (1999). Consumers and risk. In P. Bennet (Ed.), *Risk communication and public health* (p. 170). Oxford, UK: Oxford University Press.

Morgan, M. G., Fischhoff, B., Bostrom, A., & Atman, C. J. (2001). *Risk communication: A mental models approach.* Cambridge, UK: Cambridge University Press.

National Research Council (1989). *Improving risk communication.* Washington, DC: National Academy Press.

National Research Council. (1996). *Understanding risk: Informing decisions in a democratic society.* Washington, DC: National Academy Press.

Peters, R., McCallum, D., & Covello, V. T. (1997). The determinants of trust and credibility in environmental risk communication: An empirical study. *Risk Analysis, 17*(1), 43–54.

Sandman, P. M. (1989). Hazard versus outrage in the public perception of risk. In V. T. Covello, D. B. McCallum, & M. T. Pavlova (Eds.), *Effective risk communication: The role and responsibility of government and non-government organizations* (pp. 45–49). New York: Plenum Press.

Slovic, P. (1987). Perception of risk. *Science, 236*, 280–285.

Slovic, P. (Ed.). (2000). *The perception of risk.* London: Earthscan Publication.

Stallen, P. J. M., & Tomas, A. (1988). Public concerns about industrial hazards. *Risk Analysis, 8*, 235–245.

Weinstein, N. D. (1987). *Taking care: Understanding and encouraging self-protective behavior.* New York: Cambridge University Press.

5

Ethical and Legal Considerations in Postdisaster Interdisciplinary Collaborations

Anand Pandya

Introduction

Although a breakdown of communication represents one of the greatest problems in the chaos that follows disasters, the solution is not just to open up the floodgates of unrestricted sharing. It is important to recognize a more complex challenge to properly fine tune communication in a way that respects the autonomy of individuals, the rights of privacy, and the obligations of confidentiality and privilege. This chapter will elucidate these related, but distinct, concepts and describe how a lack of attention to these issues can lead to problems despite the best of intentions.

The author has worked in the aftermath of a variety of disasters beginning in 1998, when I responded to the crash of Swissair Flight 111. Later that year, I cofounded Disaster Psychiatry Outreach, a nonprofit organization dedicated to alleviating suffering in the aftermath of disaster through the expertise and good will of psychiatrists. I have subsequently helped organize the Disaster Psychiatry Outreach response to a large number of disasters including the crash of EgyptAir Flight 990 in 1999, the crash of American Airlines Flight 587 in 2001, the 9/11 attacks (including multiple sites around New York City), the South Asian tsunami of 2005, and Hurricane Katrina in 2005. Because Disaster Psychiatry Outreach is a profession-specific organization and because any reasonable disaster response requires collaboration between many different disciplines, our organization has spent a tremendous amount of time and effort in developing relationships with the other organizations that may be active as well in the aftermath of disasters. This chapter is based largely on the lessons learned from these collaborations as well as the author's training as a forensic psychiatrist.

In my experience as a disaster responder, by far the largest obstacle to effective response has been a lack of communication between different providers. Altogether too often, the rapid development of systems to respond to disasters fails to consider the range of individuals who are either active in the disaster or should be active in the disaster. Systems that traditionally work effectively in parallel without tremendous communication, such as the worlds of psychiatry and the clergy, are more likely to underestimate than overestimate the need for cross-referrals. This tendency can be exacerbated by competitive instincts that are activated by the disaster and a lack of familiarity or comfort with the areas of overlap and complementarity between these fields.

Practical Correlations

The result of communication failure can lead to substantial ethical, if not legal liabilities. The following three vignettes suggest the range of liability that can occur from such poor coordination:

Vignette 1

After a hurricane in a nearby town, a church decides to convert its basement into a temporary shelter for those who have lost their homes. Reverend Jones organizes members of the congregation to provide various services and to stay available at the church basement around the clock. Other local organizations began offering the church aid, including food, spare clothes, and daycare services for the children; and the local emergency management agency arranges a system of transportation to get people from the shelter to the local FEMA office. Rev. Jones set strict rules concerning the use of drugs and alcohol in the building or on the ground. One night, a man who appears drunk is asked to leave the building. It soon becomes clear that the person believes that he is having an argument with the President of the United States about the hurricane. He believes that the president is watching and listening to him from a satellite. The man is malodorous and drooling, and the volunteer who is in charge in the church basement concludes that this man is not drunk but quite disturbed. So, instead of being asked to leave, an ambulance is called to refer the person to a local hospital where they may be able to provide care for the individual. An hour later, the hospital calls and says that there are no psychiatric beds available in the county because of hurricane-related closures. They suggest that someone from the church should come and pick up the person. Instead, a member of the congregation who was coordinating activities at the shelter suggests that the person would be better suited at some shelter that is designed for people with severe mental illness. A week later, a newspaper publishes a story about how the church violated the Americans with Disabilities Act by not allowing individuals with mental illness to stay at their shelter.

Whether or not the person with mental illness in this vignette has a right to sue the church is less relevant. The negative effect of the publicity can be far worse than any actual monetary consequences of a suit. Several elements common to many disasters are highlighted in this vignette. First, the development of informal collaborations between public and private organizations can blur the distinction of who has responsibility for different services. Because the local government emergency management agency was arranging transportation to and from the FEMA office, the evacuees staying at the church may have developed expectations that this volunteer-run activity was somehow responsible for providing services that the church itself could not provide. Because the shelter was a new creation after a disaster, it is unlikely that Rev. Jones took the time to consult local shelters to find out how to frame rules that were considered nondiscriminatory. It is unlikely that Rev. Jones was aware of what resources were available for individuals with serious mental illness. After Hurricane Katrina, in at least one church in Baton Rouge that provided temporary shelter to evacuees from New Orleans, the local clergy discovered that there were effectively no inpatient mental health services available for individuals who were psychotic.

Because many disaster-response initiatives and many faith-based organizations rely on volunteers initially, there can be a diffusion of responsibility within an organization. The person who advised the ill individual in this vignette to go to the emergency room may not have been the person who answered the telephone when the hospital wanted to send the patient back. If the local community of disaster responders had held a meeting to discuss how to manage individuals with physical and mental illness, it is quite possible that Rev. Jones would have gone. But how likely would it be for that information to have been effectively communicated to all the individuals managing the church response every day of the week and on nights and weekends?

Vignette 2

To address the bad publicity from the newspaper coverage in Vignette 1, Rev. Jones reached out to a local psychiatric clinic and one psychiatrist there. Dr. Katz agreed to come every evening for 2 hours to help with any psychiatric issues that developed among the hurricane survivors. Over time, Dr. Katz and Rev. Jones developed a good system where different volunteers would tell Rev. Jones about people who were frequently crying or unable to sleep. Rev. Jones initially talked to these individuals and encouraged them to speak to Dr. Katz and many of them did. However, Rev. Jones was especially concerned about one lady staying in the church. The lady was a successful lawyer before the hurricane, but she lost all of her property and her firm had shut down. She would often talk about how life was not worth living since she lost her home and her job. Members of the congregation were worried that she may actually try to hurt herself as she has taken overdoses in the past. She would never go to see Dr. Katz, instead saying that the best thing that Rev. Jones could do was to pray with her. Rev. Jones did this for a week with an agreement that if she did not feel differently at the end of the week, the lady would speak to Dr. Katz. On the sixth day, the lawyer took an overdose. Rev. Jones felt manipulated and betrayed. He informed her that he felt that she would need to go to a hospital right away. The lawyer informed him that she would go on her own, but Rev. Jones did not trust her so do so, given her recent unpredictability. Instead, Rev. Jones decides to call 911. As he hung up the phone, the lawyer announced that he violated Priest–Penitent Privilege and that she would sue him for betraying her trust.

Although this is a bad situation that everyone would want to avoid, Rev. Jones in this vignette should not be intimidated by the claim of Priest–Penitent Privilege here. There is always an exception made to clergy privilege when revealing information is necessary to protect their counselees. (Also, child abuse laws preempt clergy privilege.) Privilege refers to the right of individuals to prevent certain information revealed in confidence from being revealed to the legal system. The information that a member of a congregation shares with a pastor, the information that a patient shares with a doctor or therapist, and the information that a client shares with a lawyer may all be privileged under certain circumstances. However, Rev. Jones was not disclosing information to the legal system. Therefore, this is not an issue of privilege at all. It is an issue of *confidentiality*, a different term that is often confused with privilege. Confidentiality refers to the legal and ethical obligations to not share information. Confidentiality is far broader than privilege and restricts information from being disclosed in almost all circumstances except for a few exceptions. The laws governing confidentiality may vary from jurisdiction to jurisdiction, but federal law, including the Health Insurance Portability and Accountability Act (HIPAA), provides a uniform set of protections for medical information. Although HIPAA only applies to certain broadly defined covered entities, it is increasingly becoming a universal standard that may be expected of medical records in other situations, even when it is not strictly required. However, HIPAA does not prevent individuals who are not providing any form of medical care from contacting medical personnel, and it also has exceptions for necessary disclosures to ensure safety in emergencies. Calling 911 would be such an emergency, so even if Dr. Katz had seen this patient, he would have been allowed to violate her confidentiality to get help after an overdose.

However, it is important to remember that disasters are not inherently assumed to be emergencies. Individuals retain both an expectation and legal protection to their privacy even after a disaster. As with Vignette 1, even though a lawsuit would unlikely be successful in this circumstance, we all would want to avoid this conflict. Aside from any legal obligations, we all would feel an ethical obligation not to betray the trust of individuals who we are attempting to help and who may be less likely to get necessary help in the future. This risk could be decreased if Rev. Jones created explicit expectations about how he can help and when he will need to bring in others. Having those explicit discussions are especially difficult after a disaster when there is an urge to be flexible and accommodating with people who are suffering.

Rev. Jones may have a separate concern about whether he is liable for charges of malpractice by not getting psychiatric help for the lawyer earlier. Such liability would be more clearly defined if his work with this lawyer was defined as pastoral counseling. Although most clergy develop a comfort zone dealing with a broad range of issues, empathy for victims and the urge toward heroism after a disaster may lead some pastoral counselors to stretch themselves into areas where they do not have expertise. In general, we all may have the wish to believe that we can solve things on our own, and, after a disaster when we may feel especially vulnerable, we may be especially likely to try to do whatever we can, rather than sticking to traditional boundaries. Also, because responders are often acting as volunteers and because of a positive sense of community that can develop after disasters, many may assume that there is very limited liability in these situations. However, it is important to remember that disasters are tremendously litigious situations in the United States. When disasters are the result of intentional acts (as with crimes and terrorism) or potential negligence (as with airplane crashes or industrial accidents), the victims are likely to seek redress in a court of law at some point. Even after natural disasters, it is common for victims to use lawyers to seek compensation from FEMA and insurance companies. Although most responders may not have significant direct liability, the impression may remain that all responders have some access to resources that can help a disaster victim, and thus they may all be perceived as "deep pockets" in a lawsuit-fishing expedition. At the very least, responders may expect to receive subpoenas when victims are asked to substantiate their degree of loss and suffering.

Vignette 3

Rev. Jones and Dr. Katz fine-tuned their system of referrals to avoid the problem in Vignette 2. When Rev. Jones is especially concerned about whether a survivor will see Dr. Katz, the Reverend arranges to directly introduce Dr. Katz to the survivor, thus avoiding the situation where he is left holding all the responsibility for individuals who may be deteriorating. Sometimes, Rev. Jones is able to give Dr. Katz substantial information about a person who is staying at the church and is having a problem. In one case, Dr. Katz and Rev. Jones were able to strategize on how to help a mother who was reluctant to get help for herself. The mother was concerned about the nightmares that her 10-year-old son was having, but wouldn't seek help for her own growing problems with alcohol since the hurricane. Dr. Katz agreed to meet with the mother to answer questions about her son and was eventually able to develop enough trust so that the mother could open up about her alcohol problem. A week later, the mother and son disappeared for a day and Rev. Jones called Dr. Katz to inform him. Dr. Katz called back to reassure him that they were able to visit with the son's father while his second wife was away on business. Rev. Jones was surprised to learn that the father was still alive because the mother had implied that she was widowed. When she returned to the shelter a few days later, Rev. Jones expressed his happiness that she has been doing so well and that her son was able to see his father after such a long time. He immediately realized from the look on her face that he should not have said that.

In many ways, Vignette 3 represents a good collaborative relationship between a mental health professional and a pastor. They were working as a team, but technically, there was an important wall of confidentiality that Dr. Katz needed to maintain once he developed a doctor–patient relationship. When doing outreach work after a disaster, the beginning of such a doctor–patient relationship can seem blurry. Doctors who may be comfortable working collaboratively with other disciplines within their hospitals or clinics may forget that, while their coworkers in a medical setting are all permitted to share information within a circle of confidentiality, these same rules do not apply to fellow disaster responders. In this case, the patient may have a legitimate basis for a legal claim against the doctor for sharing information about her private life without her permission.

Conclusion

In each of these three vignettes, bad outcomes resulted from some form of communication problem. In the first case, a plan for communication between the church and mental health professionals could have avoided the misperception of discrimination. In the second and third cases, survivors felt betrayed by communications from a pastor to a psychiatrist and from psychiatrist to a pastor. Thus, we must not only learn how to communicate more, but also how to communicate wisely. Because confidentiality standards and standards of care vary by jurisdiction and vary over time, there is no one perfect resource to determine whether something is legal and ethical. Even when certain practices are generally accepted as legal and ethical (as in Vignette 2), there is no guarantee that a dissatisfied individual won't create tremendous anxiety and disruption. Consider using the Internet for up-to-date rules about laws in your area. However, another resource that should be considered is your own nondisaster standard practice. How would you handle such a situation if this were not a disaster? All too often we assume that a disaster suspends all the rules when, in fact, the rules become more important than ever.

How important are these considerations? The bottom line is that there have not been systematic studies on how frequently these legal problems arise. This may prove an important area for future research. In the meanwhile, communication and an awareness of these issues is the best way to reduce distress, liability, and other bad outcomes.

For Further Study

The information provided above concerning HIPAA and the meaning of different legal terminology is based on common information available from legal dictionaries and federal Web sites. Recommended further reading in this area includes

Appelbaum, P. S., & Gutheil, T. G. (2000). *Clinical handbook of psychiatry and the law* (3rd ed.). New York: Lippincott Williams and Wilkins.
Bullis, R. K., & Mazur, C. S. (1993). *Legal issues and religious counseling.* Louisville, KY: Westminster/John Knox Press.

6

The Psychospiritual Impact of Disaster
An Overview

J. Irene Harris, Susan Thornton, and Brian Engdahl

Introduction

A most ancient and familiar story of people's struggle with faith and meaning in the face of disaster is the Book of Job. In the story, a righteous and exemplary patriarch is smitten by a series of disasters, which rob him of his property and livelihood, take his sons and daughters and families, cover him with sores and illness, and call into question his faith. He cries out to his God and struggles to make meaning of his suffering. His wife responds differently and is ready to abandon faith altogether. His friends, on the other hand, urge him, argue with him, and badger him to recognize his own sin that has brought on these disasters. Job maintains his integrity and his relationship with God. While the characters in the story come from a shared religious tradition, each individual has a different faith response to this experience of disaster.

The story is echoed throughout history and in contemporary culture. Following the destruction of the World Trade Center Twin Towers on 9/11/01, 90% turned to their faith to cope (Schuster et al., 2001). Just as those represented in the story of Job reflect varied perspectives on spirituality and disaster, research in the psychology of spirituality documents varied spiritual responses to adversity and trauma. Some describe their faith as helpful in coping, describing confidence that their Deity cares about them and will provide resources for recovery (Pargament, Koenig, Tarakeshwar & Hahn, 2002, 2004a; Strawbridge et al., 1998). Others report that their faith makes no difference in their adjustment, and still others indicate that they find their faith as a hindrance in their recovery from the trauma, viewing the incident as an expression of God's wrath or proof that a benevolent, omnipotent Deity does not exist (Elliott, 1994; Falsetti, Resick, & Davis, 2003; Fitchett, Rybarczyk, DeMarcoo, & Nicholas, 1999; Fontana & Rosenheck, 2004; Pargament et al., 2002, 2004b; Strawbridge et al., 1998).

Disasters affect communities by overwhelming their capacity to address physical and emotional needs, by destroying resources, disrupting important attachments and relationships, threatening safety, and exceeding individual and community capacity to make meaning of the events (Hobfoll et al., 2007). Most mental health research has been on the negative mental health outcomes of disaster, such as posttraumatic stress disorder, depression, and alcohol abuse (Bonanno, 2004; Brewin, Andrews, & Valentine, 2000; Kessler, Sonnegar, Bromet, Hughes, & Nelson, 1995; Ozer, Best, Lipsey, & Weiss, 2003). From the perspective of many faith communities, disaster may be viewed not only as a loss and target for problem solving but also as a challenge that can inspire growth and foster improved functioning, or "posttraumatic growth." Such growth is characterized by perceiving oneself as resilient, having more meaningful relationships with others, developing an increased appreciation for life, and experiencing enhanced spirituality (Tedeschi & Calhoun, 1996).

Background and Data

The authors for this chapter represent clinicians and a clinically trained chaplain who are involved in care of combat veterans and have both personal and professional experience with other types of disasters, including tornados, workplace violence, and a bridge collapse. Our work has involved research designed to identify aspects of spirituality that are associated with recovery from trauma, as well as aspects of spirituality that appear to *hinder* recovery from trauma. This work has grown to include the development of spiritually integrated interventions, including a program of prayer skills training to assist trauma survivors in maximizing their faith resources in recovery.

Patterns of findings in the mental health research on spirituality and trauma are emerging with increasing clarity. For example, in a study of survivors of the Oklahoma City bombing in 1995 (Pargament, Smith, Koenig, & Perez, 1998) researchers found that those accessing certain types of religious coping strategies emerged with better mental and spiritual health. These effective religious coping practices include viewing the Deity as benevolent, collaborating with the Deity in problem solving, seeking spiritual support, providing spiritual support to others, attempting to stay true to one's faith, seeking new spiritual direction, practicing forgiveness, and trying to develop a stronger relationship with the Divine (Pargament, et al., 2000; Pargament et al., 1998). On the other hand, another set of religious coping strategies were associated with reduced coping effectiveness. These strategies included viewing the Deity as punishing, attributing the stressor to the work of the devil, and viewing the community of faith as unsatisfactory (Pargament et al., 1998, 2000). Numerous other studies confirm these conclusions (Ano & Vasconcelles, 2005; Harris et al., 2008; Pargament, Koenig, Tarakeshwar, & Hahn, 2001; Pargament et al., 2004a). More importantly, they add the finding that those who experience chronic struggle or conflict in their relationship with the Divine experience poorer outcomes (Pargament et al., 2001).

Harris et al. (2008) identified two distinct religious responses to trauma. One type of response, called "Seeking Spiritual Support" was associated with higher levels of posttraumatic growth. Seeking spiritual support was characterized by the effective religious coping strategies noted above, as well as engaging in prayer to stay calm, to accept the situation, and to ask for help with coping tasks (Harris et al., 2008). The other response, called "Religious Strain," was characterized by the ineffective religious coping strategies detailed above, as well as high levels of religious fear and guilt, and feelings of alienation from the Deity. Religious Strain was associated with post-traumatic stress disorder (Harris et al., 2008). In short, research in mental health, spirituality, and disaster indicates that individuals' ways of viewing the Deity and making meaning of disaster account for different perceptions of the helpfulness of spiritual coping. This suggests that clergy, faith group leaders, and mental health professionals can effectively collaborate to assist individuals and communities in mitigating the negative psychological consequences of disaster and maximizing potential for post-traumatic growth by facilitating healthy spiritual responses to and interpretations of the event. There are many opportunities for clergy and mental health professionals to work together productively in the five essential elements of mental health disaster response: reestablishing safety, reducing emotional arousal, developing a positive perception of both individual and community capacity for coping and recovery, constructive social support, and fostering hope (Hobfoll et al., 2007).

Synthesis

Reestablishing Safety

During a disaster, access to basic resources, such as food, water, shelter, and medical care, may be disrupted. Clinics may be destroyed, travel may be difficult or impossible, and communication with clergy and mental health providers may become unreliable or unavailable. It may be possible to combine efforts to meet immediate physical safety needs with spiritual and emotional needs. For example, clergy and mental health providers can work with disaster relief providers, such as the American Red Cross and FEMA, to share the resources of the faith community; intact religious buildings may be used as sites for emergency housing, mental and physical health clinics, administrative sites for the distribution of aid, and communication centers to facilitate families finding one another. Volunteers may be recruited from within those communities. Cooperation between the faith community and sources of aid communicate to the public that those in spiritual leadership view the role of the community of faith, and the role of the Deity, as one of compassion, outreach, and help for those who suffer. Mental health providers who responded in the aftermath of Hurricane Katrina have published multiple accounts of the utility of using churches as shelters, aid distribution points, and health centers for many reasons. Churches in that area were natural settings for providing outreach, aid, and comfort to the community and became an important part of the efforts of community members to organize and assist those in greatest need (Akin-Little & Little, 2008; Smith et al., Chapter 9).

In the African American community most affected by the disaster, the church is an important community center and clergy are among the most respected leaders (Dass-Brailsford, 2008). In this situation, churches were able to address needs that were unmet by governmental responses to the disaster.

Another aspect of restoring a sense of safety is to provide accurate information about both concerns and access to resources, without rumors or catastrophized, inaccurate accounts that may exaggerate aspects of the disaster (Danieli, Engdahl, & Schlenger, 2004; Hobfoll et al., 2007). In communities that empower clergy with special respect and credibility, spiritual leaders may be the best individuals to caution survivors about attending to and spreading stories without verifying content and to assist those in the community with identifying and accessing accurate sources of information that support perceptions of safety. Clergy may have status to speak with the media to establish constructive coverage of the disaster and to collaborate with mental health professionals to facilitate use of the media and the Internet for mental health education and interventions.

Reducing Emotional Arousal

When a community faces a disaster, transient, acute distress is normal and may be adaptive in the effort to solve problems rapidly. It is important that individuals who are emotionally distressed to understand that this reaction is not "crazy" or an indication of psychopathology (Hobfoll et al., 2007). These reactions may require mental health attention if they impair basic functioning, such as eating, sleeping, and essential problem-solving tasks, but most who initially present with symptoms of post-traumatic stress disorder (PTSD) will return to normal in the coming weeks or months (Hobfoll et al., 2007). Including clergy in counseling for those with acute emotional and spiritual needs reinforces the individual's strengths and efforts toward personal growth and positive meaning-making. In many communities, seeing clergy for counseling is less stigmatizing than seeing a mental health professional and, thus, provides a means for overcoming a barrier to accessing services (Benedek, Fullerton, & Ursano, 2007; Weaver et al., 1996). Should an individual have a more protracted or serious reaction requiring inpatient care or lengthy psychotherapy, diagnostic labels may be necessary to procure funding for care. Individuals who were managing psychiatric disorders before the disaster are likely to need very specific help from mental health professionals to address stress-related symptom exacerbation, gain access to appropriate medications (which is often disrupted in a disaster), and help to cope with social and personal resource losses that affect mental health management (Resick, 2007).

Once widely practiced, Critical Incident Stress Debriefing has not fulfilled its original promise (McNally, Bryant, & Ehlers, 2003), but clergy and mental health professionals with appropriate training are positioned to provide a number of other interventions that can assist in reducing hyperarousal, including therapeutic grounding, medications, breathing techniques, yoga, imagery, meditation, and prayer (Cohen, Warneke, Fouladi, Rodriguez, & Chaoul-Reich, 2004; Foa & Rothbaum, 1998; Harris et al., 2008; Hobfoll et al., 2007; Roffe, Schmidt, & Ernst, 2005).

Research on prayer as a coping strategy indicates that those who use active coping strategies in their prayer lives emerge from stressors such as disasters with better mental health outcomes (Harris et al., 2008; Harris Schoneman, & Carrera, 2002, 2005). Clergy have opportunities to both model effective use of prayer and to assist individuals and groups to engage in prayer coping. Mental health professionals assisting clients can facilitate improvement in an individual's relationship with the Deity just as they would consider any other relationship for their clients.

It can be useful to teach survivors of a disaster about approaches to prayer that may be effective in helping them cope in the wake of disaster. While individuals from faith communities may be well versed in prayer practice, others may benefit from guidance. For example, they may consider prayer to seek assistance in accomplishing the tasks necessary to recovery from the disaster, for the ability to manage emotions well enough to help one another, for the guidance to learn and grow from this experience, and for the understanding to use aspects of the disaster to do something good in the world. Meditative and contemplative prayer practices may also assist survivors in reducing and managing stress.

Developing a Positive Perception of Individual and Community Capacity for Recovery

Use of religious communities and their resources as central points for organizing and distributing many kinds of aid does more than the work of providing aid. It also allows the individuals and groups involved to see themselves and their community as active participants in their own recovery. Mental health professionals and clergy can work together to organize groups to meet community needs. These needs may be different based on the community and disaster and may range from the distribution of drinking water to information to help rebuilding buildings. The message conveys that leaders view survivors as capable of influencing outcomes and making good recovery. This may be particularly important with children, who may feel disempowered when the adults who usually protect them could not avert danger (Hobfoll et al., 2007; Saltzman, Layne, Steinberg, & Pynoos, 2006). Groups formed to assemble hygiene kits, distribute food, organize contact information, pray for victims and survivors of the disaster, or other relevant tasks can also be provided with informal opportunities for group counseling as they work with clergy and mental health professionals joining in the task.

Building Constructive Social Support

Mental health professionals and clergy can provide opportunities for spiritual support through both formal group counseling and group activities that provide fertile ground for social support. Mental health professionals providing crisis counseling should listen to concerns about the spiritual meanings of the disaster and make appropriate referrals to clergy or chaplaincy as needed. Clergy can be trained to collaborate with mental health professionals to address negative religious coping and religious strain.

It is important to restore opportunities for the community of faith to assemble to begin seeking spiritual meaning in the disaster. This may require finding alternative sites for worship. Clergy can assist the community of faith in emerging from disaster by maintaining an intact relationship with the Deity through worship services, public memorials, and prayer groups. Clergy can model healthy approaches to using prayer to ask for assistance with the work before the community and for acceptance of the responsibility to recover and the changes this demands in the community of faith. Clergy and mental health professionals may choose to collaborate in leading small groups to allow members of the community to provide spiritual support to one another and to actively engage in prayer coping.

In communities stressed by disaster, there is an abundance of increased interpersonal conflict. Survivors of disaster may need assistance with the process of forgiveness, including forgiving the Deity or others involved in the disaster (including government and nongovernment organizations), forgiving themselves for failing to live up to their own expectations, and forgiving one another as conflicts arise. Individuals may need help in accepting their limitations as well as others' limitations.

Many spiritually committed individuals see practicing forgiveness as a serious injunction and manifestation of their faith. It is not unusual to find individuals who become distressed about their inability to forgive automatically. When clergy and mental health professionals define forgiveness as a process, rather than an event, the experience of negative emotions is no longer a reason for self-condemnation. The book *Don't Forgive Too Soon* (Linn, Linn, Linn, 1997) may be a useful resource for individuals who become distressed about their ability to forgive the Deity, the situation, others, or themselves in the wake of disaster. It may be reassuring to these believers that anger and distress are normal, that they will not resolve without time and effort, and that forgiveness can be defined as maintaining honorable behavior rather than as resolution of distress.

Providing Hope

As communities deal with the aftermath of a disaster, questions about the intentions of the Deity typically arise. For example, the impact of disaster may call into question previously held beliefs; if the Divine is benevolent and omnipotent, how could it allow such disaster and suffering? Exploring the meaning of suffering, or theodicy, is typically an important readjust-ment task for survivors of disaster. In studies of trauma survivors, certain approaches to explaining suffering have been related to poorer mental health outcomes; specifically, viewing the disaster as spiritually endowed punishment or a demonstration of Divine power and anger, attributing the disaster to one's sins, perceiving the event as a signal of the Deity's aban-donment of the believer, and relinquishing faith altogether (Pargament et al., 2003). Examples of spiritual explanations that may form the basis for hope might include perceptions of disaster as opportunities to dem-onstrate the spiritual power to make something good out of the disaster and viewing adversity as an opportunity for spiritual growth and a closer relationship with the Divine. Many clergy see discussing these concerns as an important aspect of ministry or service. Similarly, mental health professionals as well as clergy may be open to and even encourage clients to speak about these struggles. Many individuals are likely to need time, support, and opportunities to talk about their efforts to make meaning of the disaster in order to derive meanings that facilitate more posttraumatic growth and better mental health.

   In traumas and disasters, individuals and communities may be angry at a situation that is perceived to have been unjust or avoidable. In these situations, it is important for them to have safe groups or environments to deal with both their anger and the physical and psychological impact of the disaster. Some will go on to strive for positive changes, accepting the reality of what has happened and pledging themselves in a spiritual mis-sion to prevent or mitigate such events in the future.

Conclusion

Mental health research is identifying approaches to spirituality that can either help or hinder psycho spiritual recovery from a disaster. Both secu-lar and religious counselors need to be aware of the mental health implica-tions of spiritual beliefs to assist survivors in making spiritual meanings that facilitate growth and adjustment. For survivors who respond to disaster by questioning their faith or viewing the event as an indication of Divine punishment or abandonment, interventions by both clergy and mental health professionals may be helpful. Interventions and opportunities for collaboration include facilitating emergency aid for physical needs, worship and memorial services, prayer groups, mutual support and work groups, and individual counseling. Research continues on the relationships between spirituality and adjustment to trauma, and promising work is underway in interventions that will provide greater guidance in spiritual response to disasters.

References

Akin-Little, A., & Little, S. (2008). Our Katrina experience: Providing mental health services in Concordia Parish, Louisiana. *Professional Psychology: Research and Practice, 39*, 18–23.

Ano, G. G., & Vasconcelles, E. B. (2005). Religious coping and psychological adjustment to stress: A meta-analysis. *Journal of Clinical Psychology, 61*, 461–480.

Benedek, D. M., Fullerton, C. S., & Ursano, R. J. (2007) First responders: Mental health consequences of natural and human-made disasters for public health and public safety workers. *Annual Review of Public Health, 28*, 55–68.

Bonanno, G. A. (2004). Loss, trauma, and human resilience: Have we underestimated the human capacity to thrive after extremely adverse events? *American Psychologist, 59*(1), 20–28.

Brewin, C. R., Andrews, B., & Valentine, J. D. (2000). Meta-analysis of risk factors for posttraumatic stress disorder in trauma-exposed adults. *Journal of Consulting and Clinical Psychology, 68*, 748–766.

Cohen, L., Warneke, C., Fouladi, R. T., Rodriguez, M. A., & Chaoul-Reich, A. (2004). Psychological adjustment and sleep quality in a randomized trial of the effects of a Tibetan yoga intervention in patients with lymphoma. *Cancer, 100*, 2253–2260.

Danieli, Y., Engdahl, B., & Schlenger, W. (2004). The psychosocial aftermath of terrorism. In F. Moghaddam & A. Marsella (Eds.), *Understanding terrorism: Psychosocial roots, consequences, and interventions.* Washington, DC: American Psychological Association.

Dass-Brailsford, P. (2008). After the storm: Recognition, recovery, and reconstruction. *Professional Psychology: Research and Practice, 39*, 24–30.

Elliott, D. M. (1994). The impact of Christian faith on prevalence and sequelae of sexual abuse. *Journal of Interpersonal Violence, 9*, 9–108.

Falsetti, S. A., Resick, P. A., & Davis, J. L. (2003). Changes in religious beliefs following trauma. *Journal of Traumatic Stress, 16*, 391–398.

Fitchett, G., Rybarczyk, B. D., DeMarco, G. A., & Nicholas, J. J. (1999). The role of religion in medical rehabilitation outcomes: A longitudinal study. *Rehabilitation Psychology, 44*, 1–22.

Foa, E. B., & Rothbaum, B. O. (1998). *Treating the trauma of rape: Cognitive-behavioral therapy for PTSD.* New York: Guilford.

Fontana, A., & Rosenheck, R. (2004). Trauma, change in strength of religious faith, and mental health service use among veterans treated for PTSD. *The Journal of Nervous and Mental Disease, 192*, 579–584.

Harris, J. I., Erbes, C. R., Engdahl, B. E., Olson, R. H. A., Winskowski, A. M., & McMahill, J. (2008). Christian religious functioning and trauma outcomes. *Journal of Clinical Psychology, 64*, 17–29.

Harris, J. I., Schoneman, S. W., & Carrera, S. R. (2002). Approaches to religiosity related to anxiety among college students. *Mental Health, Religion & Culture, 5*, 253–265.

Harris, J. I., Schoneman, S. W., & Carrera, S. R. (2005). Preferred prayer styles and anxiety control. *Journal of Religion and Heath, 44*, 403–412.

Hobfoll, S. E., Watson, P., Bell, C. C., Bryant, R. A., Brymer, M. J., Friedman, M., et al., (2007). Five essential elements of immediate and mid-term mass trauma intervention: Empirical evidence. *Psychiatry, 70*, 283–315.

Kessler, R. C., Sonnega, A., Bromet, E., Hughes, M., & Nelson, C. B. (1995). Posttraumatic stress disorder in the National Comorbidity Survey. *Archives of General Psychiatry, 12*, 1048–1060.

Linn, D., Linn, S. F., & Linn, M. (1997). *Don't forgive too soon: Extending the two hands that heal.* Mahwah, NJ: Paulist Press.

McNally, R. J., Bryant, R. A., & Ehlers, A. (2003). Does early psychological intervention promote recovery from posttraumatic stress? *Psychological Science in the Public Interest, 4*, 45–79.

Ozer, E. J., Best, S. R., Lipsey, T. M., & Weiss, D. S. (2003). Predictors of posttraumatic stress disorder and symptoms in adults: A meta-analysis. *Psychological Bulletin, 129*, 52–73.

Pargament, K. I., Koenig, H. G., & Perez, L. M. (2000). The many methods of religious coping: Development and initial validation of the RCOPE. *Journal of Clinical Psychology, 56*, 519–543.

Pargament, K. I., Koenig, H. G., Tarakeshwar, N., & Hahn, J. (2001). Religious struggle as a predictor of mortality among medically ill elderly patients: A two-year longitudinal study. *Archives of Internal Medicine, 161*, 1881–1885.

Pargament, K. I., Koenig, H. G., Tarakeshwar, N., & Hahn, J. (2002, August 22-25). *Religious coping methods as predictors of psychological, physical, and spiritual outcomes among medically ill elderly patients: A two-year longitudinal study.* Paper presented at the annual convention of the American Psychological Association, Chicago.

Pargament, K. I., Koenig, H. G., Tarakeshwar, N., & Hahn, J. (2004a). Religious coping methods as predictors of psychological, physical and spiritual outcomes among medically ill elderly patients: A two-year longitudinal study. *Journal of Health Psychology, 9,* 713–730.

Pargament, K. I., Murray-Swank, N. A., Magyar, G. M., & Ano, G. G. (2004b). Spiritual struggle: A phenomenon of interest to psychology and religion. In W. R. Miller & H. D. Delaney (Eds.), *Judeo-Christian Perspectives on Psychology* (pp. 245–268). Washington DC: American Psychological Association.

Pargament, K. I., Smith, B. W., Koenig, H. G., & Perez, L. M. (1998). Patterns of positive and negative religious coping with major life stressors. *Journal for the Scientific Study of Religion, 37,* 710–724.

Pargament, K. I., Zinnbauer, B. J., Scott, A. B., Butter, E. M., Zerowin, J., & Stanik, P. (2003). Red flags and religious coping: Identifying some religious warning signs among people in crisis. *Journal of Clinical Psychology, 59,* 1335–1348.

Resick, P. A. (2007). Commentary on "Five essential elements of immediate and mid-term mass trauma intervention: Empirical evidence" by Hobfoll, Watson et al. *Psychiatry, 70,* 350–353.

Roffe, L., Schmidt, K., & Ernst, E. (2005). A systemic review of guided imagery as an adjuvant cancer therapy. *Psycho-Oncology, 14,* 607–617.

Saltzman, W. R., Layne, C. M., Steinberg, A. M., & Pynoos, R. S. (2006). Trauma/grief-focused group psychotherapy with adolescents. In L. A. Schein, H. I. Spitz, G. M. Bulingame, & P. R. Mushkin (Eds.), *Psychological effects of catastrophic disasters: Group approaches to treatment* (pp. 669–730). New York: Haworth.

Schuster, M. A., Stein, B. D., Jaycox, L. H., Collins, R. L., Marshall, G. N., Elliott, M. N. et al. (2001). A national survey of stress reactions after the September 11, 2001, terrorist attacks. *New England Journal of Medicine, 345,* 1507–1512.

Strawbridge, W. J., Shema, S. J., Cohen, R. D., Rogers, R. E., & Kaplan, G. A. (1998). Religiosity buffers effects of some stressors on depression but exacerbates others. *Journal of Gerontology: Social Sciences, 53B,* S118–S126.

Tedeschi, R. G., & Calhoun, L. G. (1996). The posttraumatic growth inventory: Measuring the positive legacy of trauma. *Journal of Traumatic Stress, 9,* 455–471.

Section II

Collaboration in Action: Tensions, Challenges, and Opportunities

7

Collaborating With a Community College in Post-Katrina New Orleans
Organizational and Personal Reflections

Rick Daniels

Introduction

What follows is a description of one of the most powerful experiences in my professional life. Perhaps the telling and sharing of this story will enable certain lessons to be made visible to others concerning the undertaking of collaborating with organizations that experience catastrophic disaster. This is the story of my relationship with a community college located in New Orleans, Louisiana, during the immediate aftermath of Hurricane Katrina in 2005 and which extended until the early part of 2008.

Background

To create a meaningful context for this story, it is important to provide a bit of background. The community college, prior to the storm, served approximately 12,000 students, operating from four geographical locations located within the city and the immediate surrounding areas. The college incurred tremendous loss of physical infrastructure, losing approximately 40% of its classroom space after the storm. Except for a few online classes offered by faculty members, who were at the time physically displaced, the college was basically closed but had its sights on becoming operational for the upcoming semester in January 2006. What was critical for organizational survival was the development of an ambitious plan for distance learning (designed for students who are offsite).

Prior to the storm, distance learning at this particular school was marginalized, not considered part of the mainstream. Only a few courses were offered, and those who taught online courses did so because they possessed the desire and skill. The school provided little assistance. During the fall of 2005, the school embarked on a substantive change to provide an exponential increase in distance learning courses given the substantial loss of physical classroom space. This would require a whole systems change addressing organizational capacity in regards to faculty competency, student readiness, technology infrastructure, and a culture's willingness for large-scale change.

During my initial visit in December 2005, I conversed with faculty, students, and administration to gain a sampling of experiences and perceptions about post-Katrina campus life. I attended a Substantive Change committee meeting that was tasked to explore the expansion of distance learning at the college and was asked to facilitate the session. Through this venue, I was able to gain a cross-sectional perspective of how certain factions of the college perceived the possible development and deployment of distance learning courses.

Two students approached me as I was making my way to the car in the parking lot after my third day. I was on my way to the airport to go home to Wakefield, Rhode Island. They were asking where to go to register for spring classes. These two students were standing next to a building in shambles, imploded from the storm. If a camera had taken this picture, one would see an image of destruction and renewal within the same image. This image stayed with me and continues to stay with me. It was a defining moment for me. I knew I could not leave the situation. I needed to be there to assist the rebuilding effort at the college, assisting the development of a viable distance learning strategy that can address both short- and long-term needs of the institution.

I spent over 3 years traveling from my home to New Orleans working on a pro bono consulting basis helping the development of distance learning programs that assisted in the development of organizational capacity to sustain exponential growth in this offering. Organizations, like people, can do extraordinary things in short bursts of time driven by dire need with little formal planning. Mintzberg (1994) refers to this kind of strategic thinking and action as emergent, that which is already resident in the system and can manifest itself when necessary. However, to support large, sustainable organizational change, human and structural capacity issues needed to be well thought out and executed in meaningful ways. The strategy development effort looked specifically at faculty competencies, student readiness, and organizational structure that could satisfy long-term growth and support at the college.

During the 6 months right after the storm, there was a 500% increase in online courses at the college. This was prior to any formal organizational strategy, structure, or process to support the institutionalization of distance learning. This dramatic growth preceded a well-thought-out model for both assessing and developing faculty competencies as it pertains to content development and educational delivery for the virtual classroom. Certain faculty rose to the occasion and, in many cases, with little training, took the initiative and offered distance learning courses.

In January 2005, a formal committee, the DLIT (Distance Learning and Instructional Technology) group, was created to address the strategy, structure, and process considerations. Individuals who became involved in this effort approached it from one of two perspectives. One group of individuals expressed reservations about making change as a reaction to the storm, holding onto a belief that after a certain period of time things would return to normal, and any change would make that return more difficult. The past traditions will provide a beacon, a way to sustain hope. Mintzberg (1994) suggests that formal planning is in the service of maintaining the status quo of an organization.

Review and Correlation With the Literature

Planning is fundamentally a conservative process; it acts to conserve the basic orientation of the organization, specifically, its existing categories. Thus, planning may promote change in the organization, but of a particular kind—change within the context of the organization's overall orientation, change at best in strategic positions within the overall strategic perspective. Expressed differently, planning works best when the broad outlines of a strategy are already in place, not when significant strategic change is required from the process itself. Change tends to be incremental, generic, and short term. This likely happens because incremental change occurs at the margin in limited scope and is consistent with the orientation of the organization, as is planning itself. In contrast, quantum change, which means comprehensive reorientation (Miller, 1984), disrupts all the established categories of the organization upon which planning depends. As a result, such change tends to be more resisted or more commonly ignored in the planning process (Miller, 1984).

A second group of individuals believed that massive change was the way forward in order for the organization to sustain itself. In confirmation of Mintzberg's (1994) theory of planning, this group also believed that the formal strategy work was created to slow down the emergent changes that had occurred right after the storm.

It is easy to see these two as opposing points of view; however, the challenge and the potential for positive change resides in positioning these two points of view as a constructive tension (Brown & Eisenhardt, 1998). Progressive organizations do not envision opposing points along a linear continuum, but rather they attempt to bend the line into a circle allowing these two points to touch each other. The minimal space between what were two end points are now a space for innovation and creativity. The outcome for organizational sustainability was common amongst the two groups. The imperative was to capitalize on the energy of each group, seek common ground, and bring forward the strategic offerings from each group that would serve the longer-term goal of sustainability. The group that was advocating to maintain the status quo was asked to reframe their position to the core of what is needed to sustain going forward. The group seeking massive change was challenged to think about the organizational capacity to support a large-scale increase in distance learning, in essence, balancing the long-term vision with organizational realities.

Quinn (1980) supports the notion that organizations will typically hold on to the past, as he argues that strategy is an incremental process confirming and codifying the implicit strategies residing within the organization. Incremental change supersedes transformational change, the grand ideas that are typically stated as organizational vision but are rarely achieved. Quinn (1980) commented:

> A good deal of the corporate planning I have observed is like a ritual rain dance; it has no effect on the weather that follows, but those who engage in it think it does. Moreover, it seems to me that much of the advise and instruction related to corporate planning is directed at improving the dancing, not the weather. (p. 122)

In the case of this particular college, there was little to incrementally build upon; the slate was washed clean (no pun intended). The ground was ripe for transformation. Distance learning prior to the storm was marginalized. It was now in the forefront and those who were skilled in this arena were no longer in the periphery but in the center of a critical strategic initiative.

Another tension in the system that influenced how people approached the strategy development work, somewhat contrary to the notion of constructive tension, was the schism between faculty and administration. Each facet was necessary to understand and design a whole systems solution, as distance learning touches all aspects of the college. However, these differences were seen as a barrier in both access to participate and quality of contribution. Planning meetings were held in both physical settings and virtual environments. The thinking behind this process was to accelerate the planning process by utilizing collaborative software to support planning discussions during the in-between time of physical gatherings of the planning group. It also provided an opportunity to expose individuals to distance learning technologies during the planning process.

Administration found it easier to attend the physical meetings, given that several faculty participants were teaching at the time of the physical meetings. Faculty had an easier time accessing and participating in the DLIT virtual planning environment, given their familiarity with the technology as online instructors. Faculty also expressed concerns that administrators had little experience in distance learning and, therefore, were uninformed, yet they were in a position of authority to be part of the decision-making process. Rather than focusing on these differences as diversity that could enrich the discovery, the differences were more often perceived as negative influences in moving the work forward.

This raises the consideration that at times, bringing the whole system into the room can be counter-productive. Stacey (2001) discussed the relationship of communities of practice and boundary management, in the context of what he refers to as *patching*. Patching is the organization of agents into subgroups or clusters where the number of connections between agents within a patch may be high, but the number of connections with other patches is low. This reduces the number of connections across the entire system and, therefore, tends to stabilize it enough to avoid chaotic conditions in the wider system. The system stabilizes itself by forming smaller communities. Stacey (2001) continued to point out that this dynamic has implications to organizations, as organizations tend to think of enacting policies and procedures for the whole system, or strategic planners think in terms of getting the whole system into the planning discussion, or programs need to be rolled out to the whole organization. He, therefore, contends that large-scale change and intervention may, in fact, destabilize rather than stabilize and create coherence. Rather than bringing all stakeholders into the DLIT Advisory Board structure, perhaps it would have made more sense to work with smaller subsets of the organization.

Authenticity of the work also played a pivotal role. Because many participants viewed this work as having been completed by another committee several years ago, certain participants believed that the DLIT group was formed as a political tool to demonstrate cross-functional participation to the rest of the institution, which would then possibly lead toward institutional acceptance. This perception negatively affected participation rates and participants' capacity for thinking of positive futures for distance learning. Many times, organizations convene groups to institutionalize strategies that have been already realized through emergent experience or prior strategy development activities. This typically is visible to participants and tends to disenfranchise them from the strategy experience (Mintzberg, 1994).

Another overriding dynamic visible at this time was the concept of the separation between strategic thinking and strategic planning. Mintzberg (1994) argued for a clear separation between the creation of strategic ideas and the institutionalization of those ideas into organizational process. He suggested that organizations will typically develop their strategies by going immediately to the implementation work, not taking the time to first work through strategic thinking. However, in the real world environment of this community college's strategy work, this clear delineation was not present. The strategy work was planned and architected to be respectful of this demarcation. The rules of engagement were quite explicit, and participants were frequently reminded to hold back from planning work whenever it did surface in either the physical meeting room or the online space.

This created more tension in the system as participants began to focus more on the question of why action could not be taken or began to view the thinking and conceptual work as an avoidance or getting what they referred to as the "real work" done, as evidenced by this comment of one of the participants during an interview session:

> The whole strategic planning thing, and trying to get people to participate, good luck, this is a major challenge before us. Yes, and the long term is here. This is what we are doing now. I forgot, the other day we were counting to see how we are going to proctor exams, which is going to be a nightmare. I think in the business division we have about 1,600 people in online classes. You need to deal with it now. All this conceptual stuff is nice, but hum. I was waiting to see what would happen. I guess I am waiting for direction and I haven't seen much. I need someone to tell me or e-mail me when are my final exams going to be? I have people all over the world who are supposed to be proctoring. We don't have a framework for that and that is immediate, between now and December 4th. The educational verbiage is good and fine, but it doesn't help us on a daily basis. Just like all the educational verbiage that goes on around here. That doesn't affect us.

Change goals and standards that are fine you have to do that for an educational institution. But, if I don't have a classroom, or my overhead doesn't work, or I don't have computers that work, all that stuff doesn't make a difference.

Rather than a linear progression from one stage to the next, both aspects of strategy development may need to be addressed in parallel, with each one informing the other. If participants want to and need to surface operational issues, it may be important to draw on that energy and input. Participant energy and engagement was critical to the quality of the strategy development effort. This implies that operational ideas should be captured, honored, and used in ways that make it possible to work back to strategic concepts. Conversely, if participants are offering up strategic concepts and ideas, then they should be grounded in real-world organizational implications. Strategic ideation and strategic planning need to work in an ongoing dance, each one informing the other. The real world is not so simple as to allow strategic thinking to start and stop before strategic planning begins (Daniels, 2007).

Conclusion

In conclusion, when working within an organizational system, we are working in two worlds: the organizational world and the personal world. While these two worlds are usually separated by time and place, they do influence each other. In an organizational system that is traumatized by a regional disaster, it is extremely difficult to maintain the separation of these two worlds. Individuals are dealing with issues surrounding their safety and basic necessities and are also challenged to be contributors to their organizational survival.

Shaped by both circumstance and style, individuals can and do react differently within organizations during the aftermath of a disaster. Some individuals become totally absorbed in their personal situation and are fairly absent in the day-to-day organizational efforts. Others become totally absorbed in the organization, finding a venue for creating positive change. Other individuals occupy a middle ground dealing within both worlds. As an outsider working within the system, I needed to pay attention to this dynamic. There is no right way for individuals to respond, but it was important to take notice and understand the capacity of individuals to be responsive to organizational needs.

It was important to take notice and understand individual and group orientations and capacities as they relate to serving critical organizational needs postdisaster. All individuals and groups share a desire to work toward sustaining the organization. Finding common ground and building upon the strengths that all points of view offer toward a shared desired outcome is critical during extraordinary times.

While this was a reflective piece, and lessons learned might not be generalized to other situations, perhaps the insights offered can still guide those who may find themselves in that special place, when a choice to assist is a personal nonnegotiable. At the individual level within an organizational system, understand that at times of extreme duress there will be those who will be more capable to assist, regardless of position within the hierarchy. At the organizational level, transformation is more achievable as there is less incentive to hold on to the past. Tap into the capacity of the appropriate individuals within an environment that is positioned for large-scale change. This was the post-Katrina organizational silver lining.

References

Brown, S. L., & Eisenhardt, K. M. (1998). *Competing on the edge: Strategy as structured chaos*. Boston: Harvard Business School Press.

Daniels, R. (2007). *Strategy development at Delgado Community College: The use of physical and virtual space and place—Post-Katrina New Orleans*. Santa Barbara, CA: Fielding Graduate University.

Miller, D. (1984). *Organizations: A quantum view*. Upper Saddle River, NJ: Prentice Hall College Division.

Mintzberg, H. (1994). *The rise and fall of strategic planning*: New York: The Free Press.

Quinn, J. B. (1980). *Strategies for change: Logical incrementalism*. Homewood, IL: Irwin.

Stacy, R. (2001). Complex responsive process: Learning and knowledge creation (pp. 177–178). New York: Routledge.

8

Working as an Ally to Underserved Communities
The Role of Faith, Coordination, and Partnerships in the Response to the 2001 World Trade Center Attack

Maggie Jarry

Introduction

Recovery, an increasingly important concept in mental health advocacy, is at the core of many debates in disaster work. What is recovery for one person may be different for another, and how recovery efforts reflect or reinforce predisaster inequities is a central area of concern for disaster professionals. Faith communities often channel their resources, financial and in-kind, to support the long-term recovery of disaster-affected communities. Typically, they do this by forming long-term recovery committees, otherwise know as unmet needs tables. The purpose of unmet needs tables is to consider how financial and other resources can be distributed in such a way that it does not duplicate other resources available (via the client or the community). In other words, the aid is need based, will lead to recovery (e.g., independence for the client), and does not improve the predisaster situation of the client or return the client, necessarily, to his or her predisaster level of society. In the process of assisting thousands of people from April 2002 to May 2009, participants in NYC 9/11 Unmet Needs Roundtable in New York City had many debates regarding how these principles and the philosophy of unmet needs tables should be applied.

There were days that were infuriating and there were days when the unmet needs table appeared to be the most effective tool to navigate disaster recovery. Without careful reflection, this tool can mirror or reinforce the prejudices, assumptions, and injustices of our society where the most vulnerable people are told they are not eligible for assistance. However, if used in a way that evolves with understanding of the long-term impact of disasters on individuals and how predisaster vulnerabilities lead to disaster-caused effects, unmet needs tables can be a dynamic tool to support disaster recovery in a community. When unmet needs tables are used effectively, they support the work of mental health and spiritual caregivers who then can work with people's emotional recovery because their basic needs—housing, food, medical bills—are being met.

The central question in distribution of unmet needs table aid, and disaster assistance in general, revolves around whether the individual's need is disaster caused or a preexisting condition. Imagine the following scene: In the wake of Hurricane Katrina, a woman stands on a rooftop of a house her family has owned for more than 90 years. She is African American and has lived her entire life in an area of the United States that has been neglected and poor for generations. Many of us were inundated with such images through the media after Hurricane Katrina. While much attention and discourse has been paid to the inequities of who was left or could not leave New Orleans, what many people do not consider are the questions often asked in the delivery of aid after such an event. Questions like: Is her situation disaster related or due to predisaster, systemic conditions? What is recovery for her? In some cases, a person who has experienced predisaster poverty or even a mental health diagnosis may find that developing a recovery plan will take years. The disaster survivor may find that the community expresses pity or sorrow as doors close and the survivor is told that she is not eligible for aid because her problem is systemic, preexisting the disaster, or she does not have a viable way of reaching recovery. Disaster recovery financial assistance is distributed to help a disaster-impacted person achieve a "new normal" that is not necessarily a return to or improvement of life as it was before the disaster. The subjective process of determining what is a disaster-related need, so that financial assistance can be given in support of a person's long-term recovery, is the center point of unmet needs tables and can be colored by the views of people sitting at the table.

This chapter focuses on the role of faith communities and mental health professionals in the development of financial aid assistance in response to the 2001 World Trade Center attack. With that in mind, why start this chapter with an image from Hurricane Katrina? I do so because media coverage of Hurricane Katrina helped raise America's consciousness regarding the extent that a community's predisaster situation leads to disparities in the impact that disaster will have on individual lives. However, there are few, if any, such media-generated images to summarize the invisible, underserved communities that were neglected in the immediate aftermath of the 9/11 World Trade Center attack. Many communities suffered in the shadow of the media spotlight, which focused on the families of people who died and concerns over donor intent for funds given to the American Red Cross and other major disaster recovery charities. This chapter will shed light on some of those underserved and excluded communities and how the 9/11 Roundtable became a tool for justice and aid.

So, who are the mysterious people at the unmet needs table? Who makes the decision that something is disaster or not disaster related? Often the people sitting at the unmet needs table represent faith-based, and sometimes nonfaith-based agencies, that have received donated dollars in support of the community's long-term recovery. They may be social workers, clergy, or lay people who regularly work with disaster-impacted communities. It is less likely that the people at the table will be mental health professionals; however, letters from mental health professionals on behalf of the client carry considerable weight in these discussions. Another central person at the table is the caseworker from the agency that is supporting the client in developing a recovery plan.

As well, the client participates, although they do not sit at the unmet needs table. The client is ultimately responsible for his or her own recovery and discussion at the unmet needs table, therefore, focuses on how the client's recovery plan can be supported. The person seeking assistance places an amazing level of trust in their caseworker and unmet needs table participants as they share the details of their disaster and predisaster situation, including bills, medical information, and personal history, in order to receive assistance. Depending on how information is presented and the thoroughness of case management, a request for cash assistance may be denied or accepted. In general, no one involved with disaster recovery wants to deny aid to vulnerable people, but compassion fatigue can wear down even the most kind-hearted people in disaster work and, in some cases, personal prejudice does need to be considered as decisions are made. On more than one occasion the unmet needs table that served 9/11 victims had to reflect and change its direction so that 9/11 victims we were meant to help were not arbitrarily denied aid.

Understanding the mindset and utility of these committees is imperative to mental health and spiritual care providers as they support clients who are navigating disaster aid systems. In fact, understanding the unmet needs table process can inform understanding of disaster recovery aid systems in general, as much of their criteria overlaps with American Red Cross, FEMA, and other sources of cash assistance. A shift in aid systems in the 9/11 recovery effort allowed some disaster victims to receive cash assistance as a "gift" rather than "need-based" aid, especially through the Victims Compensation program. This colored the environment of the NYC 9/11 Unmet Needs Roundtable and disaster recovery systems responding to disasters since 9/11. This, too, has led to debate among disaster professionals regarding equity and accountability in disaster recovery cash assistance. It is important to remember this concern as we focus this chapter on the role of faith communities and mental health professionals in development of the NYC 9/11 Unmet Needs Roundtable as it navigated several eras of 9/11 recovery.

Overview

The NYC 9/11 Unmet Needs Roundtable was a long-term recovery committee that existed from April 2002 to October 2008. In retrospect, the 9/11 Roundtable was one of the longest running, financially viable unmet needs tables, with the largest volume of cash assistance distributed over its lifetime compared to other tables in other disasters. While the life span of unmet needs tables can be an average of three to seven years, allowing the 9/11 Roundtable to have an average lifespan, the scope of the client populations served through this effort and the development of intensive administration systems allowed for the distribution of more dollars to individuals. The NYC 9/11 Unmet Needs Roundtable was able to inform the community at large of its work and, in doing so, made the case for continued assistance to 9/11 victims. Its administrative tools gathered aggregate data on the evolving needs of the communities being served and provided donor and caseworker accountability that built trust and appealed to new donors who wanted to help in the most effective way possible. While many agencies distributed millions of dollars to 9/11 victims, the 9/11 Roundtable stayed true to the unmet needs table tradition and painstakingly reviewed the case of individuals on a weekly basis for close to seven years. This ensured that aid was distributed based on need, not as a gift, to the most vulnerable 9/11 victims in support of their recovery.

Administrative tools developed by the 9/11 Roundtable effort included training for agency participants so that grassroots agencies and sophisticated human service organizations could have equal access to 9/11 Roundtable funds on behalf of their clients, paperwork systems to track decision making at the table so that all meeting participants could be held accountable to promises or case management suggestions made, and a database to track aid and aid requests so that evolving unmet needs could be reported back to the community in order to make unmet needs visible for advocacy efforts and continued fundraising to meet those needs. Over its lifetime, the 9/11 Roundtable assisted 4,494 families and individuals through 8,751 distinct case presentation discussions by over 80 human service agencies. To these families, slightly more than $7,340,000 was distributed from 20 donor agencies. Donors ranged from entirely faith-based donors at inception (with considerable aid from Lutheran Disaster Response, UMCOR [United Methodist Committee on Relief], the Presbytery of New York, the American Baptist and the Episcopal churches) to later gaining the support of mainstream donor agencies including the American Red Cross and Safe Horizon (formerly Victims Services).

In order to show the dynamic tool that an unmet needs table can be, this chapter reflects on the NYC 9/11 Unmet Needs Roundtable in three stages: (a) development within the 9/11 relief and short-term recovery (2001–2002), (b) scaling up to incorporation within New York Disaster Interfaith Services (2003–2005), and (c) adapting to long-term need for coordinated services when other services had ended, but new needs were emerging in the community (2005–2009).

Stage One: Development of the NYC 9/11 Unmet Needs Roundtable (2001–2002)

In the midst of the mayhem following the World Trade Center attack, hundreds of New York City's 27,474 registered nonprofit organizations responded based on their mission or expanded their vision and interpretation of their mission in order to meet the needs of people in their communities. As large and small agencies struggled to determine what their role should be, coordinative meetings expanded to include large, relief-oriented agencies and small, community-based agencies. For the general public, in the days following September 11, there were few stories covering the nuances of how "victim" was being defined and which groups were systemically excluded from aid as these definitions became codified. Many of the faith communities that typically respond to disasters—Lutheran Disaster Response, Church World Service, UMCOR—were watching the evolving landscape of aid. At first it appeared that the typical role of faith communities to provide for unmet needs and long-term recovery might not be needed as record cash donations were received. Indeed, in the first weeks of 9/11 recovery, there was a belief expressed informally between workers that there "would be no unmet needs" because of the large amount of donations received. Quickly, however, it became apparent to many that this could only be true if the definition of disaster victim was drawn so tightly that many who were clearly disaster impacted became categorized as "not direct disaster victims." Pressure from the media, especially as it attacked the American Red Cross for possible misuse of aid, and concern that aid was not being distributed quickly enough led to decisions that changed the landscape of disaster assistance in response to 9/11 and long thereafter.

Surprising to many, in the wake of the World Trade Center disaster, whole communities in New York City, many with preexisting socioeconomic vulnerabilities, found accessing disaster recovery cash assistance difficult or, in some cases, impossible. New York community-based agencies and grassroots organizations were struggling to meet the needs of people who were traumatized and increasingly depressed due to loss of jobs and fear of another terrorist attack. Clergy and lay staff of houses of worship throughout New York were also struggling to provide spiritual care despite confusion about who could be considered "direct" or "indirect" victims of the disaster. With general knowledge that assistance was being distributed at the "piers" in lower Manhattan, it took months for spiritual leaders to agree that the best use of their donated funds would be to work in collaboration through an unmet needs table. At first, there were assumptions that people would be eligible for mainstream aid. However, as Jackson Chin (personal interview, November 19, 2005) of the Puerto Rican Legal Defense and Education Fund articulated:

> What we were learning from the American Red Cross [and other agencies] was that they had very different types of criteria that then started to gel. They would say, "well, your address is above Canal Street" ... and Canal Street is not a straight line. Then all the agencies evolved to some agreement that this would be their line for who would be helped and who would not be helped. The line was drawn, but it essentially disqualified a high number of people who were within an equal distance of the World Trade Center. Because of the line, they were considered not qualified for assistance. Why is it that these people who were clearly impacted were excluded?

While this systemic exclusion of communities based on their geographic location in relationship to the World Trade Center was evolving, other concerns regarding the distribution of aid were also being discussed.

Elliot Spitzer, the New York State Attorney General, threatened to take funds away from the larger agencies, most notably the American Red Cross, Safe Horizon, and the Salvation Army, if they did not create a coordinated system for aid distribution that mitigated against duplication of aid. The most notable outcome of this threat and coordination efforts was the creation of a long-term recovery organization in December 2001 called the 9/11 United Services Group (USG) and a centralized database for case management called the Datamart.

The USG was not a long-term recovery committee; rather, it was a long-term recovery organization. This may appear to be a nuance, but there are distinct differences. The USG coordinative structure was created to manage tasks and the creation of policies between agencies, reducing duplication of services and increasing the capacity of agencies as they respond with services. Unfortunately, the only clients eligible for their case management services were those eligible for their aid, once again, individuals impacted below Canal Street. And while this resource was not led by purely secular agencies (Catholic Charities of Manhattan and Brooklyn and Queens, the United Jewish Appeal Federation, and the Salvation Army were all leading members), the role of faith communities to address unmet needs on a case-by-case basis was not incorporated in the United Services Group structurally. While the Oklahoma City unmet needs table was looked at as a potential model, there was a general sense that distributing aid on a case-by-case basis through needs assessment would overwhelm the agencies attempting to give aid. Therefore, creating, at times arbitrary, criteria that defined eligible victims and could withstand media scrutiny was considered the best route for aid distribution by these agencies.

Although the USG was an important breakthrough for disaster human services coordination, in the initial stages of implementation agencies were mandated to participate by their funder, the September 11 Fund, and almost all of the agencies involved had the same exclusionary criteria defining direct victims, and therefore eligibility and access to their programs. In time, through the leadership of Jack Krauskopf, the USG opened its doors on a functional level to include agencies participating in the NYC 9/11 Unmet Needs Roundtable. At the time that Jack took leadership of the USG, he had been a senior fellow at the Aspen Institute. But Jack had been involved in human services in New York for many years. He had been on staff when the New York City Human Resources Administration (HRA) was created in 1966 and helped create its structure, serving as special assistant to the first two heads of HRA and then as Commissioner of HRA under Mayor Koch in the early 1980's. Through his leadership, communication between agencies opened. Yet he could not overly influence the giving criteria of member agencies, many of which kept a Canal Street boundary in their criteria of "direct" victim.

In response to the evolving systems of aid distribution and in partnership with advocacy organizations like the Puerto Rican Legal Defense and Education Fund (PRLDEF) and the New York Immigration Coalition, faith communities that had received hundreds of thousands of dollars in donations began to find their individual roles in the 9/11 long-term recovery. Meetings started between representatives of Lutheran Disaster Response of New York, their case management grantee Lutheran Social Services, the New York Immigration Coalition, PRLDEF, the Urban Justice Center, and the FEMA Voluntary Agency Liaison to discuss the idea of creating an unmet needs table. As this small committee continued its meetings, strategy was discussed on several levels.

The staff of Lutheran Social Services focused on studying the case management forms used by Church World Service and UMCOR in response to other types of disasters. However, aside from Oklahoma City, this was the first time that an unmet needs table was being developed for a disaster that did not destroy people's homes, but rather their livelihood and psychological well-being. As well, in Oklahoma City many of the victims were government employees, allowing them access to different financial resources, and the number of victims and economic impact, though real, was smaller. The World Trade Center disaster in 2001 was an economic disaster, according to some estimates, destroying one fifth of the office space in Manhattan. The approach to case management, type of aid available to clients, and the concept of what a recovery plan would look like for a client had to be reconstructed.

Rather than rebuilding a roof for a family that still had a job, but whose home was destroyed by a tornado, people had to rebuild their lives after witnessing the attack and then losing their job a few days later. Thousands of people in the hotel, garment, airline, and taxi cab industries were among the first groups being told that they were not eligible for assistance because they were not "direct victims." To make this more clear, a person who lost a job below Canal Street on December 12, 2001, might have been eligible for assistance, but a hotel worker who received a letter from his or her employer on September 14, 2001, laying him or her off in midtown with explicit language that it was due to the World Trade Center attack would not have been eligible for assistance. The staff involved with developing the forms for presentation of cases at the newly forming unmet needs table had to take all of this into consideration, while the leaders in faith communities met to convince their partnering faith communities to join in this coordinated effort.

While forms were being created, the politics between faith communities also needed to be ironed out. Recognizing that donations to faith-based communities were likely intended to assist the evolving needs of the most vulnerable in disaster-impacted communities, leaders from groups such as the Council of Churches of Greater New York, the Board of Rabbis, Lutheran Disaster Response of New York, UMCOR, the Presbytery of New York, and the Islamic Circle of North America (to name only a few) met continually to discuss the best avenues to distribute aid via a collaborative approach that did not duplicate the resources already being distributed. Some mainstream churches had received substantial donations, most notably Lutheran, Episcopal, Presbyterian, Methodist, while smaller churches and other faith communities were grappling with how to serve their denominations with limited resources. This led to an uncomfortable dynamic between faith community representatives as they met on Manhattan's Upper West Side at the Interchurch Center near Columbia University (often referred to as the "God Box").

Some leaders felt that distribution of cash assistance was needed urgently (especially fearing that congregation members would backlash as the media perception of the American Red Cross began to seep into other arenas of disaster assistance). Others thought that funds should be used differently, to build resources or as mini-grants, rather than to fund individuals with cash assistance when so much was apparently being given. Others wanted funding and attended meetings to convince their peers to give them grants to assist their communities. On the Upper West side of Manhattan, these debates continued for months, while in lower Manhattan, the larger human service agencies were also learning how to work together for their communities.

In March 2002, the NYC 9/11 Unmet Needs Roundtable initial meetings were not easy. Lawyers were presenting cases from advocacy agencies and, while their clients did fit the criteria of the faith communities as disaster victims, the casework to show that the client's need could not be served by any other resource or that assistance would lead them to recovery was not complete. Participants were leaving the meetings frustrated. Lawyers who had little time for case management were becoming discouraged, concerned that the unmet needs table would not work. The faith communities that were debating their role in Upper West Manhattan were not yet convinced that the unmet needs table would be the best use of their donated funds.

To address this and recruit grassroots agencies that could do comprehensive case management, the first "training" for the unmet needs table was held in April 2002. A staff person was selected from Lutheran Social Services, funded through Lutheran Disaster Response, to manage the table, train participants, and facilitate meetings. That staff person's role developed from chair of the 9/11 Roundtable, to moderator between agency donor and case manager discussions, to becoming a function of the director of Disaster Recovery and Advocacy for the yet to-be-formed New York Disaster Interfaith Services. In the process of creating the first training, the FEMA voluntary liaison connected the new Lutheran staff person to an unmet needs table expert working for the American Red Cross in Arizona, leading to weeks of nightly 3-hour-long calls about unmet needs tables and the potential role of the faith communities to address the emerging needs of 9/11 survivors.

The process of creating the training led to development of a mission statement for the 9/11 Roundtable through discussion with the initial committee members. The 3-hour presentation served as an introduction of the concepts underlying unmet needs tables, disaster long-term recovery and the way each agency representative could work to attain assistance for their clients. The first training was held at Lutheran Social Services of New York in lower Manhattan. Attendance was great, including representatives from the mayor's Office of Emergency Management, Lutheran Disaster Response, the Puerto Rican Defense and Education Fund, Brooklyn Bureau of Community Services, Safe Horizon, and the Salvation Army (both member agencies of the USG), with approximately 50 people in attendance.

Change happened quickly in the 9/11 human services community. After the initial training, enthusiasm for the potential of the unmet needs table grew. Within weeks, the Puerto Rican Legal Defense and Education Fund had one, then two, full-time caseworkers bringing an average of six new cases to the twice-weekly meetings of the 9/11 Roundtable. The leader of Lutheran Disaster Response of New York had a functional meeting with good case presentations to invite faith-based donor partners to for observation. Within weeks, UMCOR chose to participate. Observers from the Council of Churches of Greater New York, Presbytery of New York, and Episcopal Church attended meetings and came together to become donors at the 9/11 Roundtable.

In May 2002, the chair of the 9/11 Roundtable was invited to a meeting at the Disaster Assistance Service Center, at that time managed by Safe Horizon, to answer questions about the unmet needs table. At the end of the meeting, representatives from Safe Horizon decided this could be a viable tool to address unmet needs for clients they were assisting who were "outside the box" for regular resources but still eligible for services because they had some link to 9/11 below Canal Street. This raised some concern among faith-based donors that the cases coming from these agencies would already have access to resources, but a decision was favored to allow the case managers from the United Services Group agencies to have access to the 9/11 Roundtable for case presentations. By June 2002, a breakthrough happened when the chair of the newly forming 9/11 Roundtable was invited to present information about the Roundtable to the USG case management coordination meeting. After the presentation, the 9/11 Roundtable chair from Lutheran Social Services and the partnering agency presenter from FEMA were invited to attend all case management coordination meetings at the USG. Soon after, social work supervisors from the USG facilitated NYC 9/11 Unmet Needs Roundtable in-services for all of their caseworkers. Within 2 months, 140 caseworkers had been trained by the Lutheran Disaster Response–funded staff person, and the NYC 9/11 Unmet Needs Roundtable was evolving into a steady resource for all 9/11 impacted people, regardless of their physical proximity to the disaster.

An "out-of-the-box" case was presented on behalf of the family of a 10-year-old child. On September 11, 2001, both of the child's parents were in the area of the World Trade Center. Both parents survived, but in the hours that passed waiting to hear from his parents, the child believed they were dead. This led the child to psychological distress and the child attempted suicide by jumping from a balcony. Until September 11, 2001, this family did not realize that their child might have early psychiatric problems, but even with knowledge of his parent's safety, he continued to exhibit signs of mental illness. The family was now suffering under the cost of medical bills for their child's treatment. Until September 11, this family had consider themselves middle class, but with the rising costs, they realized that they had been living paycheck to paycheck and could not survive with all of the medical bills. With the help of a good case manager, the family came up with a recovery plan, but they needed assistance with the mounting debt that they had taken on in the months after 9/11. The family's entire story was substantiated with documentation from hospitals, doctors, and other bills. This family was able to get closer to completing their long-term recovery with the help of the 9/11 Roundtable, and they were not eligible for other assistance because they did not fall into one of the common 9/11 impacted categories.

The faith communities still had concerns. Their highest accountability was to their membership, and they wanted to report back to their
membership about what they had done. They worried that, although this
was an effective tool, it would ultimately be seen as a Lutheran initiative.
They wanted to move the 9/11 Roundtable from being managed through
Lutheran Social Services to an organization that would be perceived to
be neutral. Having a functional program to run, a political will evolved
between the faith communities to create a formal structure for their coordination and collaborative efforts. With the leadership of the Council of
Churches of Greater New York, the Board of Rabbis, UMCOR, Lutheran
Disaster Response, the American Baptists, and the Presbytery of New
York (among others), New York Disaster Interfaith Services (NYDIS) was
born and formally incorporated by the end of 2002. The NYC 9/11 Unmet
needs Roundtable moved to NYDIS and its role as a tool for community-
wide disaster recovery evolved.

Stage Two: 9/11 Roundtable and New York
Disaster Interfaith Services (2003–2005)

On a few occasions, long-term recovery organizations have proved
their capacity to enhance an agency's ability to advocate for the evolving needs of communities as a disaster's full impact unfolds. The most
notable use of this tool for advocacy in 9/11 recovery was the partnering of the United Services Group, the New York Immigration Coalition
and the faith communities with other agencies to argue for expansion
of FEMA's Mortgage and Rental Assistance (MRA) program. Shortly
after the World Trade Center attack FEMA had inserted the term "direct
victim" into eligibility criteria and incorporated the use of geographic
boundaries—Houston Street and below—to determine eligibility of
"direct" victims. Many leaders expressed immediate concern that these
decisions, especially use of geographic boundaries to define individual's
eligibility for aid, created arbitrary criteria that excluded thousands of
direct victims from aid.

With an estimated 75,000 to 100,000 jobs (in New York City alone) lost
due to the World Trade Center attack during the last fiscal quarter of 2001,
FEMA's MRA program had significant impact on the lives of New Yorkers
in the wake of the World Trade Center attack. Prior to 9/11 FEMA's MRA
had been an underutilized program that had been designed to prevent eviction and foreclosure as a result of a disaster. Because of its underutilization

in past disasters, MRA had been slated for removal from FEMA's program offerings through the Disaster Mitigation Act of 2000. However, the 9/11 World Trade Center attack was an economic disaster and the scope of its impact went beyond physical loss of property and human life. Ultimately approximately 16,500 households facing foreclosure or eviction as a result of income loss due to the terrorist attacks accessed MRA assistance. Due to coordinated advocacy between human service organizations, FEMA expanded its definition of "direct" victim to include all of the residents of Manhattan and the elimination of the MRA program did not take effect until October 2002, with last distributions of aid in January 2003. The elimination of MRA from FEMA's programs remains an area of concern for New York organizations that would respond to future disasters.

While this advocacy effort eventually led to expansion of FEMA's MRA eligibility criteria so that it included all residents of Manhattan; the evolving policies of FEMA continued to exclude people living in the other four New York boroughs—Queens, Brooklyn, Staten Island, and the Bronx. Like the Canal Street boundary, the criteria for distribution of FEMA's MRA assistance continued to be a point of controversy where two people with the same disaster-caused needs could be eligible for aid if they happened to live in Harlem, or not eligible for aid, if they lived in Queens—a negligible distance of perhaps 5 to 10 miles.

Who would pay attention to such boundaries in the distribution of aid when the entire world was afraid of a next attack and mourning those who had died in the Towers? Faith communities stepped into this breach, while, as noted earlier, most of the large nonprofits distributing assistance through the United Services Group had restrictions that were, arguably, as arbitrary as those designed by FEMA. It was exactly these arbitrary and unnecessarily exclusive categories that the faith community did not abide by and these populations that the NYC 9/11 Unmet Needs Roundtable actively sought to serve.

An invaluable legacy of the NYC 9/11 Unmet Needs Roundtable is that it has allowed us to document the needs of individuals and indeed entire pockets of people who would otherwise go unnoticed and underserved because they did not fit the particular eligibility requirements of larger less flexible programs. Faith-based relief providers stepped into these breaches, putting together individual aid packages and, in some cases, entire programs or projects to reach underserved communities. At other times, faith-based agencies partnered with existing grassroots community organizations, paying for extra caseworkers, so these groups could better distribute relief. It was often faith-based organizations that identified unaddressed mental health needs and took leadership to collaborate with mental health providers to meet these needs.

As Dr. Ramon Nieves, head of Mission for the United Methodist Committee on Relief, observed: "Over 70% of our clientele at UMCOR walk in with a diagnosis of posttraumatic stress disorder (PTSD). Many do not acknowledge (or want to acknowledge) their present state of mind. They feel that if they address their financial situation, all will be well. Economic recovery is not synonymous with mental wellness." The 9/11 Roundtable was often witness to challenges of providing integrated care to those displaced by 9/11 and took leadership to address the challenge.

Through the 9/11 Roundtable, along with its continued support for 9/11 victims' recovery plans, NYDIS began administering a mental health benefit to cover the cost of mental health services that 9/11 disaster victims could not afford. (Individuals became eligible for this benefit after they had exhausted other resources including the American Red Cross mental health benefit.) An added blessing to this arrangement in terms of collaboration was that the cases of mental health clinicians began to be reviewed at NYDIS by Daniel H. Bush, a chaplain. This provided an opportunity to better coordinate the mental health and spiritual care services a person was receiving.

An example of better coordination between mental health and spiritual care was a case brought by a social worker. She was doing therapy with a Jewish man and related in her case summary that her client stopped going to Synagogue after his trauma with September 11. The therapist had not thought to contact the rabbi of the Synagogue. Daniel suggested she consider discussing the issues with the patient. With the patient's permission, perhaps she could contact the rabbi. The patient benefited from the renewed contact with his spiritual community, and this, in turn, assisted with the progress of his treatment with the social worker.

The review of these cases and the other data collected by the 9/11 Roundtable of underserved people documented unnoticed patterns, helping to inform the work of partnering agencies, opening doorways to practical and creative collaborations. For example, the coordinator of the American Red Cross Additional Assistance Program began regularly attending the 9/11 Roundtable meetings. This allowed the American Red Cross to pick up clients they missed and to learn more about those who fell slightly outside their eligibility matrix. At the same time, the presence of the American Red Cross staff person informed the 9/11 Roundtable donor agencies of a client's case status with the American Red Cross Additional Assistance program. Ideally, large agencies like American Red Cross that received the bulk of major donations would have adjusted and expanded their limited eligibility requirements based on the new data captured by the 9/11 Roundtable's documentation of pockets of underserved populations. Pressure and concern over potential media backlash continued, and despite the best intentions of staff in the core agencies, the 9/11 Roundtable remained the only viable source of assistance for people who clearly were 9/11 disaster victims but who did not fit the categories for aid developed by the American Red Cross and other agencies in the first weeks and months of 9/11 disaster relief. The American Red Cross became increasingly collaborative, however, and supported the 9/11 Roundtable efforts through grants for administrative salaries and later cash to individuals. Yet, the categories defining which 9/11 victims were eligible for aid did not change significantly over time.

Recognizing the impact of vicarious trauma and other impacts of working as a 9/11 case worker, NYDIS also used the 9/11 Roundtable as a source to fund career development and mental health support for case workers who had worked from 2001 to 2004 with 9/11 case loads as they were facing layoffs with the closing of 9/11 programs. This assistance was made available for a limited period of time and was distributed, as with all assistance, on a case-by-case basis. Faith communities continued to identify and attend to growing areas of long-term need that relief programs designed in the acute phase of a disaster were not geared to meet. For example, the Roundtable began seeing many cases of individuals who served as Ground Zero recovery workers who are now ill and being treated at Mount Sinai Medical Center. The NYDIS staff administering the 9/11 Roundtable established a collaborative relationship with the staff of the Mount Sinai Medical Screening and Treatment program, both referring clients to the program and offering assistance to recovery workers with 9/11-related illnesses who were unable to meet basic expenses. A Mount Sinai caseworker began regularly presenting cases to the 9/11 Roundtable. NYDIS also suggested to Mount Sinai that their program's mental health services be coordinated with the hospital's chaplains, a possibility that had been overlooked.

By December 2004, the landscape of 9/11 recovery had changed. The community at large was talking about "moving on" and, while many believed it was too early to close 9/11 recovery programs, pressure of public expectation led to the closing of many programs. The 9/11 Roundtable faced a crisis because without case managers, 9/11 Roundtable assistance could not be awarded to individuals. At the same time, in January 2005, the number of people in search of assistance began to steadily increase as more and more 9/11 recovery workers came forward with serious illnesses, in some cases illnesses that were leading to permanent disability or even death.

Stage Three: 9/11 Roundtable and Coordinated Services for Recovery Workers (2005–2009)

By January 2005, the NYC 9/11 Unmet Needs Roundtable had gained a reputation in the community, among service providers and clients, as a resource for assistance to 9/11 victims. As clients had continued to develop their recovery plans, some had returned to the 9/11 Roundtable two or three times requesting more assistance. In an effort to emphasize the importance of intensive case management to develop sustainable recovery plans, the Roundtable donors decided to limit funding to clients who were at the end of their recovery planning process. A client could come to the 9/11 Roundtable for assistance, in most cases, only once. The recovery plan had to be complete and viable. All other assistance had to be applied for and granted or clients had to show that they were not eligible for other assistance. For 9/11 victims who had begun their journey in September 2001, these criteria were reasonable. But, then the recovery workers began emerging with needs that had been unforeseen.

Approximately 60,000 people are believed to have served in the recovery effort of the World Trade Center site (or Ground Zero). In a report from NYDIS to the American Red Cross in written in December 2005, the following was noted:

> Since its inception in April 2002, Roundtable donors have assisted 2392 victims and recovery workers. Approximately one-third of these cases have been presented this year, with 800 cases presented and 770 funded since January 1, 2005. The overwhelming majority of individuals assisted this year are Hispanic (64%) many of whom are women between the ages of 30–50 years. Compared with inception to date demographic trends, this is an approximately fifteen (15%) percent increase in the number of Hispanic people assisted through Roundtable resources. Another large population served through the Roundtable is Polish clean-up workers, comprising nine (9%) percent of Roundtable cases since January 2005. There has also been an increase in the number of cases presented for clients with undocumented immigration status, with approximately 35% of people assisted since January identified as undocumented versus an overall 23% of Roundtable presentations for people with undocumented status.

As the needs of recovery workers increased, the concept of recovery became more complex. By the end of 2005, the majority of people seeking assistance from the 9/11 Roundtable were people who cleaned in or around the area of Ground Zero. Many had combinations of respiratory/pulmonary illnesses, muscular-skeletal injuries and mental health needs including PTSD. Up to 30% of the people suffering from these illnesses and seeking unmet needs assistance were undocumented immigrants who had cleaned the site via small cleaning companies that were created for the effort or who were in unions that, until September 11, had not been required to have their immigration status verified. Because New York City is approximately 47% foreign born or second-generation foreign born, immigrants working to clean the city were familiar to everyone involved in the recovery effort. However, the backlash against immigrants after the 9/11 attack made advocating for their needs or raising the visibility of their illnesses a slippery slope for 9/11 long-term recovery agencies. Once again, the faith communities, through NYDIS and the 9/11 Roundtable, in particular, saw this as a central role for advocacy.

One of the first steps that the 9/11 Roundtable had to take in responding to the emerging needs of the World Trade Center recovery workers was to reflect on the giving criteria of donors and return to a discussion of "what is recovery?" In this case, the decision to hold cases until their final stage of a recovery plan would have closed the door on many recovery workers who were just emerging with illnesses. For many of these recovery workers, their long-term recovery plan included accessing worker's compensation insurance from the state, a process that took an average of two years. In the meantime, these recovery workers could become homeless while receiving primary care at Mt. Sinai hospital. In many cases, the recovery workers had a career in physical labor–type jobs, so creating a sustainable recovery plan included vocational training and acceptance of their long-term disabilities. In some case, a recovery plan included end-of-life planning for the family of the recovery worker and job development for the recovery worker's spouse. In a few cases, NYDIS was called upon to provide funding for funeral expenses of a recovery worker who had died from respiratory/pulmonary illnesses. The stress of supporting this effort, with limited case managers and resources in the community, affected everyone participating in the NYC 9/11 Unmet Needs Roundtable and the staff of NYDIS.

An example of the diversity of cases coming to NYDIS and the 9/11 Roundtable in 2006 to 2008 included Mohawk Indian iron workers from Canada who had traveled to New York City immediately after 9/11 to work on clearing debris from the site. With help from the Canadian Red Cross, these Mohawk Indians were regularly traveling to New York City for treatment of World Trade Center illnesses at Mt. Sinai Hospital. The average worker in this case had limited education, perhaps high school, and had a career in ironwork that had paid $70,000 a year. On the reservation, this is good money. But recovery for these workers often meant permanent disability and few alternatives for income. In at least one case, a worker had glass in his lungs and had developed cancer. While physicians were still deciding if the emergence of cancer in recovery workers was "disaster caused," NYDIS worked with the Canadian Red Cross to develop a recovery plan for the family that included job development for the recovery worker's wife.

Not only did developing recovery plans for these clients become a complicated task, but the lack of case work agencies still active in 9/11 recovery created yet another crisis in sustaining the tool of financial assistance through the 9/11 Roundtable. By December 2005, the American Red Cross September 11 Recovery Grants had moved from funding case management to funding a limited number of agencies with direct service programs other than case management. To resolve the conflict of meeting the needs of the emerging 9/11 recovery worker population, the American Red Cross decided to partner with NYDIS, funding not only the administration of the 9/11 Roundtable, but also distributing cash assistance to individuals as a donor. In all, the American Red Cross September 11 Recovery Program distributed more than $3.5 million in cash assistance through the 9/11 Roundtable, mostly to recovery workers. But, to distribute this cash assistance to the recovery workers, NYDIS once again called upon faith communities to provide assistance to sustain case management to navigate developing recovery plans for this emerging 9/11 community. Quoting text from a 2006 report to the American Red Cross, NYDIS shared the value of partnering with faith communities:

> Anticipating this scenario, NYDIS secured funding from Episcopal Relief and Development to make four "Continuity of 9/11 Services" subgrants. These grants were given to four case management agencies in strategic locations, with special focus on the ability of each agency to serve WTC recovery workers. Through these grants and coaching from the new 9/11 Outreach Coordinator, case management agencies were able to return to case management presentations at the NYC 9/11 Unmet Needs Roundtable at the beginning of February.

At each twist and turn of 9/11 recovery, faith communities continued to rise to the call to serve the community. The NYC 9/11 Unmet Needs Roundtable adapted and responded to the needs of diverse communities. Case management and cash assistance through the NYC 9/11 Unmet Needs Roundtable moved from emergency assistance for communities being excluded from aid, to funding mental health assistance for people as other sources for mental healthcare closed their doors, to responding to the needs of WTC recovery workers who were emerging with new illnesses and who could be facing life-long or life-threatening illnesses.

The NYC 9/11 Unmet Needs Roundtable closed officially in May 2009. Closing the doors of the 9/11 Roundtable was not an indication that there was no longer a need. Indeed, NYDIS made valiant attempts to recreate some of the systems that had been available to early 9/11 victims so that the World Trade Center recovery workers could have equal access to care. In the end, resources had dwindled. But what NYDIS and the 9/11 Roundtable did was, and is, imperative for all spiritual care and mental healthcare workers: To be present with people for as long as possible, to simply be present; to acknowledge the pain of the community and, if possible, to shoulder some of the burden.

In the end, it is the community that is ultimately responsible for its recovery and the recovery of its most vulnerable members. NYDIS and the 9/11 Roundtable helped build and sustain the 9/11 human services community. Along the way, sophisticated tools for managing and adapting unmet needs-tables were developed that will hopefully be looked to as models in future disaster recovery efforts.

Conclusion

The adaptation of the unmet needs table concept to the unique needs of 9/11 victims who were economically and psychologically impacted but who had not lost physical property was yet another innovation of the World Trade Center disaster recovery effort. Before 9/11, unmet needs tables were a tool, often developed by Church World Service and UMCOR, to support the management of need-based, long-term recovery assistance with a focus on structured support in the rebuilding of homes and to replace the basic needs of families that have suffered material loss in a natural disaster. Although faith communities often use these tables as a way to coordinate the distribution of aid in a nonduplicative, case-by-case and need-based fashion, at the time of its inception in April

2002, the NYC 9/11 Unmet Needs Roundtable became the a sole source of financial assistance for basic needs—food and shelter—for thousands of New Yorkers at a time when mental health and spiritual care providers were attempting to address depression and trauma among the same populations. In April 2002, the 1-800-LIFENET crisis telephone number for New York City reported that over 40% of callers were reporting economic stress as their primary concern and their perceived cause of their depression. To address this pressing and overwhelming need, the faith communities in New York City found a central purpose and vehicle for coordination. The NYC 9/11 Unmet Needs Roundtable emerged not only as a tool to distribute assistance to vulnerable disaster victims but also as a tool for coordination and communication between agencies, faith communities, and the general public.

Accessing or not accessing these aid systems can impact the recovery and wellness of the disaster victim in care. Spiritual care and mental health practitioners have a role to play in advocating for and assisting clients in accessing the resources of these long-term recovery committees. For this reason, understanding the nuances of how a situation may be perceived as disaster or nondisaster-related is critical to the professional care given by clergy, clinical social workers, psychologists, psychiatrists, and chaplains working in the disaster recovery field. The feeling of being invalidated as a victim or survivor of the disaster has implications for mental health and spiritual care, while at the same time mental health and spiritual care givers must take an active role in advocating for their client, or the client base as a whole, to have access to disaster recovery resources.

9

On Reentering the Chapel
Models for Collaborations Between Psychiatrists, Communities of Faith, and Faith-Based Providers After Hurricane Katrina

Rebecca P. Smith, Julie Taylor, Gregory Luke Larkin, Carol S. North, Diane Ryan, and Anastasia Holmes

Introduction

Given that religious and spiritual care providers historically have been the main resource that individuals have turned to in the face of adversity or disaster, it is perhaps surprising that psychiatric training does not routinely provide instruction in the spiritual dimension of the human psychological experience of healing or in models of collaboration with providers of spiritual care. While progress has been made in psychiatry in explicitly acknowledging religious and spiritual dimensions of psychological health and mental health care, it has been slow.

It was only in 1994 that the American Psychiatric Association's *Diagnostic and Statistical Manual* included an explicit category that can be used when a mental health professional is able to recognize and acknowledge a religious or spiritual problem as the focus of their clinical attention (American Psychiatric Association, 1994). This weakness in psychiatric training places psychiatrists who wish to provide disaster mental health care at a distinct disadvantage, denying us avenues for better understanding the experiences of the disaster survivors we wish to support and impeding our ability to collaborate effectively with leaders in faith-based communities and colleagues with expertise in the provision of spiritual care. This is unfortunate because, given the incentives, what unites psychiatrists and providers of spiritual care—the desire to use our skills to provide support, comfort, and healing to disaster survivors— seems on the face of it to be stronger than what divides us.

Background

Some general consideration of the specific characteristics of the disaster of Hurricane Katrina and the affected population is instructive. After the hurricane made landfall on August 28, 2005, an area of the Gulf Coast the size of Great Britain (90,000 square miles) was declared a federal disaster area. More than 1,800 people were killed (Federal Emergency Management Agency [FEMA], 2005). The intensity of the hurricane was much discussed in the media, but actually the majority of hurricane-related casualties, evacuations, and morbidity resulted from the post-Katrina flooding of the city of New Orleans, when the city's levees were overwhelmed, rather than from the direct effects of the hurricane itself. Of the 1,800 people who were killed, 1,400 were from Louisiana. In a sense, therefore, Hurricane Katrina was less a natural disaster than a social and political one. The failure of the levees was a failure of human systems, which had long been anticipated by policymakers and communities. The population of New Orleans was knowingly, and in advance of the disaster, placed at risk. A community with significant unmet social and economic needs before the disaster was sent into a forced migration.

In one study of over 1,000 evacuees, low-income people were five times more likely to report being unable to leave (40.2%) as were people with higher incomes (6.4%). Over half (57.8%) of those with lower income who did not evacuate reported that it was due to their lack of money compared to only 1.8 to 5.1% of those with above-average income. The resulting population of evacuees suffered from preexisting chronic illness as well as postdisaster bereavement. Within one week of the hurricane, in a sample of 343 New Orleanian evacuees, 56% of adults had at least one chronic illness, 63% had at least one missing household member, and 50% suffered at least one symptom of acute stress disorder (Rodriguez et al., 2006).

For more than a month after Hurricane Katrina made landfall, an unknown number of small rural chapels were still operating in Louisiana as shelters for survivors of Hurricane Katrina who had evacuated from New Orleans.

Descriptive Experiences

In this chapter, this multidisciplinary team of authors reviews experiences drawn from the journal of a psychiatrist who volunteered to provide post-disaster mental health services in church-based shelters in Louisiana in the month after Hurricane Katrina. The psychiatrist, Rebecca P. Smith, was deployed as part of a two-person team (including one of the coeditors of this volume, Grant H. Breuner) by an organization of volunteer psychiatrists. Through providing psychiatric services in these church-based shelters in rural Louisiana, she and her teammate received an education in the depth and breadth of what faith-based communities can accomplish in caring for survivors of a disaster and were provided the opportunity to provide assistance and support as psychiatrists to these communities.

Several experiences from the first day of the response are discussed that illustrate some of the challenges faced by those in the chapels who took responsibility for trying to run the shelters, and the remarkable resilience they each displayed. In order to protect the privacy of those who received psychiatric services, details have been changed, and the clinical care provided will not be named. Finally, a piece will be provided detailing the ways in which, after the response, in the postdisaster period, collaboration continued in the form of "spiritual supervision" between a psychiatrist and a provider of spiritual care.

We believe that these experiences illustrate how, for psychiatrists, working with leaders (both formal and informal) in faith-based communities can provide unprecedented opportunities to remove barriers to care and expand opportunities for us as psychiatrists to foster health and healing after a disaster. The pieces also illustrate how interdisciplinary collaboration between psychiatrists and spiritual care providers can promote morale and a renewed sense of competence and hope for each in ways that are often very surprising.

"Entering the Chapel": Providing Services in Church-Based Shelters After Hurricane Katrina

Discussion of the response to Hurricane Katrina involving services provided in rural church-based shelters may at first seem hard to reconcile with the immense scale of Hurricane Katrina, the largest disaster in U.S. history. Before visiting these church-based shelters, it was difficult to understand how the members of these small communities of faith had arrived at the idea that they could open their doors and make a difference. After meeting them, however, it was completely clear that the size of the disaster didn't matter; the idea that people were in dire need meant that the churches had to respond and figure out how to make the responses work. A parishioner volunteering at the first chapel-based shelter we visited summed it up this way: "For me as a part of our church, the way I see it. … there's no job too big, no job too small. So I come here every day and do what I can."

On September 21, 2005, the numerous volunteers who descended on the Baton Rouge area included a two-person team of volunteer psychiatrists from New York City. They had been deployed through a not-for-profit organization of volunteer psychiatrists at the request of the community's public mental health authorities who had found out about the organization and stated they needed volunteer psychiatrists.

After meeting with the local public health authorities, and registering their credentials, they were told that several chapel-based shelters had requested mental health services, "in particular, psychiatrists." No information was available about what sorts of services were needed. The psychiatrists were asked to check in with the leadership of the chapel, ask what was needed, provide triage and services, and report back. None of the local mental health authorities had visited these chapels and so little was known about the specific nature of their operations and needs. The following is excerpted from the journal of one of the psychiatrists:

> The first chapel was a forty-five minute drive away. Once we arrived, we stood outside looking in. Just figuring out how to go in and introduce ourselves was a challenge.
>
> The process of entering a hospital or psychiatric clinic or office differs fundamentally from the process of entering a chapel. Ordinarily, a psychiatrist doesn't think much about the process of entering a hospital or a clinic. However, coming into a chapel in order to provide psychiatric services requires some thought. It is a house of worship and, therefore, it is important to be mindful as one enters to make an effort to go slowly, to acknowledge people, and to be alert for ways to show respect for the space and for the people who may be inside. The process of having mindfully entered the chapel formed the rest of our efforts for the day, and probably helped us more than we realize.
>
> Once we got inside, there was a lobby area with 10 people, all sad-looking, sitting in fold-up chairs, not talking. There were three little girls, probably aged six to eight, running around playing in the lobby. An elderly woman seated at a table appeared to be a receptionist, and was also watching the three girls. She brought us to the person identified as being in charge of the shelter. She

introduced herself and described herself as "the one running the shelter part of things because I'm unemployed, and have had relevant experience, having raised 12 children, and I've been through some things in life … I understand these people." She had been working 7 days a week since the hurricane struck to try to help run things at the church. She was remarkably calm and focused, given this history. I asked her for some background on the shelter, some sense of the scale of the operation. She said that they currently had "about 50" people in the shelter, but had had as many as 200 two weeks earlier: "Many people left, it's been hard to keep track." She had identified three individuals that she felt were in need of psychiatric evaluation.

In addition to identifying individuals in need of evaluation, she made a point of asking us to spend some time with the pastor of the church when he arrived. He took us on a tour of the chapel and then brought us back into his office. We spent over an hour with him. It was important that both of us were there; in a sense it seemed more like we were bearing witness. He asked if we were psychiatrists, and then when we assured him that we were, he closed the door and said he had several things to tell us. He spoke slowly and was very somber. He told us that the main thing he had learned from having more than 50 people living in his chapel was that food and shelter were not actually the most important things these people needed—it was social services. "When I heard about the hurricane and the levees breaking … I thought, we must open our doors to those people and take them in. … I figured we'd have five or six people for a few days." He shook his head and there was silence in the room. He then asked about his own symptoms of sleeplessness, anxiety, and depression and wanted to know if they were normal or if he should worry. We were able to reassure him. At the end of our conversation, he looked relaxed and much less somber; he'd clearly managed to feel supported by our presence.

My colleague told him how glad we were to have been able to spend time with him and asked him, "Why were you able to talk to us? And you asked if we were psychiatrists. What was it that mattered about that?" He said that he felt that he wanted to talk to people from outside his community who he could trust, who would not judge him or the efforts the chapel had made. He said that he felt that, as psychiatrists, we "probably know what social problems are and what it's like to not have enough to give to people. …"

The second shelter we visited, we arrived around dinnertime. We were welcomed in by a crowd of evacuees and parishioners who quickly put together paper plates with barbecued chicken on them and put them in our hands. The church seemed like a gymnasium inside, with one area with sleeping bags and little suitcases arranged next to each other in neat rows, and another area with long tables and folding chairs. We spoke with the person in charge of the shelter, a retired tradesman, who was quite energized to see us. "I'm so glad you are here. We have a fellow here, a very nice fellow, I like him, but he is on medications and he clearly has some mental disorder. … I'm glad you are here so we can get him to the kind of place where he can get the care he needs, a hospital or something. He's very nice. We have a retired nurse in our parish, she's over there at that table helping the old people with medications, but she doesn't know about mental diseases." We evaluated him, a fellow with a history of chronic mental illness who had been alone in his apartment in New Orleans when it had flooded. He was stable, friendly, and not in acute distress, though he spoke in sentences that were somewhat disorganized. He showed us that he had medications with him, but had not been taking them. We were able to understand why the shelter director liked him; he had an endearing charm, and vulnerability that made one instinctively want to take care of him. This situation appeared stable for the moment. We had to work with the shelter leader to help him understand and accept that we had no solution to this problem: There was not a hospital we could arrange that would take in this fellow, and, in fact, that this would be true even if the hurricane had not occurred. The shelter director understood quickly and was very responsive to our efforts to reassure him that, in the short term, this fellow did not appear to pose a risk and was much more likely to do well with regular medication. The shelter director walked over with us and we met briefly with him and the nurse and talked with both of them about the specific medications. The fellow offered to take them every morning if the nurse would keep them for him, which was mutually recognized as the best that could be done under the circumstances.

The individuals described above each illustrate aspects of the resilience of individuals who provided postdisaster services in faith-based communities in Louisiana after Hurricane Katrina. The parishioner at the first chapel was expert at triage; her experience raising 12 children had prepared her well. Therefore, in addition to trying to identify people in need of psychiatric evaluation, she was also mindful of the needs of her colleagues, and was able to identify an opportunity for us to provide support to her pastor. She possessed the implicit skills to connect people who are there to provide support to people who need it, a skill that is invaluable after a disaster.

The pastor who can admit to his own need for comfort, when confronted with feeling of inadequacy in the face of social problems, sets an example of self-care that every disaster mental health and spiritual care provider can relate to and by which they can be inspired. At the second chapel, the shelter leader was able to gracefully accept that there was no immediate solution to his problem and to facilitate communication about how to work within these limitations in the short term. Such acceptance and willingness to work constructively in the face of disappointment is very adaptive in any postdisaster mental health setting and sets an example for professional spiritual and psychiatric care providers.

The Evolution of a Model for "Spiritual Supervision" Between a Chaplain and a Psychiatrist

Much writing about disaster mental health concerns characterizes what happens during the actual disaster response. Therefore, it is easy to overlook the opportunities for building collaboration during disaster preparedness phases (pre- and postdisaster). While interdisciplinary exchanges are often accomplished in the context of formal "debriefings" or "defusings" postdisaster, it is helpful as well to seek out informal avenues for discussion and exploration of the experiences one has when providing postdisaster care. In an informal one-on-one setting, a different sort of exchange can take place. The following describes how the psychiatrist in the excerpt above sought informal assistance from a colleague with expertise in the provision of disaster spiritual care and a new collaboration was initiated.

Ultimately, several months after Hurricane Katrina, the psychiatrist approached a chaplain she knew from disaster preparedness exercises and responses, with whom she had volunteered earlier in the week in a local response. She asked if the chaplain would be willing to meet and provide consultation and feedback about how to deepen her understanding of experiences of faith after a disaster. They discussed several experiences, including one that the psychiatrist had while providing support to survivors of Hurricane Katrina who were living in church based shelters a month after the hurricane.

One of the survivors approached her and said he had a question he wanted to ask a psychiatrist. He identified himself as a person of faith. He said he wanted to talk to her about being troubled by how best to handle his experience of doubting the existence of God and being angry with God after Hurricane Katrina. He was unsure whether to pray for restoration of his faith, and asked whether she thought it would be mentally healthy for him to do this, or whether it would be, as he put it, masochistic. They spoke together and explored his ambivalence about whether it made sense for him to pray for the restoration of his belief. Ultimately, at the conclusion of the conversation, he informed her he had decided it did make sense for him to pray for the restoration of his faith.

This experience left the psychiatrist wanting to know more about the experience of faith after disasters. The chaplain was able to provide the psychiatrist with information characterizing the psychological experience of faith, and, in particular, that this experience often involves doubt in the existence of God as well as passionate feelings including anger and gratitude. This helped the psychiatrist develop an increased tolerance for ambiguity and uncertainty around different dimensions of the experience of faith, and an improved feeling of confidence about discussion of spiritual experiences. Whether considered from a psychological or a theological perspective, this exchange raises a number of fascinating questions: Once a person feels that he or she has lost their faith that God exists, what is it like to pray to have it restored? If one no longer believes in God, then what does it mean to pray? If one does pray for restoration of belief, doesn't this suggest that, in fact, belief is still there?

These and other questions initiated the process the two colleagues termed "spiritual supervision." In the first iteration of this model, the chaplain agreed to offer her expertise and knowledge about spiritual concerns to help the psychiatrist understand how to support the efforts of survivors, who identify as people of faith, tap into spiritual resources recovery from psychiatric symptoms and emotional distress. Creating a meeting time for "spiritual supervision" permitted these colleagues to collaborate in an ongoing exploration of the intersection between mental health care and spiritual care.

Conclusion

This discussion has come to include all of the coauthors and is ongoing. It is clear to all of the authors that ongoing consultation between disaster spiritual care and disaster mental health colleagues can help psychiatrists integrate the knowledge about spiritual care into their understanding of disaster mental health care and broaden the specific roles psychiatrists can play in promoting healing after a disaster. Ultimately, the current focus on differentiating approaches to "disaster mental health care" and "disaster spiritual care" must not be allowed to obscure the fact that both derive from a human tradition thousands of years old, which has its origins in houses of worship.

References

American Psychiatric Association. (Ed.). (1994). *Diagnostic and statistical manual of mental disorders* (4th ed.). Washington, DC: Author.

Federal Emergency Management Agency (FEMA). (2005). *Hurricane Katrina current location report: Reports of missing and deceased*. Washington, DC: Author.

Rodriguez, S. R., Tocco, J. S., Mallonee, S., Smithee, L., Cathey, T., & Bradley, K. (2006). Rapid needs assessment of Hurricane Katrina evacuees—Oklahoma, September 2005. *Prehospital Disaster Medicine, 21*(6), 390–395.

10

Collaboration in Working With Children Affected by Disaster

Daniel Gensler

Introduction

When disaster strikes a community, children suffer along with adults. By now, we have developed a number of concepts to understand children's reactions to disaster. In this chapter, I describe these ideas and then give two examples in which the ideas are used during interventions at the community level. Both examples occurred after 9/11: working with schools whose students were affected and working with a company whose employees included parents who were killed. This chapter is written from the point of view of a mental health provider. I illustrate ways of collaborating with schools and corporations from this perspective, using fundamental principles for working with children. Our vision for intervention did not include working with clergy and they were not involved. This limitation was unfortunate both for their likely contribution to the work with children and parents after disaster and for the continuity they would probably have provided within the families' religious communities after the mental health interventions came to an end.

I focus on collaboration with schools and corporations because of the impact on me of the attack on New York that occurred on September 11, 2001 (Gensler et al., 2002). I was working in Manhattan that day and spent much of the next 3 years responding in different settings to the effects of the disaster. Nearly all the work was collaborative, involving workshops, training, briefing, debriefing, group work, and family work. Interventions were offered through a variety of organizations: the police department, graduate and postgraduate training institutes, a social service agency, a conference of school superintendents, representatives of a consortium of over 100 public schools, pupil personnel at public schools, and a large company that was located in the World Trade Center. The community setting and collaborative nature of most of this work held my interest as I worked through my own reactions to September 11.

Background

Resilience and Risk

Before a trauma or disaster, children can be more at risk or more resilient. Many factors increase children's resilience, as highlighted in Table 10.1.

Because of the prevalence of such resilience factors, most children may have a brief acute stress reaction after a trauma but do not go on to develop posttraumatic stress disorder (PTSD).

Other factors increase a child's vulnerability to breakdown after a disaster, as indicated in Table 10.2. Together these risk factors affect trauma response through a child's physiological reaction, emotional and cognitive processing, and ability to enlist social support and help after a disaster.

Kinds of Trauma During Disaster

After horrible experiences, acute stress disorders are common, dissipating within a few weeks. Most children are resilient enough, and are faced with tolerable enough stresses, to return to their previous level of functioning

TABLE 10.1   Factors Contributing to Resilience in Children

Preexisting secure attachments.
A tendency to appraise situations optimistically—to see adversity as limited or temporary and not one's own fault.
A tendency to seek adult support outside the family.
Compassion for suffering and an inclination to help others as a way of coping.
Tolerable levels of anxiety and effective ways of self-soothing.
A tendency to activity and a sense of the efficacy of one's actions.
A belief in the right to survive and an ability to imagine a happier future.
The ability to detach and deny for periods of time.

TABLE 10.2   Risk Factors for Children in Disaster

Circumstances that prevent parents from providing opportunities for secure attachments to their children, such as parental depression, anxiety, or parents' own posttraumatic stress disorder.

A pattern of avoidant attachment rather than secure attachment (such children might appear indifferent, or inhibited, with only superficial compliance or concern).

Prior trauma (neglect, abuse, violence, or loss).

Preexisting mood disorders or anxiety disorders because such children may be more likely to appraise disastrous situations pessimistically, seeing adversity as widespread, lasting, and one's own fault.

Not having words for feelings (alexithymia), leading to avoidance or hyperarousal.

Lower cognitive ability and consequent trouble coping with trauma.

Intense physiological reactivity (heightened startle response, slow extinction of physiological reactions) and consequent trouble modulating the physiological arousal that comes with trauma.

Tendency to dissociate in the period immediate after the trauma or to become afraid of the bodily reaction to the shock of the trauma (e.g., rapid heartbeat), with trouble returning to prior level of functioning quickly (Pynoos, Steinber, & Goenjian, 1996).

within that time. When stress reactions last longer than a month, the catastrophic nature of the stress has overwhelmed the child's resilience, so that the child cannot restore psychological or biological calm more quickly. Here, the acute stress disorder becomes a lasting posttraumatic stress disorder (PTSD), including dissociation, persistent reexperiencing, avoidance, and arousal (DSM-IV). PTSD also involves intense psychological distress and physiological reactivity on exposure to cues that resemble an aspect of the traumatic event (traumatic reminders). Among children, there is often a sense of a foreshortened future and a restricted range of affect.

In understanding of trauma and children, there are other kinds of distinctions. There is simple trauma, but also trauma complicated by grief, as when a loved one died during a disaster. There is single trauma, or a series of traumas, each one traumatic itself but also reminding the child of the previous traumas. A series of traumas can lead to a chronic stress disorder.

Secondary Adversity

After a disaster, children can suffer adversities that are secondary to the traumatic event. They may undergo medical, surgical, or rehabilitative treatment; relocation or resettlement; change in caretaking; a drop in family finances; worsening of school performance; unwanted questions from peers and others; stigma due to scars or deformities; compromised parental function, such as increased maternal depression; increase in family violence or substance abuse during a posttrauma period; and so forth.

Cognitive and Physiological Effects

Traumas such as disasters have other effects that vary with age and stage of development, including effects on memory, cognition, and physiological functioning. Regarding memory, young children may recall events with a distortion of the sequence to developmentally normal immaturity in temporal memory (Pynoos et al., 1996). Disasters elicit many feelings at once, and young children may later recall the experience inadequately because of lack of familiarity of being aware of having two emotions at the same time. Young children's memory may focus on single images, sounds, or smells (such as cries for help of a family member) but not on internal sensations, feelings, thoughts. A child's recall of the story may be laced with intervention fantasies, and so the narrative may involve altering events, interrupting the action of the trauma, reversing negative consequences, or retaliations that in fact never occurred.

Experiencing a disaster can also interfere with a child's verbal coherence. First memories of the trauma are often fragmented and sensory. Children's narratives are also influenced by parental coconstructions. These interferences with narrative coherence can lead on to trouble with communicating, writing, and reading comprehension and with consequent school trouble. Other common reactions include interference with concentration and focused attention and greater irritability, leading to trouble with peers and with learning.

Yet another effect of disaster is on children's physiological functioning. While it is hard to distinguish preexisting factors from psychophysiological outcomes of PTSD, it is clear that most children who experience trauma have more intense reactions to sound afterward, with greater trouble controlling the startle reflex. Extinction of autonomic responses is impaired after trauma. Trauma also disturbs sleep, especially non-REM sleep, leading to disturbances, such as sleep walking, calling out while sleeping, motor restlessness, and night terror. Not getting a good night's sleep leads, in turn, to daytime difficulty in concentration and attention and to greater irritability, which can affect family life, peer relations, and learning ability (Yehuda, 1999).

Developmental Consequences

Trauma can have more lasting effects on cognition, affect regulation, relations with parents, and relations with peers, as seen in Table 10.3.

TABLE 10.3   Developmental Consequences of Trauma for Children

---

Interference with narrative, verbal coherence, memory, and concentration can have long-term academic effects.

The negative effect of trauma on modulating aggression can lead to disturbance in regulation of emotions across development.

Not feeling protected by parents from the effects of a disaster, a young child's trust in parental effectiveness and helpfulness is compromised; so is a parent's confidence in his or her own ability to help the child.

Disaster can cause problems with relations with peers all through child development.

School-Based Initiatives for Children Regarding Disasters

Several kinds of school-based interventions are possible and helpful for mental health professionals to work on. These include prevention (preparation, teacher training), screening and early intervention immediately after a disaster, reduction of traumatic reminders of the disaster, reduction of school-based developmental consequences, arranging for school-wide acts for safety and commemoration, and communications with parents with referrals for treatment.

Yet achieving a collaboration between mental health professionals and the schools is often difficult. At times of crisis, people turn to the roles and systems for communication and influence with which they are most familiar and tend to feel overwhelmed at first by offers of help from the outside. Principals may reject the offer of help, stating that their school-based support teams are sufficient to deal with the disaster. Offers of help from outside a school are accepted under three conditions: (a) if there have been preliminary collaborative efforts that have succeeded in making the "outsider" someone the leaders of the school think to call upon, (b) if the principal or superintendent has an unusual ability to think creatively, and (c) if the disaster becomes unremitting and overwhelming.

Even when the first of these conditions has occurred, the rate of turnover of principals in many schools is so great that the principal with whom the mental health professional has established a collaborative relation may have left by the time a disaster occurs. Further, in a large metropolitan area like New York, there can be insufficient integration of services. To get reimbursed by insurance for services, many professionals must define the children they serve as "patients" and see them in their offices rather than at schools.

To address such difficulties, mental health professionals can try going above the principal to a system-wide intervention or going below the principal to a grassroots intervention. I have found that the former has drawbacks, and the latter is more likely to work if a contact person can be selected who will stay in that school year after year.

Regarding the first approach, a number of us at the White Institute's Trauma Response Service planned over several years after 9/11 to collaborate with a consortium that represented over 100 public schools in New York City. The effort was quite exciting because of the large number of schools that potentially were going to be involved in receiving training in psychological preparedness for disasters (this training is described in more detail below). Yet the effort failed due to an unnecessary internal difference in budget expectations, which was based on insufficient internal communication on our part regarding the minimum budgetary needs for the project.

The second, grassroots approach was more successful, as we worked with a grade school in our neighborhood for some time. Prior to 9/11, we had consulted with that school, provided therapy for its students, and offered workshops for its teachers. After 9/11, the principal rebuffed our offers for help and left at the end of the year anyway. However, because of a key preexisting contact with the school psychologist, we continued to be a helpful presence for that school, offering onsite consultation as well as therapy services at our clinic. Such contacts and preexisting relationships must be built over long periods of time and are an important part of being prepared to deal with disasters when they occur.

Once there is an entry point in a school, whether through the system, the principal, or a grass-roots contact, school staff should receive training in recognizing signs of trauma in students, both for existing situations and for future disasters. This basic psychoeducational approach facilitates collaboration by providing common ground required for clear understanding and discussion. Communication should be kept open among teachers, aides, and school-based support staff regarding such students. Staff should keep lists of children who have risk factors for developing PTSD; such lists can be developed through teacher reporting and peer screening. In one school, this goal was compromised by the administration's concern over legal liability for intervention once a student was identified as needing help, compared to the supposed legal innocence of not knowing about a problem. A solution here can be for the concerned individual (parent, school personnel) to consult with lawyers and clergy in the community on the legal and moral aspects of this issue or to join the school board and to urge the administration to listen to all sides of the issue. In addition, peer screening programs can run up against norms against tattling. In that case, social education programs can be developed, with the help of mental health professionals and spiritual care providers, to address moral issues around helping versus tattling.

Schools should be guided to decide on and implement procedures intended to create a number of desirable outcomes after a disaster, such as

- Plans for emergency pickup of children from the school.
- Communication with students regarding the nature of the disaster as it occurs and regarding reasons for steps taken to ensure their safety.
- Decisions about limiting the exposure of students in school to television, radio, and Internet, especially in grade school.
- Efforts to maintain a sense of calm.

Conflict can arise when school staff cannot keep to familiar procedures. For example, some school security officials were upset on 9/11 when parents picking up their children in the middle of the day ignored procedures for signing children out. The parents' well-intended actions made the school staff feel all the more helpless as their authority and roles were ignored. To handle this common problem, school administration officials should meet with all school staff in the days immediately after the disaster, with the goal of briefing the staff on what happened and debriefing them on their reactions. Staff should be given the chance to express their emotional reactions to not being able to act within their usual roles, and these reactions should be normalized and respected.

Collective Events in the School-Based Setting

Students also need briefing and debriefing in the first days after the disaster. Public expression of feelings, including grief, fear, and anger, can be valuable. Such public expression can occur through commemorations, assemblies, collages, volunteer work, and political activities for older students. Themes concerning the disaster can be worked into the curriculum, contests, performances, puppet shows, masks, music, art, essays, and theater. Staff and students who showed courage and compassion during the trauma can be commended in various ways.

Yet the value of public commemoration and expression of feeling must be balanced with the other important agenda of minimizing reminders of the trauma. Reminders of the disaster can retraumatize students, raising autonomic reactions and causing flashbacks. After the initial round of intense focus on what happened and how students reacted, normal routines should resume. Also, in the days after the disaster, school staff should be watching out for copycat incidents and posttraumatic play in which the disaster is played out in dangerous ways. Finally, school staff should be attentive to the need to make referrals of at-risk students and their families to counseling services inside and outside the school.

Community-Based Initiatives for Children Regarding Disasters

For mental health professionals who want to help children outside of the school setting after a disaster, there is no time to wait for a treatment relationship to begin in the traditional way, with a client approaching a therapist. Parents, children, and adolescents can be approached at help centers that often spring up near the site of the disaster, organized by local groups, the Red Cross, or the Federal Emergency Management Agency (FEMA). After the attack on the World Trade Center in September 2001, for example, this kind of center was created at Pier 94 in downtown Manhattan (Coates, Schechter, & First, 2003). With children, the use of drawings, collages, and other forms of art was especially helpful in finding a way to express the horror of the disaster. It was useful to have a separate area set aside for these activities, providing a protected environment for the children.

Another way to help children and families at the community level after a disaster is to solicit large corporations and businesses to aid in the effort. Affected companies need to mourn the loss of colleagues, employees, and leaders. Staff members need to adjust to new locations, relationships, roles, and challenges. Many employees and executives are parents who bring their stress home. Some employees may be bereaved because of the disaster, and some may have been killed, leaving spouses and children bereaved at home. For surviving staff who are left with their families intact, guilt and concern over these families interferes with morale and productivity at work. These problems refer to an enormous need.

To illustrate, I describe my own work collaborating with other colleagues as we helped one such company. After the terrorist attacks on September 11, an organizational consultant began working with a company that had been located in the World Trade Center and organized a small team of mental health professionals to join him. A year later, the group broadened its focus to include the families of employees who had been killed, and I joined the collaborative project to add to the ability to respond to the needs of children. I made home visits all over the greater New York area to bereaved parents and children who had been identified as particularly in need. The parent (usually a mother) let the children know that my presence was important, and I found that I had as much of the kids' attention as possible. My presence usually created an atmosphere similar to that brought by a nurse coming into a room where someone is sick, bringing fresh air and matter-of-fact answers. I also brought hope and rekindled the process of mourning, insofar as I evoked images of the lost parent.

We also sponsored retreats, community-based day-long workshops and information sessions, working with other companies who wanted to support the families from this company. Offering this kind of support had a mixed appeal; some parents welcomed it and some rejected it. There were no fees paid because the collaborative group was supported by a foundation created for this purpose by and for the company that had been so damaged on 9/11. There was often a personal kind of guilt that the professional felt when the relationship ended because it was the professional who had started the relationship and urged the parent (usually a mother) or child to open up. Reaching out may also have kept the surviving parents in a passive and dependent role, compared to the more common activity involved when a client seeks out a professional.

We arranged three annual weekend retreats. These retreats were for families who had lost a parent, including surviving spouses and children of all ages. One third of the families in this category accepted our invitation. Others were interested and unavailable that weekend, while others did not want to attend. We chose a place that afforded childcare, recreation, and meeting rooms. We wanted to allow time for families to be together and to be on their own; to let children be with other children who shared their experience to reduce isolation; and to let parents meet together for support as single parents, for help with grief and mourning, and for company with other parents who also went through the disaster.

Work With the Children

The children saw that we were engaging their parents emotionally around issues that had to do with the deceased parent. In that way, we were temporarily, for the child, replacing the dead parent emotionally. This kind of stepping in freed the children to play, feeling that for the moment we were taking care of their parents' grief. The children felt during the retreat as if they temporarily had regained a lost or important connection with the deceased parent, as we engaged the surviving parent and also the children. We also encouraged the children to engage each other because these children had parents who had worked together in the same company and had not survived the disaster. This offered a respite from the burden of mourning through a different kind of connection over grief. In fact, after the weekend retreats, some of the children had periods of agitation, because of having to give up that temporarily regained connection.

We organized children's workshops according to age, with meetings for both the younger children and the older children. We used drawing, mutual storytelling, social dreams, and discussion to break the ice and allow expression of feeling and memory. The parents of the younger children's group watched in the background. They were impressed and sometimes surprised at how expressive their children were in their drawings and stories. We felt the same way. The imaginative stories were full of themes of children getting lost, relying on other people for help to find their way, finding ways to help themselves, and making friends and meeting enemies along the way. The children were engaged and on occasion embellished each other's stories. None left after the break in the middle of the session. They took to the drawing exercises readily, using facial expressions and weather images to depict the sadness they felt after their mothers or fathers were killed. References to the lost parent or to his or her death were expressed in private symbols or in obvious symbols (like a rescue helicopter hovering over a big building). One 4-year-old's picture of her family's tension after 9/11 was of a monster. Another little girl's picture of running shoes opened up a memory from the day of the attack: yelling to her father over the phone to run away from the burning building, but realizing that he had left his running shoes at home.

We had children tell their dreams, one after the other, and heard many anxious ones. This kind of exercise, called *social dreaming*, was easy for younger children (ages 3 to 7) but harder for older children. The older children and teens were more guarded, having come to rely on the repression of feeling. They also felt the developmentally normal wish not to stand out in front of their peers as someone who couldn't handle intense feeling. Among the teenagers, some of the boys felt that they were now the man of the house, and others had become rebellious and difficult. Many of the girls had become more affectionate with their mothers. All the sibling systems seemed closer than before. There was a particular difficulty for boys who had lost their fathers and for girls who had lost their mothers.

Children were ambivalent about their single parent getting back into life (working, dating, socializing, enjoying recreational activities). They wanted this kind of transition to a new level of normalcy, yet they also did not want their parent to get back into life (the child feeling jealous and resentful of this), feeling that this would betray the dead parent in some way.

Work With the Parents

In workshops with parents, we spoke about how to handle children's fears concerning bad things happening again and how to reassure when safety cannot be guaranteed. We introduced the concept of probable safety and of danger that was possible though unlikely as a way to speak with reassurance and honesty with their children. Parents realized the mixed messages they were giving their children about safety, such as saying, "You're not allowed to go to school on your bike" (communicating their fear of another loss) but also saying, "God wouldn't do that to me twice."

Parents asked about getting help for their children and whether they should do it now or wait until the children expressed problems. Several had already brought their children and other family members for therapy. Parents were often unsure whether to interpret their children's problematic behaviors and attitudes and feelings as reactions to losing their father or mother on 9/11 or as reactions to other matters that would have happened even without the trauma (such as siblings fighting or a parent going away overnight). Parents also had to deal with their children's resentment of their dating or with their children's longing for a new parent to replace the lost one ("I want a new daddy") when the parent was not yet ready. We were able to encourage parents who were avoiding reference to the dead parent to find ways to refer to him or her. We explained that they could let their children identify with the dead parent and value him or her, telling the child that they were like the parent and valuing stories about that parent.

We also helped parents examine how to help their children and themselves to manage the public image of losing a mother or father or spouse on 9/11. Many parents spoke of the exhaustion of being a single parent, compounded by the public nature of their loss. When news media and teachers and chance comments referred to the events of 9/11, feelings of painful loss were revived. Their children sometimes did not know how to respond to other children's comments and sometimes did not realize the effect of their own comments, such as telling another child at a birthday party, "My father died on 9/11. Did yours?" We spoke about ways parents could help teachers speak with their children, such as explaining to another child that Susan's father had died and that was why he was not there on a parent–teacher day. Parents also needed help managing other people's comments to them. They were angry over pity or false empathy ("I know how you feel") when the person had no idea how they felt, or poorly timed condolences, or comparisons to much more trivial difficulties that the other person was suffering. They struggled with their anger when the other person changed the subject to the other person's concern, ignoring their upset while pretending to be caring. There was much discussion on having to teach people how to give and not give condolences. We did not discuss religion or faith directly, but there was occasional reference to God and to the degree of adversity one person would be allowed to suffer.

Parents needed help dealing with their own parents and their in-laws, especially around arrangements for funerals and memorials. Each disaster creates its own problems in this area. For us, a particular problem occurred when parents of someone who had died on 9/11 unexpectedly attended a discussion group primarily for the spouses. Bereaved widows and widowers shared the agony of learning that body parts of one's spouse were discovered months or years after September 2001, but the subject of the disposal of body parts was addressed differently by parents of the deceased. In one discussion, the parents of the deceased were entitled and bitter in their feelings, while the spouses felt intense pain and awkwardness, and these different kinds of voices clashed.

The bereaved spouses also realized that many of them were trying to imagine the last moments of their loved ones. They shared their anger and their guilt over this anger regarding the decisions and actions that worsened the outcome on that day. They looked for someone to blame. We also discussed their evaluations of how much progress they had made, compared to how much progress they and others thought they should have made, in coming to terms with the loss of their spouses. They wanted to compare their experience to surviving spouses of victims of other disasters.

The number of families participating dwindled each year. At the third retreat, we asked them to take over the task of organizing the next one. They did not, and the project ended. In hindsight, the provision of such support by many professionals collaborating together to help these families served a valuable purpose during the first years after the 9/11 attacks. As the parents put their lives back together, their need for us diminished. In turn, we became less inclined to provide collaborative support without being asked.

Conclusion

Reviewing this experience, it is apparent that prior contact with schools or corporations creates trust and familiarity and allows access and involvement after a disaster that is much harder to achieve with no prior contact. Regarding preventive intervention, creating and maintaining contacts for ongoing consultation with community institutions, such as schools or companies, is invaluable in the event of a disaster. Similar value can be found in the cultivation of relationships between groups of mental health professionals on the one hand and churches and synagogues on the other to open doors and keep them open during the time after a disaster.

During interventions, there are advantages to having several adults lead group discussions. For us, when one facilitator could not find a way to interrupt an unfortunate direction in the conversation, another was able tactfully to lead the conversation elsewhere. This is an important point in understanding how people may effectively work together in a chaotic environment, by the implicit or stated agreement to share leadership roles and tasks.

Internal collaboration and open communication is essential to interact effectively with external groups like schools or corporations, even as this internal collaboration develops in conjunction with needs presented by these groups. Projects can fail if the collaborative team is in conflict about matters such as budget, roles, and authority to make decisions.

Collaborative projects on behalf of children after a disaster need someone to organize the effort, whether a professional or a parent. There also comes a time for the project to end. After our collaborative project with the company so damaged on 9/11 finally came to an end, parents continued to receive support through ongoing community, company, or church involvements and through support groups and church-based activities that had preceded our own intervention but were enriched by the experiences we had offered.

References

Coates, S., Schechter, D., & First, E. (2003). Brief interventions with traumatized children and families after September 11. In S. Coates, J. Rosenthal, & D. Schechter (Eds.), *September 11: Trauma and human bonds* (pp. 23–49). Hillsdale, NJ: The Analytic Press.

Gensler, D., Goldman, D., Goldman, D., Gordon, R., Prince, R., & Rosenbach, N. (2002). Voices from New York: September, 11, 2001. *Contemporary Psychoanalysis, 38,* 77–99.

Pynoos, R. S., Steinberg, A. M., & Goenjian, A. (1996). Traumatic stress in childhood and adolescence: Recent developments and current controversies. In B. A. Van Der Kolk, A. C. McFarlane, & L. Weisaeth (Eds.), *Traumatic stress: The effects of overwhelming experience on mind, body, and society* (pp. 331–358). New York: Guilford.

Yehuda, R. (Ed.). (1999). *Risk factors for posttraumatic stress disorders.* Washington, DC: American Psychiatric Press.

11

Making Referrals
Effective Collaboration Between Mental Health and Spiritual Care Practitioners

Patricia Berliner, Diane Ryan, and Julie Taylor

Introduction

Although mental health workers and spiritual care providers have worked together for many years to meet the needs of local communities, disaster response, as an organized discipline, is a relatively new specialty for both groups. Being present to those affected by tragedy is a finely calibrated effort, a multidisciplinary process in which each piece must fit together appropriately, comfortably, and effectively within the whole.

Background

In the United States, major developments in collaboration between mental health and spiritual care providers in response to major tragedies followed several aviation incidents within a short period of time: the US Air Flight 427 disaster in Pittsburg, Pennsylvania, in September 1994, the ValuJet air crash in the Florida Everglades in May 1996, and the July 1996 TWA Flight 800 disaster in Long Island, New York. Each time, people from near and far converged on the sites of these disasters, offering their concern and willingness to help in any way they could. Although their concern was heartfelt and well meaning, many of the volunteers were not experienced or trained in disaster response.

Pat Berliner was one of the first responders to TWA 800. She lives near Kennedy Airport and, as a member of the New York State Psychological Association Disaster Response Network, was asked to report to the Ramada Inn where both the Command Center and the accommodations for the families were set up. It was a mass of activity, seeming chaos and sadness, and the first major disaster she had experienced.

When Pat arrived at the hotel, she walked into a mass of people. Command stations for police, firefighters, and media shared the limited space in the first floor lobby and banquet hall along with family members, flight crew, and responders. At the same time, guests of the hotel walked in and out of the lobby, the restaurant, and the courtyard. After getting her bearings, Pat went over to a young couple, standing alone in the courtyard. They had lost their daughter, one of the students from Pennsylvania who was on a school trip to France. Pat went over to them, standing with them quietly, until they began to talk about their loss. They were gracious, scared, devastated people. In the midst of talking quietly, two eager young volunteers came bounding over, announcing that they were counselors and asking inappropriate questions in an inappropriate manner. Pat quietly told them that she and the family were talking and that they might want to see who else could use some help. Soon after that, two members of the staff of the Travel Agency, which booked the flight, came over to her and said they didn't know what to do. They were afraid that they would be seen as enemies but wanted to let the families know that they cared about them in their grief. They, too, needed to find a way to grieve. Pat suggested that their company might provide a scholarship to the school in the names of the children. They were relieved to have something concrete to offer.

At lunchtime, Pat was in the lobby, waiting for lunch to be served to the staff and volunteers. One very prominent member of the mental health community was standing in front of her, speaking loudly with other colleagues about her planned trip to Hawaii. Pat was aghast at this and left to be with members of the families and the TWA personnel, who were there to support them.

As the day went on, volunteers kept arriving. Nuns who were pastoral counselors, clergy of various denominations, social workers, psychologists, counselors (credentialed and noncredentialed), all wanting to help, all not knowing quite what to do, some very well qualified, some not at all. Screening of these volunteers was next to impossible. Because of this response and several additional aviation incidents that occurred within a short period of time with similar complications, there was a call for legislative guidelines outlining the ways families would be provided services in future incidents.

The Aviation Family Disaster Assistance Act of 1996 mandated the National Transportation Safety Board to designate a human services agency to be responsible for the provision of care to friends and families of aviation disaster victims. The American Red Cross was the agency identified. Because of the requirement for the American Red Cross to coordinate and manage the organizations and personnel that provide counseling, spiritual and other support services, disaster mental health workers and spiritual care providers began working together with greater frequency. Fairly quickly, they recognized that collaboration with one another allowed for more comprehensive care for those in need. From lessons learned at this and the many other disasters, which have occurred since then, and the implementation of guidelines developed together, the building of a partnership between spiritual care and mental health in the United States expanded dramatically across the nation and across the globe.

The Hawaiian Red Cross disaster mental health program has collaborated with disaster spiritual care for many years, most notably in the Hurricane Iniki response in September 1992, the Sacred Falls landslide in May 1999, and the mass casualty shooting at the Xerox building in November 1999 evidence the effectiveness of the interdisciplinary team. In New York, the relationship between spiritual care providers from Disaster Chaplaincy Services and disaster mental health workers from the American Red Cross in Greater New York was solidified during many months of working side by side during the 9/11 World Trade Center disaster response. Both at the site and at local centers set up around the area, many of which were places of worship, trained spiritual care, mental health teams, as well as great numbers of spontaneous volunteers offered services in a multiplicity of areas, working together to provide whatever physical, emotional, and spiritual comfort they could. Since that time, the two response groups have worked together regularly at fatal fires, transportation incidents, and other disaster events in which people are experiencing emotional and spiritual distress.

Data

In diasaster work, there are many challenges inherent in collaboration between two distinct disciplines. Mental health workers and spiritual care providers have different orientations and speak different "professional languages." Confusion and misunderstandings are not uncommon. Conflicts with role differentiation, terminology, authority, boundaries, trust, and communication must be identified by those willing to resolve them and resolved by those able to work together. Sometimes being well intentioned, eager to be of service, and concerned about the well-being of those we are serving can become testy. Everyone brings something from his or her own history to the situation at hand. Everyone wants to be as helpful as possible. Mental health workers do not always trust that spiritual care providers will recognize that sometimes people's emotional and psychological needs go beyond what the spiritual care provider can handle. Spiritual care providers, in turn, may feel that their skills are not valued and, at times, are negated by the mental health professionals. In the midst of disorganized chaos, the organizational structure of disaster response threatens to break down. This is exactly the worst time for this to happen.

In contrast, those seeking true collaboration recognize that a disaster site is no place for competition and that no one discipline is the final authority. Rather, those groups designated as leads retain equal status in the partnership. In the ideal world, disaster operations in which mental health providers report to a mental health lead, spiritual care providers report to a spiritual care lead, and the two leads collaborate as equals reporting to a job director is the most effective model. When the two leads do not collaborate and instead one or both communicate only to the job director, the chaos inherent in any disaster situation is exacerbated, duplication of effort occurs, and the relationship between the two leads becomes strained and characterized by mistrust. The result of this is that clients do not receive the best care as energy and efforts are diverted to the relationship difficulties of the two disciplines.

In communities, and among representative organizations where developing effective collaboration between mental health and spiritual care has been a priority, the relationship between the disciplines could be likened to a dance. With individual clients and sometimes communities, there are times when one leads, another follows, the roles can change, and the movement is fluid. There needs to be an implicit trust that, when one group takes the lead, the other will stand by to assist as needed. This trust develops as with any other relationship, across time and experience together as each discipline learns that the other has an inclusive, open, and nonterritorial framework.

Each disaster is different, although always chaotic and ripe for communication gaps. When individual responders have been well prepared, in both the theoretical and response level, and when the leads and team members of partner groups know each other well, the movements can be choreographed quickly without the need for lengthy discussion. This occurs only after repeated positive experiences with each other, when both partners have a sense of each other's response patterns and movements. Until such a sense of other is developed, it is essential for the two groups to frequently communicate about each discipline's assessment of individuals and the community affected and together develop an effective service delivery plan to meet emotional and spiritual needs.

In the dance of disaster response, disaster spiritual care providers take the lead when communities with a religious affiliation or strong ties to their faith are affected, when the affected are those who are not comfortable speaking with mental health professionals, and in working with cultures that historically have a comfort level with clergy and are wary of mental health workers, such as first responders.

A Red Cross national poll taken by Caravan ORC International in October 2001 surveyed over 1,000 adults and found that 60% of the population reported a preference to speak with people of faith rather than mental health personnel. Other studies have found that "in small communities, clergy often coordinate disaster relief efforts due to their longstanding leadership roles in those communities" (Koenig, 2007, p. 921).

When a death has occurred, spiritual care and mental health workers both provide support during death notifications and escort families to the morgue for body identification. Experience has shown that when people are in that vulnerable state, they often find great comfort in the presence of a faith leader. Even when people are mad at God, often they will seek out someone they see as a representative of a faith to yell at, question, demand answers from, or even blame.

For those impacted by disaster who are wary of religion or who have no religious affiliation, if there is a need for a mental health evaluation of a client and in disasters affecting a population with known mental illness, mental health practitioners take the lead and spiritual care providers are available to assist them. For example, at the March 2008 crane collapse in Manhattan, Julie Taylor assessed the spiritual needs, and Diane Ryan assessed the emotional needs of the families of those missing and deceased as well as the residents evacuated from the affected buildings. A service delivery plan was mutually developed and the mental health and spiritual care teams were briefed on the operational plan for the next few days. Throughout the first 12 hours of the operation, Diane and Julie were in frequent communication as the needs of those affected changed. Together, the team consoled families through death notifications and morgue escorts, working with animal control agencies to assist those with pets remaining in vacated buildings, and supporting those who learned they could not reoccupy their dwelling for some time.

No matter what disaster discipline practitioners identify with, each must be skilled in crisis intervention and embrace the art of compassionate presence, which is the ability to be with those in their suffering and be of comfort without trying to fix situations or provide answers. "Very rarely is what we say the most important thing, it's really the fact that we are there. That we are willing to sit and not walk away from the pain and anguish of what comes along in life. We sit, we accompany, we companion with folks the worst days of their lives" (Taylor & Ryan, 2007, pp. 66–67).

It is common in disaster work to find people who are licensed in a mental health discipline and trained as a spiritual care provider. When volunteering to work at a disaster site, it is imperative that the multi-qualified worker identify which capacity he or she will be serving for the particular response and that the work is done within the parameters of that discipline.

In areas of the United States that are active in preparedness activities, there is now a movement toward members of related response disciplines coming together before a disaster happens. Preincident relationships are essential to strong collaboration and must include opportunities for regular trainings, meetings, drills, and exercises and social events at which people can get to know each other in a relaxed environment. This nondisaster collaboration brings opportunities to learn one another's language, establishes communication and prepares a foundation for trust. Awareness of what each group brings to the table can open both to a mutuality of learning and cross-training between disciplines.

Communicating and collaborating with communities impacted by tragedy is always more effective when it is driven by those who do not appear to be "outsiders." Given the diverse populations within our country and our local communities, disaster mental health and spiritual care teams must be culturally, racially, ethnically, religiously, and linguistically diverse. Often, spiritual care teams will have practitioners who can address the needs of people with different cultural backgrounds, faith beliefs, languages, and cultural needs. This is not always true for mental health teams and is another example of the strength of a collaborative team approach.

One tenet of spiritual care providers is that "we help the healing process best when we seek the help of others and build partnerships within the communities we are deployed to help heal" (Ashley et al., 2008, p. 232). Referrals between disaster mental health workers and disaster spiritual care workers occur during all phases of a disaster (warning/threat, rescue, honeymoon, disillusionment, recovery) as practitioners triage and assess emotional and spiritual stress. Mental health and spiritual care workers must have a working knowledge of each groups' skill sets in order to competently triage and assess for referral.

Because disaster work is based on the concept that most people have a basic resiliency and with appropriate support during times of disaster will activate their own coping skills to manage the crisis, it is of major importance that mental health and spiritual care providers resist the urge to fix the problems of disaster victims. The goal in most situations is to help those affected determine options that are congruent with their culture, background and belief system, and then support them as they identify resources and begin making decisions on their recovery.

To best help the healing process, both mental health and spiritual care responders often refer those affected by disaster to local mental health and/or spiritual care workers who can provide long-term follow-up care. Generally, disaster mental health workers refer individuals for long-term mental health care and disaster spiritual care workers refer those in need of faith-based services, such as pastoral counseling, religious services and rituals, etc. Because it is most helpful if the worker can refer to practitioners in the area who are known for their expertise, each disaster worker should also have access to resources and referrals within the local area. Additionally, many communities have local Critical Incident Stress Management (CISM) teams comprised of peers, chaplains, and mental health personnel who work, train, and respond together regularly. For organizations that work with CISM teams, this can be another valuable resource for collaboration, particularly if you are coming in from the "outside."

We recognize that partnership between disaster mental health workers and spiritual care providers is most successful when each group benefits from the contributions and support of the other. For example, it was a very moving experience when the American Red Cross in Greater New York mental health volunteers provided end-of-assignment support to Disaster Chaplaincy Services personnel after they had blessed the remains at Ground Zero/World Trade Center site during the 9-month disaster recovery operation. In another situation of grief, when a Red Cross staff member was unable to attend the overseas funeral of her beloved aunt, a Disaster Chaplaincy Services member came in to perform a private service for her and several close colleagues at the precise time that her aunt was being buried. This generous gesture and ritual experience helped ease the grief of the Red Cross staff member by providing an opportunity for her to feel connected to her family oversees as they, together, honored and mourned her aunt.

Synthesis

The examples and guidelines we have offered are meant to be an introduction to the mission and work of disaster mental health workers and spiritual care partners. We hope that they have given a sense of the "behind the scenes" collaboration, trust and support that make possible the work we do for the people in our communities at times of suffering and loss. We who share a sacred trust reverence the privilege of being able to help bring healing to the pain, hope in despair and some semblance of normality to the lives of victims of disaster and tragedy, whether that be one person or a nation.

Conclusion

Because this model has proven to be effective, other disaster organizations in the United States have begun to develop their own collaborative forums between mental health and spiritual care providers. The work of team building that has already been done is extraordinary, but many practical challenges remain, including finding new funding resources to create disaster chaplaincy groups. Another major goal is identifying creative ways in which mental health and spiritual care teams can implement and extend the networking process. We trust that we will continue to move forward and that, with and from our work, will come new groups, new volunteers, and new resources to meet the needs of people who suffer disastrous losses.

References

Ashley, W. W. C., Samet, R. L., Radillo, R., Ali, U. N. A., Billings, D., & Davidowitz-Farkas, Z. (2008). Cultural and religious considerations. In *Disaster spiritual care: Practical clergy responses to community, regional and national tragedy.* Woodstock, VT: Skylight Paths Publishing Company.

Caravan ORC International (2001). American Red Cross national poll, October 5–8.

Koenig, H. (2007). Introduction: Spirituality and catastrophe. *Southern Medical Journal, 100*(9), 921.
Taylor, J., & Ryan, D. (Winter 2007). Roles in respite centers: Peers, chaplains, and mental health. *International Journal of Emergency Mental Health.* Abstract of a presentation at the ICISF 9th World Conference, Baltimore, MD (February 16) 9(1): 66–67.

Further Readings

American Red Cross. (2001). *The ripple effect from Ground Zero. Coping with mental health needs in time of tragedy and terror.* Washington, DC: ARC Presentation.
American Red Cross (2007, March 14). *Chapter mental health team and disaster chaplaincy services solidify their ongoing partnership.* Press release.
Danieli, Y. (2001). ISTSS members participate in recovery efforts in New York and Washington, DC. *Traumatic Stress Points,* 15(4), 4.
Guinta, R. (2002). *God@ground zero. How good overcame evil one heart at a time.* Nashville, TN: Integrity.
Halpern, J., & Tramontin, M. (2007). *Disaster mental health theory and practice.* Belmont, CA: Thomson Brooks/Cole.
Keyayan, V. A., & Napoli, J. C. (2005). *Resiliency in the face of disaster and terrorism: 10 things to do to survive.* Fawnskin, CA: Personhood Press.
Koenig, H. (2006). *Keeping faith when disaster strikes. In the wake of disaster: Religious responses to terrorism and catastrophe.* Radnor, PA: Templeton Foundation Press.
Miller, M. (2003). Working in the midst of unfolding trauma and traumatic loss: Training as a collective process of support. *Psychoanalytic Social Work, 10*(1), 7–25.
Moghaddam, F., & Marsella, A. (Eds.). (2004). *Understanding terrorism: Psychological roots, consequences and interventions.* Washington, DC: American Psychological Association.
Myers, D., & Wee, D. F. (2005). *Disaster mental health services.* London: Brunner–Routledge.
Norris, F., Friedman, N., Watson, P., Byrne, C., Diaz, E., & Kanisty, K. (2002). 60,000 disaster victims speak: Part I. An empirical review of the empirical literature. *Psychiatry, 65*(3), 207–239.
Roberts, S., & Ashley, W. W. C. (Eds.). (2008). *Disaster spiritual care. Practical clergy responses to community, regional and national tragedy.* Woodstock, VT: Skylight Paths Publishing.
Webber, J., Bass, D., & Yap, R. (Eds.). (2005). *A counselor's guide to preparing and responding.* Alexandria, VA: American Counseling Association Foundation.

12

"To Do No Harm" Spiritual Care and Ethnomedical Competence

Four Cases of Psychosocial Trauma Recovery for the 2004 Tsunami and 2005 Earthquake in South Asia

Siddharth Ashvin Shah

Indeed there was a near melee of activity from the large number of agencies who rushed to the region, albeit most of them without any previous experience of a country like Sri Lanka, its culture and background problems. Many came specifically to provide mental health assistance to the "traumatized victims" of the tsunami. But the question is: Were such communities seeking mental health and psychosocial assistance framed in this way? The impressions gained from field-level discussions are that they were not. They did not want counseling, instead pointing to their shattered homes and livelihoods. The children were observed to be sad, and a few with nightmares, but well functioning and keen to have their schools rebuilt. (Jayawickrama, 2006, p. 2)

Introduction

How can spiritual care be appropriately and safely integrated into psychosocial trauma recovery work? What constitutes "appropriateness" vis-à-vis the diversity of psychological, social, and medical tasks that need to be accomplished in global disaster relief? In order to respond to such questions, this chapter will present a framework involving refashioned categories and new terminology in hopes of bringing to life the pitfalls and potential solutions of global trauma work. Such pitfalls and a review of past recommendations will be outlined. Next, four case studies of collaboration from South Asia will be discussed through fieldwork vignettes and interview material. The chapter's synthesis will involve methods and support for applying spiritual care techniques in ways that offer healing in diverse domains of health. "Appropriateness" will be discussed by maintaining that there is a cost–benefit determination that takes into account psychosocial benefits at the lowest cost (including cultural costs) to the disaster-affected society. The chapter will end on its message that collaborations happen best within democratic and symmetric relationships of stakeholders innovating optimal interventions.

From a category standpoint, spiritual care techniques are among the many ethnomedical techniques within the larger domain of *integrative medicine** that, when blended with the domains of public health and group psychology, make up integrative psychosocial resilience (IPR) (Figure 12.1).

IPR brackets our attention on healing the psychosocial wounds of disaster (and excludes other important relief functions, such as food, water, sanitation, disease prevention, structural repair, communications, and security). The designation *ethnomedical* incorporates the view that all healing practices are configured by the context in which they were created and the context in which they are currently

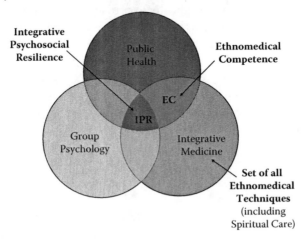

Figure 12.1 Model of integrative psychosocial resilence

---

* Integrative medicine: A set of all empirically efficacious ethnomedical techniques for healing and curing human suffering. It includes spiritual care, traditional medical systems, and allopathy (modern biomedicine). Modern psychiatry with its pharmaceutical methods and psychotherapy methods is viewed as one subset of ethnomedical techniques among many others.

being applied. *Ethnomedical competence* (EC) is the capacity to discern appropriate blends of techniques that meet public health needs for particular situations. Appropriate blends are ones that deliver substantial benefits while doing minimal harm (including minimization of costs). While maintaining an evidence-informed stance on effectiveness and safety, EC views Western and non-Western techniques as equally respected partners.

BOX 1: CULTIVATING ETHNOMEDICAL COMPETENCE

1. Utilize literature review, anthropology, and related disciplines in order to arrive at a more accurate view of affected persons, preliminary therapeutic goals, and list of possible interventions.
2. With the community, learn about local idioms of distress, negotiate mutually agreeable goals, and prepare to exercise maximal flexibility consistent with those goals. Balance cultural power so that all parties collaborate in democratic and symmetrical learning environments. Consider utilizing a consultant with ethnomedical experience to provide perspective and cultural skill sets.
3. Study applicable culturally embedded, local healing interventions. Ascertain how culturally embedded interventions are (or are not) being utilized.
4. Take a step back to view the entire field of possible interventions (Western, local, and nonlocal/non-Western) and choose a set of interventions on the basis of feasibility, efficacy, "doing no harm," and cost.
5. Work within a plan of integrated services. Expand program monitoring/evaluation terms and outcome studies so that the measured parameters take local signs of distress into account.

Why even bother to create so many categories with new terminology? These categories aspire to take into account the increasing academic critique (Jayawickrama, 2006; Shah, 2006, 2007a; Summerfield, 2005) against the individual-focused, pathology-oriented, psychological protocols that are applied by outsiders coming to Asian disasters with the intent of doing good. Many Asian-centric relief authorities prefer psychosocial conceptualizations of trauma intervention in order to respect the dynamic relationship between psychological states and social realities—recognizing that strengths and vulnerabilities in either will coinfluence the other. Psychosocial programs show "commitment to nonmedical approaches and distance from the field of mental health, which is seen as too controlled by physicians and too closely associated with the ills of an overly biopsychiatric approach" (van Ommeren, Saxena, & Saraceno, 2005, p. 71). The blending of integrative medicine, public health, and group psychology into IPR is a framework to mitigate the challenges that are inevitable in doing cross-cultural and transnational psychosocial work.

Background Obstacles and Challenges

In order to prevent an overly biopsychiatric approach, IPR is a framework that accommodates the blending of psychosocial interventions. Still, psychosocial interventions can be ill-fitting if local interventions are ignored or Western interventions are not culturally adapted. Epistemologically, it makes a world of difference that widely accepted interventions and protocols are developed largely by those in Western settings, validated through randomized control trials with Anglo-European populations seeking generalizability, and configured by the philosophical underpinnings of modernism, positivism, and logocentrism. Part of the cultural cost to a non-Westernized person who avails herself of a Western intervention is that a survivor must work (and possibly lose parts of herself) to adopt a self-concept that fits the intervention's terms of reference. Operationally, these interventions are then superimposed (taken "off the shelf") or lightly adapted for use cross-culturally and transnationally with the hope that they bring benefit (and they often do) without considering a wider palette of interventions that would better take into account the local population (as possibly bringing substantially more benefit). With a view toward mitigating these challenges, warnings from leaders in the field include the following:

> **BOX 2: CHALLENGES TO CROSS-CULTURAL AND TRANSNATIONAL TRAUMA INTERVENTIONS**
>
> 1. A World Health Organization (WHO) bulletin: "We need to remember that the Western mental health discourse introduces core components of Western culture, including a theory of human nature, a definition of personhood, a sense of time and memory, and a secular source of moral authority. None of this is universal" (Summerfield, 2005, p. 76).
> 2. "Off the shelf" intervention materials are difficult to use in diverse settings because they are unknowingly embedded with cultural

expectations and unsubstantiated assumptions (Norris & Alegría, 2006; Vega, 1992).

3. "Attempts from outside Aceh to 'train' various community leaders in how they might respond to widespread psychological distress at a community level, using western constructs of community reconstruction and development, may be misguided and will probably be unwelcome" (WHO, 2005, p. 4).

4. "Standardized instruments are useful for evaluating outcomes in relation to standard psychosocial interventions, but they may not encompass local constructions of mental distress, reasons for seeking traditional healing, or definitions of successful treatment, which may be grounded in spiritual cosmologies" (Patel, Kirkwood, & Weiss, 2005).

5. A Sri Lankan academic, Janaka Jayawickrama (2006), offers this analysis: "… unplanned and uncoordinated humanitarian assistance without a clear vision may create as much distress as the disaster. To categorize affected communities as 'traumatized' and in need of psychological or psychosocial support—and on the basis of assumptions that owe nothing to the voices of the people themselves—is to miss important opportunities to provide humanitarian assistance that will be valued by recipients."

Clearly, spiritual care interventions are vulnerable to the above pitfalls, especially if the field of spiritual care pursues generalizability and protocol-driven interventions. If, however, spiritual care aligns itself appropriately with local traditions and holistic healers—while evolving practice norms—it can stimulate highly relevant IPR, while minimizing harm. With this in mind, what follows are relevant recommendations from different sources:

BOX 3: RECOMMENDATIONS FOR UTILIZING RELIGIOUS, SPIRITUAL, AND TRADITIONAL VIEWS IN DISASTER

1. The religious construction of meaning surrounding the disaster may mean that efforts to deal with psychological and social consequences of the disaster in ways that are not consonant with such religious and cultural values and beliefs (e.g., trauma-focused counseling, psychiatric approaches) will be both ineffective and unacceptable. (WHO, 2005)

2. Authors Carballo, Heal, and Hernandez (2005, p. 398) observed improved resilience in tsunami-affected populations utilizing spiritual grounding and religious leaders. They suggest the following: "Some of

those affected by the Tsunami may react poorly to alien approaches ... external (as well as internal) groups must always pay careful attention to local cultures, religions, and traditional ways of coping with incidents, such as the tsunami."

3. "Traditional healers are culturally and linguistically similar to their clients, share the cosmology of their clients, and generally have a holistic approach to healing especially useful to conflict-affected populations who may suffer a variety of traumatic impacts and symptoms, including emotional, psychological, physical/somatic, social, and spiritual ones" (de Jong, 2007, p. 217).

4. "From a public health perspective, traditional healers often have the advantage that they are easily accessible from a cultural and geographic point of view" (de Jong, 2007, p. 217).

There is great scope for IPR appropriately applied (i.e., ethnomedically competent) spiritual care and preexisting rituals retooled (or retraditioned) to fit disaster contexts. As the primary mechanism (under the United Nations' resolutions 46/182 and 48/57) for interagency coordination of humanitarian assistance, the Inter-Agency Standing Committee (IASC) has laid out important guidelines for psychosocial best practices:

BOX 4: THE IASC'S GUIDELINES ON MENTAL HEALTH AND PSYCHOSOCIAL SUPPORT IN EMERGENCY SETTINGS

Encourages relief workers to interface with appropriate spiritual practices and local healers. Relevant warnings and recommendations from IASC's *Guidelines* include:

1. Engaging with local religion or culture often challenges nonlocal relief workers to consider world views very different from their own. Because some local practices cause harm (for example, in contexts where spirituality and religion are politicized), humanitarian workers should think critically and support local practices and resources only if they fit with international standards of human rights. (IASC, 2007, Action Sheet 5.3)

2. Ignoring such healing practices, on the other hand, can prolong distress and potentially cause harm by marginalizing helpful cultural ways of coping. In many contexts, working with religious leaders and resources is an essential part of emergency psychosocial support. (IASC, 2007, Action Sheet 5.3)

3. Blending therapies in order to arrive at ethnomedically competent integrative psychosocial resilience is encouraged in Action Sheet 5.3 as well:

"Accept existing mixed practices (e.g., local and Westernized) where appropriate" (IASC, 2007, p. 108).

4. Even when allopathic health services are available, local populations may prefer to turn to local and traditional help for mental and physical health issues. Such help may be cheaper, more accessible, more socially acceptable and less stigmatizing and, in some cases, may be potentially effective. (IASC, 2007, Action Sheet 6.4)

5. Before supporting or collaborating with traditional cleansing or healing practices, it is essential to determine what those practices involve and whether they are potentially beneficial, harmful, or neutral. (IASC, 2007, Action Sheet 6.4)

When attempting to offer sustainable disaster work in South Asia, I have learned the power of engaging experienced nongovernmental organizations (international iNGOs or national NGOs) in mediating collaborations:

1. They often have the trust of the people because the staff has taken the time to learn local realities.

2. They form a cadre of barefoot counselors providing psychosocial first aid and making referrals.

3. They provide feedback on the merits and demerits of outsiders providing services.

Indeed, with regard to No. 3 above—feedback that [we] outsiders are ethically called upon to solicit—there have been several NGO communications (Jayawickrama, 2006; Shah, 2006) about wrong-headed interventions brought from the West. Such feedback has also been reported by WHO officials (Summerfield, 2005; van Ommeren et al., 2005).

In order to regulate well-intentioned, but inappropriate, interventions from iNGOs and NGOs, governments can play significant protective roles. For example, when tsunami relief efforts by iNGOs and NGOs appeared to be lopsided in favor of donor stakeholders versus practical needs on the ground, the government of India took steps that "mandated consulting the affected people in relief efforts, refusing any measures to be permitted that are donor-driven and disturb the way of life of the people" (Prashantham, 2008, p. 201). A proactive stance for outsiders is to recognize that some degree of "pushback" is inherent to aid relationships (Shah, 2007a) and that pushback can be magnified in cross-cultural encounters. Furthermore, beyond simply anticipating pushback, mechanisms of communication and feedback must be put in place to solicit dissatisfaction from the field to repair and adapt operations so that a program evolves with real-time, real-life concerns.

From a trauma research standpoint, Hobfall (1998) and Draguns (2004) both conclude that a review of past studies suggests the effectiveness of viewing all individuals through the lens of broader familial, interpersonal, and social contexts. Going one step farther than the de facto practice of cultural competence (Shah, 2007a), EC affirms that not only must we take into account multiple contexts to understand the traumatized self-concept but that once we see the traumatized self-concept through many lenses, it is important to develop IPR (a blend of appropriate techniques from a wide palette to achieve optimal results). Within South Asian populations, spiritual care techniques tend to be prevalent and well received. In the next section, I will present four cases of blending spiritual care within IPR delivery in South Asian disasters.

Data on Collaborations

Tsunami in India (Acute Phase)

Entering tsunami relief efforts, I was facilitated by preexisting relationships. In this context, *preexisting* could signify any of the following in varying degrees: confidence, empathy, faith, and positive expectations. On the day of the tsunami, December 26, 2004, I contacted a handful of NGOs that knew me, and I let them know what I could offer. I was ready to provide consultancy to relief agencies on psychosocial first aid (PFA) and neuropsychoeducation* of vicarious trauma and self-care (hereafter "VT/SC education"[†]).

Indicorps, an iNGO located in Ahmedabad, had the most actionable ideas for my involvement. My preexisting relationship with this iNGO was as an "alongside," meaning that I was a standing resource and consultant for addressing Indicorps staff stress and behavioral health concerns. Indicorps leadership put me in touch with their partners in Chennai, the metropolis from where major NGOs in South India staged their operations. On the subject of anything psychosocial, I was prepared to get responses

---

* Classical psychoeducation (teachings to deal with a psychological condition) plus education on the neurobiology of stress/distress/trauma/anxiety/depression. Neuropsychoeducation is taught in the spirit of democratizing health by teaching cognitive mastery and behavioral regulation.

† Vicarious trauma is also known as "secondary traumatic stress" in the academic literature. Education on vicarious trauma involving self-care and resilience also aids in the prevention of burnout, which is a related phenomenon of exhaustion occurring as a result of harsh working conditions.

such as: "We cannot stop our acute rescue operations for anything mental health right now." Regarding VT/SC education, I was prepared for: "We cannot see the priority of taking care of unaffected rescue workers when so many affected people need aid." However, after two NGOs heard my description, they stated that they recognized the VT phenomenon in their midst. They had a sense of urgency for which I was unprepared, saying, "We cannot afford not to have such training" and "We have college student volunteers working who have never encountered such tragedy, and they have pained eyes as they work."

On December 30, four days after the tsunami, I arrived in Chennai. Through interviews with fieldwork supervisors, I made an assessment of first responder work exhaustion and current self-care protocols. In one organization, Association for India's Development (AID), college students had arrived by busloads to help clear dead bodies and clean debris. One supervisor was visibly worried that many of the fieldworkers were working without breaks and close to exhaustion because "the devastation was so great and there was too much to do." From what I could gather, aside from AID workers being told that they should rest, there were no formal self-care protocols.

On December 31, I conducted a half-day training for AID fieldwork supervisors and upper management in its Chennai headquarters. The training covered the following:

1. VT/SC education (Bride, 2004; Jayawickrama, 2007; Pearlman & Caringi, (2008); Rothschild, 2006; Shah, 2007b; Young, Ford, & Wilson, 2008)
2. Reviewing individuals' currently used relaxation and expressive techniques; inquiring what other techniques would be culturally compatible
3. Simple mind–body relaxation techniques and leading practice sessions on systematic relaxation (e.g., breathing techniques)
4. Discussion on initiating/maintaining simple SC practices in the field (e.g., buddy system, reminders to breathe for relaxation)

Early in our training, one manager shared with the group how daily morning yoga, even during these days of crisis, was a factor in her resilience. From my point of view, this was an important revelation because it reinforced a link between disaster resilience and a common, nonforeign self-care practice. We explored what it would be like to do yoga postures with the explicit intention of preventing VT. I led a segment in which we practiced Nadi Shuddhi (a yoga practice of alternate nostril breathing) as a method for detoxifying especially emotional moments. Similarly, I presented other ways to link disaster resilience and common practices, such as: "What would it be like to have a peaceful meal (and any preceding prayer) infused with the explicit intention of building resilience vis-à-vis a disaster?" In teaching systematic, intentional relaxation, I suggested that people adopt a regular activity or technique that has resilience as its central purpose. This is in contrast to practices like "vegging" in front of a television or exercising or napping that are passively relaxing for some people.

January 1st, on the request of other voluntary agencies, I was asked to travel to Nagapattinam, the region of India most devastated—in lives lost, witnesses and survivors, and infrastructure destroyed. There I taught PFA to workers from NGOs and promoted PFA at a meeting coordinating government and NGO activities.

In the villages of Nagapattinam, I was asked repeatedly whether I wanted to get groups of survivors together in order to discuss what happened during the tsunami. In my assessment, this was a problematic way to proceed. First, this would resemble a critical incident stress debriefing (CISD), and although CISD may be beneficial for first responders, such as firefighters who have been trained to use CISD after tragedies, the research evidence shows that convening CISD-naïve groups of survivors to discuss a tragedy in the acute phase of horror is likely to be nonbeneficial or harmful (Gist & Devilly, 2002; Rose, Bisson, & Wessely, 2006; van Emmerik, Kamphuis, Hulsbosch, & Emmelkamp, 2002). Second, in the villages to which I would have exposure, survivors were milling about or parts of fluid groups; any group that we wished to repeat the next day would be made up of different people. Thus, the stability of the group composition would be compromised, and I as an outsider "swooping in" for a few sessions and "swooping out" may add another layer of disruption, abandonment, and "disaster tourism."*

On two occasions, when the request came from the victims themselves, I did agree to conduct PFA groups with primarily affected people. We would start with two to three people, and then others would drift over in what appeared to be either curiosity or emotional need.

---

* Disaster tourism is driven by curiosity and not any relief objective. Swooping in/out has a relief objective but with a transitory quality. Swooping in/out may bring benefits, but it must be counterbalanced with any harm accrued by disaster victims having to repeat their stories and grieve the loss of a caring presence. As disaster-related phenomenon that well-intentioned people participate in, disaster tourism and swooping in/out have not been adequately discussed in the literature. The ethics (dilemmas, line-drawing, harms, recommendations) of such phenomena require deeper treatment elsewhere.

In one case, we were under a tree and news traveled fast that a "psychological" session was happening. In these sessions, I allowed survivors to ventilate, and I normalized traumatic reactions (survivor's guilt, insomnia, and emotional numbness being among the reactions that people shared openly.)

Finally, traditional, time-honored healing practices involving touch, laying on of hands, and energy psychology appeared to be in demand by primary victims. During this project, my EC was not robust, and I did not make an assessment of how traditional healers were being utilized in Nagapattinam. Ranjan, a traditional healer, mentor, and friend with whom I had been traveling—after finding no opportunities through me and my PFA training work—took his own initiative and began providing healing sessions in the same room with volunteer psychiatrists. His services were touted by consumers who found a form of healing that resulted in restfulness and comfort. A line of consumers formed for Ranjan's 10- to 25-minute healing sessions, and this line continued to grow during the days of his stay in Nagapattinam. As mentioned in another piece (Shah, 2007a), by not partnering with Ranjan from the beginning in more integrative work, I believe I missed an important EC opportunity. Yet, like flowing water's ability to find lower ground and eventually meet up with other bodies of water, the healing work of Ranjan found its way to the tsunami-affected without much institutional backing.

Tsunami in Sri Lanka (Subacute Phase)

I interviewed Harshada David Wagner (personal interview, March 5, 2008), a New York City–based meditation teacher who innovated and implemented psychospiritual aid beginning 2 weeks post–tsunami. While his Sri Lankan pediatrician wife provided medical aid, Wagner worked via Banyan Education (his consulting firm). The following are excerpts from the interview prefaced with headings describing important psychosocial and spiritual resiliency principles that worked for the disaster setting:

1. Partnering with local workers to channel, amplify, and adapt interventions. Locals "take the temperature" of the larger community and culturally adapt the work in concentric circles:

   Arriving January 12, we developed a 6-week project involving youth and parents in a number of little coastal villages around the town of Akarapattu, in Ampara District on the Eastern coast.

It is a mostly Tamil Hindu enclave with some parts under LTTE control. When we got to Ampara District, Oxfam-Australia immediately connected us with a team of locals between the ages of 18 and 24 that became our crew there. These eight team members implemented our ideas, spoke the local language, and had interpersonal connections; and they were all tsunami-affected themselves. By the end of our work there, we felt that our team members were really the people that we ended up giving the most interventions to. We would debrief together. We would socialize. So I did more explicitly spiritual work with them rather than the larger community.

And that was very important because the work happened in concentric circles. First, the local team was enrolled in what we wanted to do. Then as they interfaced with the larger community, they informed us as to the needs, the rhythm of the place, and the vibration of the local people. And, then they were responsible for rolling out the interventions.

2. Integrating psychological work into a nonforeign spiritual activity:

I taught people to meditate. I sat in meditation with people who wanted to do it in community. I would have what you might say were spiritually therapeutic conversations* in the process.

3. Enlistment in recovery efforts (well-described as a best practice in the disaster literature) with an additional spiritual frame that supported the reframing of victim-hood into survivor-hood:

Then it was healing to do Karma Yoga.† Right from the beginning it became very clear that my team experienced healing by being part of our project. Seeing themselves not as victims, but as people who had something to offer. We were very conscious of that, and we would talk about it. As a spiritual practice, we would talk about the psychospiritual dynamics of Karma yoga.

4. Cultural concept (for Hindus, a guest is equal to a deity) retooled for recovery:

The other major intervention, well if you had to give it a name you might call it dhrishti.‡ These people coming to the clinics

---

* *Satsang* (being together in the presence of truth): The practice of spiritual practitioners discussing their experiences/struggles/joys with their teacher in a group so that the listeners benefit from the exchange as well.

† Karma Yoga can be thought of as the practice of serving others without any expectation of benefits for oneself.

‡ Dhristi is a special way of seeing that allows the seer to perceive the divinity in the seen entity.

see themselves as victims, as everything they had being taken away from them. We wanted to reinforce that we all have a lot of value inside of us even if so much physical had been taken away. I taught our teams, medical especially, to treat everyone as gods and goddesses. They would not be treated as villagers are in Sri Lanka when they came to the clinic. I taught the team to give villagers an honored seat and to treat them with the respect reserved for deities. Villagers really noticed this love and reverence, and they responded.

5. Symbolically compatible, ethnically homogenous, and nonevangelical environments:

Also, Anu, my wife, is a Hindu doctor in an area of mostly Hindu villagers surrounded by Christian doctors supported by missionary organizations, almost militantly evangelical. Our medical clinic had Hindu deities hanging on the door and a brown-faced doctor. Villagers felt more religiously comfortable.

6. Rituals or ordinary practices retooled for recovery:

In play therapy, dancing was a huge thing. What we found worked with the kids to raise their energy and spirits was Sri Lankan pop music, which they adore. We would pull up with a van rigged with big speakers, and kids would flock to that van. And that dancing is what they would always do, so they took to it so naturally. We often danced with them. Even if we didn't dance, we were holding the space there, just like with play therapy and satsang. From my point-of-view, it was one of the most freeing things that they did.

In Sri Lanka, it is traditional for parents to watch, and not join in with, kids playing. As we did play therapy, dancing, and sports, select parents would be nearby watching. The parents would tell us that "it makes such a difference to hear the sounds of kids playing." So then we would purposely set up our Happiness Clinic in proximity to despairing adults to have the highest impact.

Earthquake in Pakistan (Subacute Phase)

Two months after the earthquake, I led a team of psychotherapists to teach PFA, EC, and VT/SC education to nearly 200 relief workers in Islamabad, Mansehra, and Muzaffarabad. Through the coordination of an educational NGO, Idara-e-Taleem-o-Agahi, these trainings brought together national staff workers from governmental agencies (government of Pakistan), NGOs (ITA, Rozan), iNGOs (World Vision, Save the Children), and UNICEF.

Before arrival in Pakistan, I asked Khalida Sheikh, our team's Pakistani–British psychotherapist, what Muslims may do spiritually to bring comfort in times of tragedy (personal correspondence, 2005). She replied that a Muslim may repeat silently the *Darood Sharif* (or, *Durood Shareef*), a spiritual formula well known to orthodox Muslims linking a person to Allah and inducing peace. Furthermore, she informed me of a mystical practice using imagery and meditation called *Muraqba*.

We adapted and piloted a 12-minute script of vocal instructions (Sheikh & Shah, 2005). Our pilot subject found the script agreeable and suggested some word changes for superior results. Our trainees and their beneficiaries were predominantly Muslim, still, we inquired whether a relaxation technique using *Darood Sharif* and *Muraqba* would be welcome. Even though the individuals had varying degrees of religiosity and types of spiritual practice, everyone agreed to try the *Noor* Meditation.

BOX 5: *NOOR MURAQBA* MEDITATION

1. Two minutes of progressive relaxation coordinated with inhalation and exhalation
2. Two minutes of reciting a spiritual formula, such as *Darood Sharif*; or a repeating a phrase like *Allah Hoo* coordinated with inhalation and exhalation
3. Five minutes of *Muraqba*-guided imagery involving *Noor* (Divine Light) making its way over each portion of the body and then gently interpenetrating muscles, organs, and "spirit." *Noor* is a prevalent positive symbol in Islamic mythology. Participants are told that this Divine Light is healing and that contact with it gives a sense of peace and deep comfort.

Throughout the PFA, EC, and VT/SC education modules, we attempted to work the boundary across different care provision traditions—bringing in useful Western views while leveraging and respecting local customs.

Those who gave verbal feedback expressed that being in touch with one's own spirituality was itself a therapeutic tool in their inner healing. The following are other subjective feedback transcribed from evaluation forms:

- I get very tired easily and feel mentally fatigued. Today's sessions have made me realize that to become an effective caregiver, I need to take care of my own mental, psychological, and emotional needs. I found learning breathing techniques and muraqba exercises very useful.

- I wish that these sessions were offered soon after the earthquake to all the relief workers.
- The skills I learned today I will pass them on to other people in the community who suffered a great deal due to the earthquake.
- Relaxation exercises should be produced on CD and computer so everyone could learn how to relax.
- The session on alternative healing methods was very useful. The discussions we had and the exercises we shared were very simple and beneficial.

Finally, I inquired about traditional healing practices or local healers that might be of use to the relief efforts. The NGO and iNGO staff were unaware of accessible practices or healers. When my queries were met with a lack of interest or inquisitiveness, I decided not to pursue this line of inquiry.

Tsunami in Sri Lanka (Chronic, in Between, Phase)

Harshada David Wagner was invited by a development NGO, Foundation of Goodness (FG), in Seenigama to return one year after the tsunami to build resiliency within a mixed group of Sinhala Buddhist workers— most were first responders to the tsunami, some were new FG members. Wagner invited me to teach Laughter Yoga during the daylong training in which he would teach meditation, physical activities, and group reflection. While Laughter Yoga was unknown to FG, methods of yoga were not foreign. My hope was to provide an intervention that would be consistent with the recommendation that culturally based rituals and traditions be retooled as the basis for innovative interventions (Norris & Alegría, 2006).

Laughter Yoga involves three major components that I have adapted for use in disaster resiliency for workers:

1. Instructions to laugh in various ways (e.g., milkshake, cell phone, lion, and electric) so that the physiological act of laughing, through a neurological feedback loop, induces a psychological state of well-being and joy.
2. Interactive group activities that stimulate further laughter through being socially contagious; some interactions ask that people act out social "values" (e.g., handshake, shyness, appreciation).
3. Breathing activities from yoga traditions. In addition to the other deep breathing techniques taught during a Laughter Yoga session, laughter

itself spontaneously induces breathing in a way that lengthens the exhalation. Prolonging exhalation engages the vagus nerve and parasympathetic nervous system enough to reduce heart rate and bring about a subjective feeling of calm (Hobfoll et al., 2007; Sakakibara & Hayano, 1996; van Dixhoorn, 1998).

Our sessions of Laughter Yoga were loud, enthusiastic, and sometimes challenging. Laughter activities appeared to reinforce playfulness and interconnectedness in a novel way that was linked to yoga traditions.

Synthesis

**BOX 6: INTEGRATIVE PSYCHOSOCIAL
RESILIENCE: SEVEN PROJECT STEPS**

1. Inventory of team capacities and determining optimal scope of work
2. Communicate with networks, build collaborations, delineate scope of work
3. Onsite assessment, development of ethnomedically competent services, exit strategy determination
4. Service provision
5. Monitoring/outcomes measurement, monitoring team for burnout/ vicarious trauma
6. Returning to and refining Steps 1, 2, 3, 4, and 5 as appropriate
7. Closing work processes, exit

Of note, the four IPR cases described in this chapter do not represent-complete applications of the above seven project steps. While subjective evaluations were collected, objective or pre- and postoutcome measurements were lacking. This is a major gap in monitoring and evaluation, and projects should strive to close this gap not only to ensure the quality of its services for immediate beneficiaries but also because reliable objective data can provide a guide (with evidence-based recommendations and warnings) to the field of psychosocial relief work.

With varying degrees of success, the above four IPR cases strove for EC. However, in order to make key EC processes more transparent, the following section describes EC rationale correlated to the IPR cases.

BOX 7: EC–IPR CASE CORRELATIONS

1. As an American physician, I remained more inclined to have contact (educational or therapeutic) with relief workers rather than primary victims for the following reasons:
   - The emotional vulnerability/susceptibility of workers is frequently less than that of primarily affected victims. Even if I was working in one of the South Asian languages I speak fluently, I believe I am always capable of teaching something culturally inappropriate, and workers are in a better position to say, "Stop, this is not working." Such a structural power gradient is due to at least two factors: class differences (in which poorer, disenfranchised beneficiaries are likely to affirm whatever is being offered to them without contradicting the speaker) and voluntary agency work culture (in which staff are exposed to or thrive upon a culture of debate and resistance).
   - Workers can determine what parts of my education/therapies are applicable to primary victims. Workers thus act as an additional tier of cultural adaptation—adding to EC. This process is displayed in the feedback from the Pakistani trainee who said, "... skills I learned today I will pass them on to other people in the community who suffered a great deal due to the earthquake." Conversely, a worker can protect primary victims from any interventions that might clash with the cultural context.
2. When my queries for local healers or traditional healing practices were met with a lack of interest or inquisitiveness, I decided not to pursue this line of inquiry in acute or subacute phases. While not inappropriate to ask in any phase, a more aggressive pursuit should be deferred for chronic or in between phases. Action Sheet 6.4 of the IASC (2007, p. 137) *Guidelines* advises: "Information may not be immediately volunteered when people fear disapproval from outsiders or consider the practices to be secret or accessible only to those sanctioned by the community."
3. While I have intuited that it is inappropriate to use Laughter Yoga with disaster survivors or with workers in the acute/subacute phases, it has been well received when I do it for disaster worker capacity building or burnout prevention in chronic or in between phases.
4. In the Pakistani case, we proceeded to make compressed digital (mp3) recordings of the *"Noor" Muraqba* Meditation so that workers could email it to each other.
5. Evangelism, as hinted upon in the Sri Lankan case, should be checked in disaster zones. Action Sheet 6.4 of the IASC (2007, p. 138) *Guidelines* addresses this in the following way: "International and national 'outsiders' should take a nonjudgmental, respectful approach that emphasizes

interest in understanding local religious and spiritual beliefs and potential cooperation with the local way of working. Emergencies should never be used to promote outsiders' religious or spiritual beliefs." Thus, spiritual care practitioners have an opportunity to build institutional trust and integrity with heterodox and religiously other communities by checking any quid pro quo interaction that could come off as "relief in exchange for conversion."

6. In the Indian case of conducting PFA groups out in the open, the physical boundaries of the group should have been enforced in order to prevent adverse exposure of unwitting listeners (cf. CISD articles by Gist & Devilly, 2002; Rose et al., 2006; van Emmerik et al., 2002).

In the midst of multiple lists of multiple recommendations here, it is crucial to remember that our goal is empowering individuals for a sense of control over their lives and fostering resiliency, which includes helping individuals to enhance functioning and helping communities to identify and mobilize their natural resources (Hobfoll et al., 2007; Norris & Alegría, 2006; Solomon, 2003).

Academic and fieldwork support for IPR approaches as outlined above are increasing. Examples include Transcultural Psychosocial Organization's methodology described by Eisenbruch, de Jong, and van de Put (2004, p. 124) integrating "as far as possible traditional, local, and Western healing methods." Compared to medically oriented programs, open-minded spiritual care programs may have more liberty or comfort or more access in applying ethnomedical techniques, such as breathing relaxation, spiritual formulae, or "self-dialogue through the repetition of a word or verse" (de Jong, 2002, p. 79). In one of the most authoritative reviews of what empirically helps in mass trauma, Hobfoll et al. (2007, p. 290) cited multiple articles in the literature giving support to diverse ethnomedical techniques, for example: "Yoga also calms individuals and lowers their anxiety when facing traumatic circumstances, while muscle relaxation and mindfulness treatments that help people gain control over their anxiety are being applied that draw from Asian culture and meditation."

Conclusion

Two questions came at the beginning of this chapter. First of all, how can spiritual care be appropriately and safely integrated into psychosocial trauma recovery work? The Seven Project Steps (Box 6), four IPR cases in South Asia, and the overall IPR framework are responses to this first question. And then, what constitutes "appropriateness" vis-à-vis the diversity of psychological, social, and medical tasks that need to be accomplished in disaster relief? Boxes 1, 2, 3, 4, and 7 are responses to this second question.

Among the ethnomedical components of integrative medicine, spiritual care is no less valid than modern psychiatry; it only needs to be deployed in a way that ensures EC. Mental health practitioners who work within the psychosocial model are increasingly looking to local culture for clues and strengths for appropriate blends. And often, spiritual care and mental health are housed in the same practitioner or program. Such integration frequently gives rise to important hybrids of practice that will be exceedingly relevant to EC and IPR.

There are both good indicators and unclear signs regarding spiritual care and retooling religious traditions. In Sri Lanka, in conjunction with an NGO named Sarvodaya, a U.S.-based colleague, Gaea Logan (personal communication, July 6, 2008), evaluated subjective outcomes among a group of women who had participated in Psycho–Spiritual Healing Project, which included therapeutic play, physical activity, group discussion, experientials, and meditation. The consensus was that meditation had been "the most useful and most calming." In the Pakistani and Indian cases above, I solicited feedback from trainees and most people gave the trainings glowing reviews. From a scientific evidence point-of-view, however, post hoc analysis of such feedback will not go very far. In my cases, even with great urging, no one provided negative feedback—a skew that may be a function of the goodwill created between trainers and trainees.

The "appropriateness" question may be solved by a complicated cost-benefit calculation that recognizes intangibles and involves diverse stakeholders. Experience shows that an overly biopsychiatric approach predicated on generalizability misses important cultural specificity and angers some stakeholders. Experience also shows that psychosocial interventions with multiple therapeutic mechanisms given by well-meaning cultural relativists tend to produce positive feedback but no scientifically convincing measurements of effectiveness. Improving our knowledge on both sides of this equation is crucial. Collaborations with disaster-affected stakeholders and disinterested researchers together will advance our field of work. Gradual approximations with EC will help to unpack the many layers of complexities involved with people's trauma and the interventions that we develop to support recovery.

In closing, I want to express my gratitude to the people of South Asia for their willingness to teach me expanded notions of psychosocial resilience. Reading into this chapter's opening excerpt from Jayawickrama, there may be situations in which "traumatized victims" want neither mental health interventions nor spiritual care interventions. Some people may simply want restoration of tangible conditions (livelihood, schools) so that they can control their destinies and address their inner lives in collaboration with the people of their choice.

For those people, however, who are open to global exchanges of a psychosocial nature, I will propose we work according to one last guideline: planetarity.* While not congruent with our current notions of globalization, the flattening of the Earth, or being green, my usage of planetarity is an ethical call for how different people/nations relate to one another, and when necessary, help one another in times of crisis. With regard to psychosocial trauma, planetarity stimulates opportunities for democratic and symmetric relationships of stakeholders innovating optimal interventions. New species of interventions—ones that no one can imagine just yet—may arise in response to such calls as long as we have open minds, nondomineering work processes, and curious spirits.

References

Bride, B. (2004). The impact of providing psychosocial services to traumatized populations. *Trauma and Crisis: An International Journal, 7*, 29–46.

Carballo, M., Heal, B., & Hernandez, M. (2005). Psychosocial aspects of the tsunami. *Journal of the Royal Society of Medicine, 98*, 396–399.

de Jong, J. T. V. M. (2002). Public mental health, traumatic stress and human rights violations in low-income countries: A culturally appropriate model in times of conflict, disaster and peace. In J. T. V. M. de Jong (Ed.), *Trauma, war and violence: Public mental health in sociocultural context* (p. 1–91). New York: Plenum-Kluwer.

de Jong, J. T. V. M. (2007). Nongovernmental organizations and the role of the mental health professional. In R. J. Ursano, C. S. Fullerton, L. Weisaeth, & B. Raphael (Eds.), *Textbook of disaster psychiatry* (pp. 206–224). Cambridge, UK: Cambridge University Press.

Draguns, J. G. (2004). From speculation through description toward investigation: A prospective glimpse at cultural research in psychotherapy. In U. Gielen, J. Fish, & J. Draguns (Eds.), *Handbook of culture, therapy, and healing* (pp. 369–387). Mahwah, NJ: Lawrence Erlbaum Assoicates.

---

* From Gayatri Chakravorty Spivak (2003): A sociohistorical call for people to be ethically responsible for each other.

Eisenbruch, M., de Jong, J. T. V. M., & van de Put, W. (2004). Bringing order out of chaos: A culturally competent approach to managing the problems of refugees and victims of organized violence. *Journal of Traumatic Stress, 17*(2), 123–131.

Gist, R., & Devilly, G. J. (2002). Post-trauma debriefing: The road too frequently travelled. *The Lancet, 360*(9335), 741–742.

Hobfoll, S. (1998). *Stress, culture, and community: The psychology and philosophy of stress.* New York: Plenum Press.

Hobfoll, S. E., Watson, P., Bell, C. C., Bryant, R. A., Brymer, M. J., Friedman, M. J., et al. (2007). Five essential elements of immediate and mid-term mass trauma intervention: Empirical evidence. *Psychiatry, 70*(4), 283–315.

Inter-Agency Standing Committee (IASC) (2007). *IASC guidelines on mental health and psychosocial support in emergency settings.* Geneva: Author.

Jayawickrama, J. (2006). Taking people for a ride: The Sri Lankan example of tsunami affected communities and experience of mental health interventions. In D. Khoosal & D. Summerfield (Eds.). *Bulletin of transcultural special interest group of Royal College of Psychiatrists* (pp. 2–10), London. Retrieved from, http://www.rcpsych.ac.uk/pdf/TSIG%20BulletinWinter%202006.pdf

Jayawickrama, J. (2007). *Concepts of care: A workbook for community practitioners.* Geneva, Switzerland: Community Development Gender Equality and Children Section Community Developmentt Unit of UNHCR in ongong parternship with Newcastle upon Tyne: UK; Community Mental Health and Wellbeing Programme, Diaster and Development Centre School of Applied Sciences, Northunbria University.

Norris, F. H. & Alegría, M. (2006). Promoting disaster recovery in ethnic-minority individuals and communities. In E. C. Richie, P. J. Watson, & M. J. Friedman (Eds.). *Interventions following mass violence and disasters: Strategies for mental health practice* (pp. 319–342). New York: Guilford.

Patel, V., Kirkwood, B., Weiss, H., Pednekar, S., Fernandes, J., Pereira, B., et al. (2005). Chronic fatigue in developing countries: A population survey of women in India. *British Medical Journal, 330*, 1190–1193.

Pearlman, L. A. & Caringi, J. (2008). Vicarious traumatization and complex trauma. In C. A. Courtois & J. D. Ford (Eds.). *Complex traumatic stress disorders: An evidence-based clinician's guide.* New York: Guilford.

Prashantham, B. J. (2008). Asian Indians: Cultural considerations for disaster workers. In A. J. Marsella, J. L. Johnson, P. Watson, & J. Gryczynski (Eds.), *Ethnocultural perspectives on disaster and trauma* (pp. 175–207). New York: Springer Science.

Rose, S., Bisson, J., & Wessely, S. (2006). Does brief psychological debriefing help manage psychological distress after trauma and prevent post traumatic stress disorder? *The Cochrane Database of Systematic Reviews: Evidence Update.* Liverpool, UK: Effective Health Care Alliance Programme.

Rothschild, B. (2006). *Help for the helper: The psychophysiology of compassion fatigue and vicarious trauma.* New York: W.W. Norton.

Sakakibara, M., & Hayano, J. (1996). Effect of slowed respiration on cardiac para-sympathetic response to threat. *Psychosomatic Medicine, 58*, 32–37.

Shah, S. A. (2006). Resistance to cross-cultural psychosocial efforts in disaster and trauma: Recommendations for ethnomedical competence. *The Australasian Journal of Disaster and Trauma Studies, 2*. Retrieved July 7, 2008, from http://trauma.massey.ac.nz/issues/2006-2/shah.htm

Shah, S.A. (2007a). Ethnomedical best practices for international psychosocial efforts in disaster and trauma. In E. Tang & J. Wilson (Eds.), *Cross-cultural assessment of psychological trauma and PTSD* (pp. 51–64). New York: Springer Verlag.

Shah, S. A. (2007b). Secondary traumatic stress: Prevalence for humanitarian aid workers. *Traumatology, 13*(1), 59–70.

Solomon, S. (2003). Introduction. In B. L. Green, M.J. Friedman, J. T. V. M. de Jong, S. D. Solomon, T. M. Keane, J. A. Fairbank, et al. (Eds.), *Trauma interventions in war and peace: Prevention, practice, and policy* (pp. 3–16). New York: Kluwer/Plenum Press.

Spivak, G. C. (2003). *Death of a discipline*. New York: Columbia University Press.

Summerfield, D. (2005). What exactly is emergency or disaster "mental health"? *Bulletin of the World Health Organization, 83*(1), 76–77.

van Dixhoorn, J. (1998). Cardiorespiratory effects of breathing and relaxation instruction in myocardial infarction patients. *Biological Psychology, 49*(1–2), 123–135.

van Emmerik, A. P. A, Kamphuis, J. H., Hulsbosch, A. M., & Emmelkamp, P. M. G. (2002). Single session debriefing after psychological trauma: A meta-analysis. *The Lancet, 360*(9335), 766–771.

van Ommeren, M., Saxena, S., & Saraceno B. (2005). Mental and social health during and after acute emergencies: emerging consensus? *Bulletin of the World Health Organization, 83*(1), 71.

Vega, W. (1992). Theoretical and pragmatic implications of cultural diversity for community research. *American Journal of Community Psychology, 20*, 375–392.

World Health Organization (2005). *WHO recommendations for mental health in Aceh, Department of Mental Health and Substance Abuse*. Geneva: Author.

Young, B. H., Ford, J. D., & Wilson, P. (2008). Disaster rescue and response workers. In A.J. Marsella, J.L. Johnson, P. Watson, & J. Gryczynski (Eds.), *Ethnocultural perspectives on disaster and trauma* (pp. 395–398). New York: Springer Science.

Section III

Collaboratively Nurturing Resilience After Catastrophic Trauma

13

Rituals, Routines, and Resilience

Koshin Paley Ellison and Craig L. Katz

Introduction

This chapter is written in two distinct parts, one from the perspective of a spiritual care provider and the other from that of a psychiatrist. This format was initially born of the practicalities of two busy coauthors who have not previously collaborated in any way, whether in writings or in disaster response. But, we ultimately chose to retain this division because it seems to reflect many of the differences between clergy and psychiatrists. We suspect bear upon not just the topic of rituals but on the possibilities of collaboration between the two fields in disaster response. Between the writing of the two of us lie different voices, different focuses, and even different sources. In this pairing, where one refers to poetry, the other cites scientific journals. It seemed nearly impossible to merge our perspectives and writings without diminishing the force of what we each had to say. Our approaches to understanding disaster-related rituals are not in any way at odds, and there are no counterpoints to be made. Nor do they readily interlock like pieces of a puzzle. It would be best to say they hover around each other like two birds, sharing the harmony of a common purpose and hope. Themes of meaning, connection, and containment run throughout this duet on rituals and disaster.

A Spiritual Care Perspective
Koshin Paley Ellison

What do routines, rituals, and resilience have to do with providing care and taking care of ourselves? What do they have to teach us as ways to approach disasters? From my combined experiences and trainings as a Zen Buddhist priest, social worker, poet, chaplain, chaplain supervisor, and psychotherapist, they have much to offer. My Zen Buddhist practice truly informs and imbues the rest. We train to continually return to the transitory nature of all things. This is not a nihilistic view or practice but a great sense of opening to a larger sense of the world, going beyond our small isolated selves to a sense of connectedness. I have practiced for many years with allowing myself to see the preciousness of life and how an intrinsic part of this is how life blooms and fades, sometimes violent, sometimes neutral, sometimes with ease.

My first direct teaching of this came from attending the week-long bearing-witness retreats at Auschwitz–Birkenau. I wanted to go to a place of personal and collective devastation in the context of a yearly ritual of a spiritual retreat. For a week each November, the retreat of international and interfaith group convenes at the camp. The ritual consists of memorial services at the crematories and day-long sitting in meditation at the selection site where people were unloaded from the cattle cars. All day and into early evening, the people in the meditation circle chanted the names of the dead. For the sake of focus of this short essay, I will not go into detail of this powerful ritual. I will say that it was my first experience of how ritual can transform something that is contracted within me (like my own ignorant and abstract hatred of Germans and Poles) that after 5 years of attending and participating in this group ritual has allowed me to become more resilient. By resilient, I mean I am able to see my own hatred and bigotry as part of my personal life and as a part of human nature. The camp itself offered up a valuable image of the negative Shadow that can exist in my life and all of our lives. It was at Auschwitz that I vowed to serve in the world to help others integrate their darkness with their whole sense of self.

As I write this, I think of the Cambodians under siege during the time of Pol Pot's killing fields. Many families were being slaughtered, and each thought they themselves were likely to be next. There are numerous accounts of mass groups of people gathering together in the Buddhist temples and chanting together: "Hatred never ceases by hatred, but by love alone will there be healing. This is the ancient and eternal law." I have always been so inspired by this story. I believe that this is what we were practicing in a functional way in those retreats in Auschwitz. We were practicing working with the collective trauma of the human disaster of Aushwitz and seeing that it is not separate from ourselves. Each of us has a killing aspect. Each of us has rage and intolerance. The ritual is about acknowledging this in each of us. Learning to love those parts of ourselves and the world is the path. As a psychotherapist and chaplain, I have witnessed countless accounts of people suppressing those parts of themselves and I have witnessed the individual and collective damage this inflicts. Maybe by ritual it may look like the poem, "miss rosie," by the august poet Lucille Clifton:

> when i watch you
> wrapped up like garbage
> sitting, surrounded by the smell
> of too old potato peels
> or
> when i watch you
> in your old man's shoes
> with the little toe cut out
> sitting, waiting for your mind
> like next week's grocery
> i say
> when i watch you
> you wet brown bag of a woman
> who used to be the best looking gal in georgia
> used to be called the Georgia Rose
> i stand up
> through your destruction
> i stand up

Sometimes it looks like the ritual of noticing the aspects of our world and acknowledging that person, situation, emotion, or event as a part of ourselves. Like Clifton, we too can stand up and be fully present of this aspect. Life does not happen in one approach, and for this reason, resilience and flexibility can be most helpful in determining what is truly needed. Like at the Auschwitz retreat, we start with not knowing and letting go of our fixed ideas. Then, we can bear witness to what is arising in that particular moment, and then we practice allowing loving action to flow from that moment. Like the people in Cambodia, they practice remembering the true death of a man or woman is the denial of his or her humanity and the wholeness of our interconnectedness. How might this kind of ritual be helpful in disasters?

The O-Bon Ceremony

From my interest in Zen Practice and how to learn from bearing witness to suffering and disasters created by people, in July 2001 I traveled to Hiroshima to train in a Zen temple, interview survivors of the atomic bomb about their experience of resilience, and participate in their O-Bon ceremony on August 6. Sixty-six thousand people died in August 1945, when the atomic bomb was dropped. Each day I practiced meditation and ritual at the temple, then I would head to "ground zero" to interview survivors. Through the interviews with survivors, it became clear through shared answers that those who were able to heal and become whole again were able to do this through shifting their understanding from the victim to just a person to whom something terrible had happened as one event in a full life. They were able to put it in context. When I asked them what was helpful in their healing, the answers were also incredibly similar: to tell their story and be heard at the yearly O-Bon ceremony. By telling their story, they meant the whole story—the event, the story they created, and the life they created from it.

One woman told me the story of being a little girl and losing everyone she loved. She herself was badly scarred and deformed from the blast. It was through the consistent loving actions of the temple priest who counseled and prayed with her that she began to see that her other life faded and she began to find the life of a young woman who deeply appreciated that the cherry blossoms bloomed again and again, year upon year. Each year at O-Bon, she gathers with her fellow *hibaksha* (ones affected by the blast) and tells stories and chant together, and they write poems on paper, light lanterns, and set them into the river.

The O-Bon ceremony is a Japanese Buddhist custom to honor the deceased spirits of one's ancestors. This Buddhist custom has evolved into a family reunion holiday during which people return to ancestral family places and visit and clean their ancestors' graves. Each morning I would see families in the temple graveyard talking and cleaning graves in the temple cemetery. While traditionally the festival of O-Bon lasts for 3 days; these 3 days are not listed as public holidays, but it is customary that people are given leave from work. What a delightful and respectful aspect of a culture to honor time to connect with their grief and memory. O-Bon is a shortened form of the legendary *Ullambana* festival. It is Sanskrit for "hanging upside down" and implies great suffering. The Japanese believe they should ameliorate the suffering of the Ullambana. O-Bon culminates with the *Toro Nagashi*, or the floating of lanterns. Paper lanterns are painted in ink with the names and offerings for the dead, illuminated with candles, and then floated down rivers symbolically signaling the ancestral spirits' return to the world of the dead. On August 6, hundreds of thousands of people gathered on the banks of the Otagawa River, held memorial services, and, in the evening, painted lanterns and floated them in the river. That night, I stood and chanted with a number of the men and women I had interviewed and watched the darkened river became a river of light.

Three weeks upon my return, two planes were crashed into the World Trade Centers, claiming close to 3,000 lives. The world had one reflective day of wondering what this means to our lives, and then the government turned reactive and went to war. What was missing was a national and city time to grieve and reflect. A year later, T.K. Nakagaki, a Jodo Shinshu priest from the New York Buddhist Church, organized an O-Bon ceremony on one of the piers on the Hudson River. Hundreds gathered to chant together, participate in a memorial service, and paint hundreds of lanterns with the names of the dead from 9/11 and beyond. The lanterns were then sent out into the river.

What does this routine ritual have to do with flexibility? It is a teaching that time is needed to gather together and create ceremony and ritual in a regular way to honor the parts of us that have died or been destroyed. When this doesn't happen, we can't gather together to tell our stories, ritualize the moment, and connect to that which we have lost. In my experience as a chaplain and psychotherapist, it has been essential to clients' and patients' healing process to have a set ritual of remembrance. It becomes a touchstone of their year. Without such a time, they tend to drift in the sea. Each loss, each disaster, and each change echoes each loss. How do we create a container through ritual to hold this so that we as a culture can become totally alive? What I mean by fully alive is to be connected to a larger order of being. This differs from a psychological sense of aliveness in that typically, although it is changing, psychological aliveness tends to be limited to that person's specific life. What is of interest to me is the confluence of psychology and Buddhism and how there is a new blossoming and commingling. The O-Bon ceremony is one such ritual.

The wonderful haiku poet, Basho, wrote:

In a village with no temple bell—
What do the people do?—
Twilight in spring

Sometimes I feel the psychological view is this village without a temple. Yet, as Basho says, what do the people do? How to we function without an organizing spiritual principle. I believe that we need to have some ritual to call us together to remember what it is to be alive with all our suffering, grief, and joy.

A Psychiatry Perspective
Craig L. Katz, M.D.

My perspective on disasters and rituals arises from my experience in co-founding and leading, in various capacities, an organization devoted to utilizing psychiatrists to reduce suffering in the aftermath of disaster, Disaster Psychiatry Outreach (DPO). I have had the opportunity to participate in every disaster to which our organization has responded since its founding in 1998, ranging from aviation disasters, such as the 1998 crash of Swissair Flight 111, to terrorist attacks like 9/11, to natural disasters, such as the 2008 Sichuan earthquake in China. I have witnessed the role of rituals and routines across disasters, cultures, and countries and believe they are a central aspect of the psychological and spiritual experience of recovery.

Related to but apart from my volunteer work in disasters has been my role in developing and directing a mental health program to meet the long-term needs of rescue and recovery workers who worked or volunteered at Ground Zero in New York City (Katz, Smith, Silverton, et al., 2006). This has been part of my day-to-day work life since July 2002. Therefore, it is with telling irony that, as I sit writing this chapter, I am missing "World Trade Center Responder Day," an all-day event to commemorate the efforts of 9/11 responders and how those efforts may have changed their lives in ways both good and bad. It is taking place around Ground Zero and includes a "speak out" for responders to share their experiences, as well as spiritual activities. My mental health colleagues and I were invited to provide professional support to attendees, but I am not there. My absence from this ritual exemplifies the complexity of how the field of mental health, especially psychiatrists, deals with rituals. As I will discuss further below, Responder Day, like other rituals, feels necessary but entirely foreign.

In what follows, I will elaborate on the ambivalent relationship between psychiatry and rituals and try to begin to sketch a picture of a less-conflicted future.

Background

Ritual has been defined as a ceremonial act or as an act or series of acts regularly repeated in a set and precise manner (Merriam-Webster OnLine). A more detailed definition from within the field of psychiatry is as follows: "Rituals are group methods that serve to maintain a culture's social structure and its norms, strengthen the bonds of individuals to their communities, assist adaptation (to change or crises), manage fear and anxiety, and ward off threats" (Danieli & Nader, 2006).

Psychiatry has historically viewed rituals as problematic, if not as outright pathology. Sigmund Freud, who has influenced the field of psychiatry as much as anyone in the last century, famously wrote about the pathologic proneness to repetition seen in many of his patients (Strachey, 1914). The repetition compulsion represents a tendency for people to unknowingly repeat problematic experiences from their past, especially the formative years of their childhood, in present-day experiences. They are unaware of how they repeatedly experience current relationships in terms of key past relationships and, thereby, distort them in such a way as to be unable to participate in them in a maximally healthy and fulfilling manner. Patients repeat instead of remembering, and it is the psychotherapist's role to get them to understand how their forgotten past compels them to fruitless repetition. It is not hard to see how Freud's discussion of the ignorance and dysfunction that are the bookends to repetition could have contributed to a long tradition of psychiatrist's seeing repetitions, like rituals, as indicators of something being wrong with someone. At the least, we can see the roots of why the field may not embrace routine and ritual.

Freud even wrote about the parallels between obsessive patients' proneness to routines and rituals and the psychological processes underlying religious ritual (Strachey, 1907). He suggested that the rigid routines and ceremonies of neurotic patients (e.g., how fastidiously they wash or where they invariably sit in their home) differed from religious ceremony because the latter at least was full of symbolism and meaning, whereas neurotic obsessions are more of a "half comic and half tragic" form of "private religion." Even with this distinction drawn, however, it is hard not to come away from Freud's comparison of obsessive and religious rituals with a sense that rituals of any kind occur within a mental blind spot. They are performed for unconscious reasons, representing an ultimately dysfunctional way of managing anxiety over one's impulses.

Ritual-like behavior also abounds in modern day definitions of psychiatric illnesses, as laid out in the main text of psychiatric diagnosis, the American Psychiatric Association's (APA) *Diagnostic and Statistical Manual* (2000). Autistic disorder includes engaging in repetitive patterns of behavior, including "nonfunctional routines or rituals." Obsessive–compulsive disorder can include compulsions, which are repetitive behaviors or mental acts that could include praying, that the sufferer feels rigidly driven to perform as a means of allaying their anxieties. Although not part of the definition of the disorders, proneness to bizarre routines or rituals may also be seen in psychotic conditions like schizophrenia or a related condition, schizotypal personality disorder.

Psychiatrists, therefore, typically work within a tradition that is at least wary of rituals. Ritual and ceremony are largely absent from the practice of psychiatry (Johnson, Feldman, Lubin, & Southwick, 1995). When I have been asked to participate in ceremonies, such as World Trade Center Responder Day, it is, therefore, not surprising that I cannot locate any professional landmarks from which to launch my involvement. Colleagues and I have been asked in the past to advise organizers of memorial services for events as disparate as aviation disasters or 9/11. But, we are lost in these circumstances, lacking for expertise to offer and often relegated to hovering in the shadows of such events as virtual voyeurs seeking purpose in a foreign land. Perhaps not coincidentally, a 2007 study found that, compared to other physicians, psychiatrists were more likely to describe themselves as having no religious affiliation, preferred to consider themselves "spiritual" rather than "religious," and are less likely to use religion to cope (Curlin et al., 2007).

The Evidence

If there were ever a place in which psychiatrists should feel comfortable with rituals, however, it is precisely that of disasters. Disasters and trauma disconnect people from one another and from their past and future. Routines are destroyed along with lives and cherished belongings. Questions of purpose and meaning inevitably arise as stricken communities struggle to find hope amid death and destruction. In the face of these many psychological challenges, it would seem, then, that rituals should be just what the "doctor ordered," as they are activities that explicitly seek to enhance community bonds, strengthen its structure, enhance adaptation, and deal with anxiety or fear.

Rituals and ceremonies, in fact, can be put to therapeutic use. Johson et al. have written about the three effects that ceremonies can have in helping patients with posttraumatic stress disorder (PTSD; Johson et al., 1995). There is good reason to believe that these effects can be generalized to traumatized populations, irrespective of whether PTSD is at issue. First, rituals compartmentalize the trauma, creating a safe and contained space within which to face the emotions of the experience without flooding the rest of life. Second, these events not only recognize the trauma but also become metaphors for transformation and change. Third, rituals and ceremonies embody attachment to the family, the community, and society at large, reflecting a shared journey away from what happened. They based these observations on four ceremonies they have used to assist combat veterans and their families to recover from the psychic wounds of war:

1. An opening ceremony welcoming patients and their families into their months-long treatment program
2. A family night ceremony that emphasizes sharing of feelings and forgiveness of pain caused by the veteran and their PTSD
3. A ceremony for the dead that memorializes dead combat buddies
4. A "crossing over ceremony" that marks the patients' completion of the program

Thai Buddhism's view of the afterlife played a role in how people dealt with the staggering loss of human life that resulted from the 2004 tsunami that struck Thailand (Sorajjakool, 2007). In Thai Buddhism, the spirits of the recently deceased are thought to wander around as ghosts seeking rebirth. Monks chant special prayers to help the dead to relinquish their connections with those who survive them and the places they lived so that they can indeed be reborn. Psychologically, ghosts represent an unresolved loss. Rebirth can occur into a "happy place" or a "world of suffering," and those who have earned sufficient merits in their prior life will be reborn into the happy place as a human or an angel. Large-scale memorial services following the tsunami, therefore, focused on survivors, through the chanting of monks, passing on merits to the deceased, enabling them to stop wandering as ghosts and to be reborn in a happy way. In this way, Buddhist ritual enabled large-scale grieving to occur, letting the living let go of the deceased as much as the deceased to let go of the living.

Rituals may also reduce anxiety, a common emotion after disaster, even apart from whether someone has an underlying psychiatric condition. One study compared a group of Catholic college students who engaged in weekly recitation of the Rosary with another group of students from the same college who watched a religious content video (Anastasi & Newberg, 2008). The anxiety state of the Rosary group reduced significantly after the prayers, whereas that of the video group did not. And, even though the groups' respective anxiety levels were the same before the exercises, the Rosary group's anxiety level was significantly less than that of the video group afterward. The authors suggested that the ritual quality of the Rosary, which they suggest has the highest ritual versus religious content ratio of any aspect of Catholic ceremonies, had antianxiety qualities. Ritualistic repetition soothes, a finding Freud would likely have agreed with, albeit with significant qualifications.

Implications

Resilience has become an important concept by which to understand the human relationship to trauma. It has been variously described as reflecting an individual's ability to withstand the effects of trauma or disaster, whether by having the capacity to (a) remain unaffected, (b) readily bounce back from whatever effects there are, or (c) bounce back to a new way of being that is shaped positively more so than negatively (e.g., wiser and more interesting). These ideas can be captured in corresponding images of a tree that is unbending in the face of a hurricane's winds, that bends but returns to upright, or that bends and returns to a new posture that is no longer upright but no less stable. Insofar as disasters constitute traumas at the level of the community, these images of resilience apply to communities as much as individuals.

Reason, as well as the limited number of studies available in the published literature, suggests that rituals promote resilience. Their shear occurrence probably even embodies resilience—a community comes together and, thereby, shows itself that it is still standing and still functioning in unison. Psychiatry has long been attuned to unhealthy aspects of rituals but has far to go in trying to understand what are healthy, resilience-enhancing aspects of rituals, at least as regards disasters and probably even the daily stresses of life. Yet, the positive elements of rituals in the face of disaster seem evident enough and the occurrence of rituals natural enough to not have to reduce rituals to a clinical activity. So, why get psychiatrists involved at all?

The answer to this, at the least, is because psychiatry stands to benefit from becoming involved, or at least aware, of activities like rituals that foster meaning when life seems to have lost meaning and purpose. Under any circumstances, one of the hardest things to do as a psychiatrist is to lend a patient passion and purpose. After disasters, this is an especially daunting challenge. I am still haunted by my memory of the words of a survivor of the 2004 tsunami who I met in a rural northeastern region of Sri Lanka: "I lost my wife, my daughter, my boat for fishing, and even, literally, the shirt off of my back. I have no spirit. Life has lost its meaning. What is there?" Considering prescribing this clearly and understandably depressed man antidepressant medication seemed especially disproportionate to these existential concerns.

We know that the "avoidant" symptoms of PTSD, in particular, are often harbingers of a poor prognosis, being among the most enduring of all PTSD symptoms even when treatment has been beneficial. These include feeling painfully detached from life, experiencing less emotional depth and having a tenuous connection to one's future. Insofar as rituals have an apparent function of fostering meaning, they may constitute an important tool in a range of interventions psychiatrists recommend to a disaster survivor.

Psychiatry may well have something to offer to ritualistic practices as well. There can be a collective dialogue about what constitutes the purpose, in psychological and spiritual terms, of rituals. This naturally involves studying how to capture, as exactly as is possible, what it is about rituals that is effective. Next, we can investigate what factors contribute to this effectiveness. These may include factors as far ranging as the size of ceremonies, their location relative to the disaster site, their timing relative to the event, and even their frequency. Ultimately, it should then be possible to generate guidelines, borne of collaboration between the spiritual and mental health care realms, for when and how to initiate postdisaster rituals. Indeed, it is perhaps time to generate these guidelines through joint dialogue, while we await whatever further answers clinical science can offer on the subject.

Conclusion

Rituals are a central aspect of spiritual practice but far afield from the practice of psychiatry. The examples from survivors of Auschwitz, Pol Pot's killing fields, Hiroshima, and 9/11 reflect how rituals appear to play an important role in aiding the postdisaster search for meaning amid the seemingly unfathomable, enhancing cohesion among fractured communities, and containing difficult-to-bear emotions. These are all goals that disaster psychiatry shares with spiritual care. Where their differences lie is in the methods, at least as regards rituals. These differences can be used to the mutual benefit of each field. Spiritual care providers can turn to the scientific eye of psychiatry to improve their understanding and implementation of rituals to best accomplish their goals. Psychiatry stands to benefit from becoming more familiar with rituals and including them in their typically multipronged approach to trauma and disaster. And, ultimately, survivors of disaster will surely be the beneficiaries of the two fields' working together.

Spiritual References

Basho, M., *Japanese haiku*. Retrieved from http://www.sacred-texts.com
Clifton, L., *Miss Rosie*. Retrieved from http://www.poemhunter.com/poem/miss-rosie

Psychiatry References

American Psychiatric Association. (2000). *Diagnostic and statistical manual of mental disorders* 4th ed., text revision. Washington, DC: Author.

Anastasi, M., & Newberg, A. (2008). A preliminary study of the acute effects of religious ritual and anxiety. *Journal of Alternative and Complementary Medicine, 14*(2), 163–165.

Curlin, F. A., Odell, S. V., Lawrence, R. E., Chin, M. H., Lantos, J. D., Meador, K. G., et al. (2007). The relationship between psychiatry and religion among U.S. physicians. *Psychiatric Services, 58*(9), 1193–1198.

Danieli, Y., & Nader, K. (2006). Respecting cultural, religious, and ethnic differences in the prevention and treatment of psychological sequelae. In L. Schein, H. Spitz, G. Burligame, & P. Muskin (Eds.), *Group approaches to terrorist disasters* (pp. 203–234). New York: Haworth Press.

Johson, D. R., Feldman, S. C., Lubin, H., & Southwick, S. M. (1995). The therapeutic use of ritual and ceremony in the treatment of post-traumatic stress disorder. *Journal of Traumatic Stress, 8*(2), 283–298.

Katz, C. L., Smith, R. P., Silverton, M., Holmes, A., Bravo, C., Jones, K., et al. (2006). A mental health program for Ground Zero rescue and recovery workers: Cases and observations. *Psychiatric Services, 57*(9), 1335–1338.

Merriam-Webster OnLine. Retrieved June 14, 2008, from http://www.merriam-webster.com/dictionary.

Sorajjakool, S. (2007). Tsunami and ghost stories in Thailand: Exploring the psychology of ghosts and religious rituals within the context of Thai Buddhism. *Journal of Pastoral Care Counsel*, *61*(4), 343–349.

Strachey, J. (1950). Obsessive actions and religious practices. In *The standard edition of the complete psychological works of Sigmund Freud: Volume 9 (1906-08). Jensen's 'Gradiva' and other works* (pp. 115–128). New York: W. W. Norton & Company.

Strachey, J. (1950). Remembering, repeating and working-through (Further recommendations on the technique of psycho-analysis II). In *The standard edition of the complete psychological works of Sigmund Freud: Volume 12 (1911-1913). The case of Schreber, papers on technique and other works* (pp. 145–156). New York: W. W. Norton & Company.

14

Fundamentals of Working With (Re)traumatized Populations

Yael Danieli

Introduction

This book is about collaboration between mental health and spiritual care providers working in disasters, and this chapter is included to provide a background for understanding how disasters may "reactivate" various prior forms of trauma so that disaster responders will be prepared to understand how the crisis they are responding to may be complicated by the presence of unresolved previous traumatic experience. In this chapter, I use *retraumatization* to denote all the categories mentioned below.

Retraumatization is defined herein as one's reaction to a traumatic exposure that is colored, intensified, amplified, or shaped by one's reactions and adaptational style (Danieli, 1985) to previous traumatic experiences. In the literature and in differing contexts, one can find this phenomenon and its effects variously referred to as additive or cumulative trauma, revictimization, reactivation, reexperiencing, and reliving.

A potentially useful distinction is among retraumatization denoting (a) the same trauma repeated over and over again, such as in recurring instances of child abuse and rape; (b) the occurrence of a *new and different* trauma from the past, original one, such as a flood happening to an adult who had been exposed to abuse as a child (see Moinzadeh, 1998); and (c) normative life transitions or events that are experienced as traumatic by previously traumatized individuals, such as the reaction of a genocide survivor mother to her adult daughter leaving for college, a torture survivor's panic in response to a necessary medical examination, or WW II veterans or Holocaust survivors' responses to retirement (Danieli, 1994a, 1994b). Retraumatization has also been referred to in the context of a therapeutic or other helping relationships, or in a research context as possibly provoking traumatic reactions by untimely and insensitive inquiries.

A brief overview about trauma and posttraumatic stress disorder (PTSD) symptomatology (see *Diagnostic and Statistical Manual of Mental Disorders,* 4th ed., American Psychiatric Association, 1994, for the full criteria) sheds light on the many components of the experiential process of repetitive reenactment and ripple effect of trauma. Specifically, Criterion B for the diagnosis of 309.81 posttraumatic stress disorder in particular (see below) acknowledges the *internal* dimension of (re)traumatization in both adults and children, while Criteria C and D describe their internal attempt at coping with this (self-)retraumatization.

Criterion B: The traumatic event is persistently reexperienced in at least one (or more) of the following ways:

1. Recurrent and intrusive distressing recollections of the event, including images, thoughts, or perceptions.
   Note: In young children, repetitive play may occur in which themes or aspects of the trauma are expressed.
2. Recurrent distressing dreams of the event.
   Note: In children, there may be frightening dreams without recognizable content.
3. Acting or feeling as if the event were recurring (includes a sense of reliving the experience, illusions, hallucinations, and dissociative flashback episodes, including those that occur on awakening or when intoxicated).
   Note: In young children, trauma-specific reenactment may occur.
4. Intense psychological distress at exposure to internal or external cues that symbolize or resemble an aspect of the traumatic event.
5. Physiological reactivity on exposure to internal or external cues that symbolize or resemble an aspect of the traumatic event.

Criterion C: Persistent avoidance of stimuli associated with the trauma and numbing of general responsiveness (not present before the trauma), as indicated by three (or more) of the following:

1. Efforts to avoid thoughts, feelings, or conversations associated with the trauma
2. Efforts to avoid activities, places, or people that arouse recollections of the trauma

3. Inability to recall an important aspect of the trauma
4. Markedly diminished interest or participation in significant activities
5. Feeling of detachment or estrangement from others
6. Restricted range of affect (e.g., unable to have loving feelings)
7. Sense of foreshortened future (e.g., does not expect to have a career, marriage, children, or a normal life span)

Criterion D: Persistent symptoms of increased arousal (not present before the trauma), as indicated by two (or more) of the following:

1. Difficulty falling or staying asleep
2. Irritability or outbursts of anger
3. Difficulty concentrating
4. Hypervigilance
5. Exaggerated startle response

A particularly salient example is of the many survivors of previous trauma living in the United States who were particularly shaken by the terrorist attacks on September 11, 2001, because, until then, they had viewed America as their "last place of safety." As part of their adaptation to prior massive trauma, it was inconceivable to them that the United States, in general, and New York, in particular, could be a place of vulnerability or that they would be unsafe again, here. For some, specific features of the terrorist attacks served as triggers, as well as aspects that were symbolic of past trauma, and then reactivated past symptoms (e.g., incineration for Holocaust survivors and their offspring, or absence of remains for relatives of the "disappeared" from some Latin American countries and from Bosnia and Herzegovina; see also, e.g., Kinzie, Boehnlein, Riley, & Sparr, 2002). American former prisoners of war (POWs), having lived through the attack on Pearl Harbor, combat, and imprisonment, and who were already well aware of life's unpredictability and fragility, were also affected by 9/11. Rodman and Engdahl (2002) found a small but significant increase in PTSD-related distress among 117 WWII and Korean War POWs surveyed in July 2002, indicating that the past can symbolically come alive in the face of present distress, despite the passage of time.

Trautman and colleagues (2002) similarly report that PTSD symptomatology from prior trauma in Asian and Middle Eastern immigrants was most predictive of initial physiologic and emotional response to the Oklahoma City 1995 bombing and of later bomb-related PTSD symptoms. They also found that bomb-related PTSD symptoms increased with age and were inversely related to age at the time of prior trauma. Their results underscore the importance of providing long-term disaster assistance to immigrants with prior trauma (see Mollica, McInnes, Poole, & Tor, 1998, in the context of cumulative trauma in particular).

Similar findings are reported in children and adolescents with PTSD; for example, in Kenya (Pfefferbaum et al., 2003), particularly in the context of cumulative stress or multiple or prolonged stressors/traumata such as in Sri Lanka, where children were exposed to family violence, war, and the tsunami (Catani, Jacob, Schauer, Kohila, & Neuner, 2008; Schauer, Catani, Ruf, & Elbert, 2006). This was also evident in Native American adolescents in substance abuse treatment (Deters, Novina, Fickenscher, & Beals, 2006), and Cuban children and adolescents after release from a refugee camp (Rothe et al., 2002).

The literature invokes both psychological (Breslau & Anthony, 2007; Johnsen, Eid, Laberg, & Thayer, 2002; Moinzadeh, 1998; Solomon & Prager, 1992) and biological (e.g., Yehuda, Morris, Labinsky, Zamelman, & Schmeidler, 2007) mechanisms to explain the process of retraumatization. Moreover, these seem to operate both within the directly traumatized generation for a lifetime, and multigenerationally—between the traumatized generation and generations to come. Within the directly traumatized generation, Solomon and Prager (1992) found that the sense of a previous similar experience did not affect the response of the non-Holocaust survivors to the first Gulf war, while it amplified the distress of the survivors. Furthermore, the first neurobiological study of Holocaust survivors provides evidence that the biological abnormalities in younger PTSD patients persist in elderly survivors (Yehuda, Southwick, Nussbaum, Wahby, Giller, & Manson, 1990; see also van Kammen et al., 1990).

Regarding intergenerational retraumatization, Solomon found that children of survivors of the Nazi Holocaust who failed to cope during the Lebanon war suffered deeper and more intense distress than those who are not children of survivors (see also Rosenheck and Fontana, 1998, on Vietnam veterans in the United States, and Nader, 1998, on children exposed to a violent event). Yehuda et al. (1998) demonstrated empirically that offspring of Holocaust survivors appear to have a similar neuroendocrine status to that of Holocaust survivors with PTSD, and that they may be more psychologically and biologically vulnerable to stress and trauma than controls. Concluding that the "intergenerational syndrome" may have a phenomenology and neurobiology similar to that of PTSD, Yehuda et al. (1998) also found that low cortisol levels in offspring of Holocaust survivors are associated with their tendency to indicate distress about the trauma of the Holocaust and to have PTSD symptoms in response to Holocaust-related events for which they are aware. That is, when traumatized, children of survivors of the Holocaust (born after World War II) responded as if the trauma had happened to them rather than to their parents before they were born. More recently, lower cortisol levels were found in women who were pregnant and directly exposed to the 9/11 terrorist attacks. Strikingly, babies of mothers who developed PTSD also showed low salivary cortisol levels in the first year of life (Yehuda et al., 2005).

These findings suggest that, in the face of retraumatization, including repetition of prior trauma and new traumatic experience, individuals with a history of prior trauma will require specialized, long-term attention from both spiritual care and mental health providers. Although this in no way suggests that those without prior trauma history do not require attention, it does emphasize that resilience may be compromised by a history of trauma. Thus, retraumatization occurs when a person who had been traumatized in the past is exposed to further trauma or responds to even an ordinary life event (possibly a reminder of the prior trauma) in a traumatic fashion. This effect is in addition to any concrete insults to resilience, such as loss of financial, social, and/or community support.

Massive trauma causes such diverse and complex destructive effects on the body, psyche, family, and community that only a multidimensional, multidisciplinary integrative framework (Danieli, 1998) is adequate to describe and understand it and treat its consequences. Every individual's identity involves a complex interplay of multiple systems including biological and intrapsychic; interpersonal including the familial, social, and communal; ethnic, cultural, ethical, religious, spiritual, and natural; educational/occupational; and material/economic, legal, environmental, political, national, and international dimensions. These systems interact and intermingle over the life span, creating a sense of continuity from past through present to the future. Ideally, when fully functional, one should have free psychological access to and movement within all of these identity systems. Each system is the focus of one or more disciplines that may overlap and interact, such as biology, psychology, sociology, economics, law, anthropology, religious studies and theology, and philosophy. Each discipline has its own views of human nature and it is those that inform what the professional thinks and does. The focus of this book on the indispensable collaboration between mental health and clergy professionals in the aftermath of both human-made and natural disasters, thus necessitates the mutual exploration by professionals of both disciplines (that, in reality, encompass numerous different "schools") of the differing views of human

nature held by them so that they would be able to understand their varying professionals' recommendations and choices of action. As an example
from a related field, one cannot but follow Esposito's (2006) recommendation to nurses who "unknowingly encounter survivors of sexual assault
every day in clinics, ambulatory care centers, emergency departments,
and inpatient units. These patients may have a variety of acute and chronic
physical or emotional conditions, which include migraine headaches, gas-
trointestinal disturbances, depression, or substance abuse. While these
presenting problems are addressed, the underlying cause may be missed."
Emphasizing that "healthcare visits can be reminders of a sexual assault,"
she suggests that "nurses can ask questions, listen to patients, and be sensitive to potential indicators of abuse, which all can assist patients who have
a history of sexual assault toward an emotional healing process" (p. 69; see
also Mezey, Bacchus, Bewley, & White, 2005) on health professionals in
the context of maternity care and Cloitre, Cohen, Edelman, & Han, 2001,
as related to medical problems and care).

Trauma Exposure and "Fixity"

Trauma exposure can cause a rupture, a possible regression, and a state
of being "stuck" or "frozen," which I have termed *fixity*. The free flowing
state of smoothly negotiated, multiple identity dimensions associated with
healthy adaptation to a complex and changing world becomes rigidified
and less functional. The intent, place, time, frequency, duration, intensity,
extent, and meaning of the trauma for the individual, and the survival
strategies used to adapt to it, will determine the degree of rupture and
the severity of the fixity. Although there is a dizzying array of complexly
interacting factors determining the severity and the heterogeneous ways
individuals are affected, it is beyond the scope of this chapter to describe
a predictive model. However, when working with affected individuals, it
is necessary to explore the above-mentioned factors, as appropriate for the
setting and, with appropriate supervision, to clarify and evaluate these
factors as they pertain to the individuals with whom you work.

Fixity can be intensified, in particular, by the *conspiracy of silence*
(Danieli, 1982, 1998), the survivors' reaction to the societal—including
healthcare and other professionals—indifference, avoidance, repression,
and denial of the survivors' trauma experiences (Symonds, 1980). The
effect of this strong taboo against speaking cannot be overemphasized.
Society's initial emotional outburst, coupled with a socially constructed

demand for rapid return to apparent normality, is an important example of how the societal need to return to normality may interfere with the needs of its individual members. This *conspiracy of silence* is detrimental to the survivors' familial and sociocultural (re)integration by intensifying their already profound sense of isolation and mistrust of society. It further impedes the possibility of their intrapsychic integration and healing and makes the task of mourning their losses impossible. Fixity may render *chronic* the immediate reactions to trauma (e.g., acute stress disorder) and, in the extreme, become life-long (Danieli, 1997) *post-trauma/victimization adaptational styles* (Danieli, 1985). This occurs when survival strategies generalize to a way of life and become an integral part of one's personality, repertoire of defense, or character armor. Fixity may cause subsequent trauma to be more damaging, increasing the probability of a maladaptive response to subsequent traumatic events, such as disasters. As mentioned above, there are both psychological and biological foundations for this increase in vulnerability due to fixity, which are beyond the scope of this discussion.

The current diagnostic framework, while an improvement over prior conceptualizations, is still evolving and is as yet incomplete, unfortunately often to the detriment of those we seek to help. Recognition of the possible long-term impact of trauma on one's personality and adaptation and the *intergenerational* transmission of victimization-related pathology still await explicit inclusion in future editions of the diagnostic nomenclature.

Importantly, and often overlooked, conceptualizing disaster work as repairing the rupture and thereby freeing the flow usually does not mean "going back to normal." Clinging to or encouraging the possibility of "returning to normal" may indicate denial of the survivors' experiences and, thereby, intensify fixity and delay the posttraumatic healing process.

Based on extensive international experience (Danieli, Rodley, & Weisacth, 1996) and my "Trauma and the Continuity of Self: A Multidimensional, Multidisciplinary, Integrative (TCMI) Framework" (Danieli, 1998; Danieli, Engdahl, & Schlenger, 2003; Danieli, Brom, & Sills, 2005), immediately following 9/11, I (Danieli, 2001) suggested that, more than ever, issues related to the time dimension (process, rather than short-term, premature, but superficially reassuring resolution) emerged as paramount. First was the imperative to resist the culturally prevalent impulse to do *something, anything*, to find quick fixes, to focus on outcome rather than process, to all too swiftly look for closure, and flee "back to normal," leaving important psychological, emotional, and spiritual work unfinished. Second, acknowledging that there will be long-term, even multigenerational, effects of the disaster and of the immediate interventions, addressing the importance of and necessity for sustained commitment to budgeting for and working in the long term, and examining systematically every short-term decision from a long-term perspective—no easy task. I also noted the necessity of considering *at-risk times* (e.g., family holidays, anniversaries, and specific age groups) as well as the *at-risk group*, when working with those afflicted by disasters, tragedies, and other traumas (see also Chen et al., 2007; Galea et al., 2004; Pantin, Schwartz, Prado, Feaster, & Szapocznik, 2003; Sutker, Corigan, Sundgaard-Riise, Uddor, & Allain, 2002). The long-term perspective also allows for ongoing evaluation of the differing effects of interventions on various groups and communities and of the determination of yet unmet needs that may require further plans and related funding, though the sad and challenging reality is that resources are often not allocated to address these important long-term consequences and needs. In fact, in itself, the very lack of appropriate resources may become a source of retraumatization or prolongation of the trauma, a disaster in its own right, induced by the preceding insult.

Integration of the trauma must take place in *all* of life's relevant (ruptured) systems and cannot be accomplished by the individual alone. Systems can change and recover independently of other systems. It may be easier to begin to restore the religious community through the comfort of its rituals before a trauma is accepted and integrated into the psyche.

Rupture repair may be needed in all systems of the survivor, in his or her community and nation, and in his or her place in the international community. To fulfill the reparative and preventive goals of trauma recovery, perspective, and integration through awareness of all the events leading to, during, and after the trauma and their related meanings and containment of all feelings and choices associated with it must be established so that one's sense of continuity and belongingness is restored. To be healing and even self-actualizing, the integration of traumatic experiences must be examined from the perspective of the *totality* of the trauma survivors' and family and community members' lives.

This places the challenge of coordination of and collaboration among all helpers and of providing them with specialized training so they themselves don't suffer *event countertransference* (Danieli, 1982b, 1988b); that is, the therapists' reactions to patients' stories of their traumatic events rather than to the patients' behavior. This phenomenon is variously described in the literature as *vicarious traumatization* (Pearlman & Saakvitne, 1995), *secondary traumatic stress* (Hudnall Stamm, 1995), *burnout* (Maslach, 1982), or *compassion fatigue* (Figley, 1995). A recent book, *Sharing the*

Front Line and the Back Hills (Danieli, 2002), addressed the costs paid by protectors and providers and the responsibilities of their organizations to train and support them before, during, and after their missions. Exposure to trauma has been shown to affect the interveners in multiple ways, both directly (sharing the same environment with the victims) and indirectly (listening to victims' accounts of their experiences in the context of attempting to help them or taking their testimonies). Thus, all those who help victims on the front lines are at high risk for double exposure and should receive specialized training to help the individuals they serve but also in self-care.

Vulnerability and Resilience

The literature is in disagreement regarding the impact of prior trauma on subsequent trauma for affected individuals. Two contrasting perspectives exist. The first, the vulnerability perspective, holds that prior trauma left permanent psychic damage that render survivors more vulnerable when subsequently faced with extreme stress (see above). The second, the resilience perspective (Harel, Kahana, & Kaliana, 1993; Helmreich, 1992; Kaminer & Lavie, 1991; Leon et al., 1981; Shanan, 1989; Whiteman, 1993) postulates that coping well with initial trauma will strengthen resistance to the effects of future trauma (see, for example, findings by Keppel-Benson, Ollendick, & Benson, 2002) about posttraumatic stress in children following motor vehicle accidents). In other words, survivors of previous trauma will manifest more resilience when faced with adversity. In a sense, people who may succumb to the trauma's effects can be contrasted with those who do not. The latter may well be described as resilient or more resistant to the negative effects of trauma. Both perspectives recognize individual differences in response to trauma, that exposure to massive trauma may overwhelm predisposition and previous experience, and that posttrauma environmental factors play important roles in adaptation (see also Eberly et al., 1991; Engdahl et al., 1993; Ursano, 1990). As I have argued, rather than artificially dichotomize vulnerability versus resilience—both of which coexist in each individual, depending on the particular dimensions ruptured by the trauma—one must be cognizant of how both may be at play in those with whom we work.

Similarly, while some of the literature on children of survivors reports good adjustment (e.g., Leon et al., 1981), Solomon, Kotler, & Milkulincer, (1988) demonstrated in them a special vulnerability to traumatic stress.

Despite optimistic views of adaptation, even survivors in the "those who made it" category (Danieli, 1985) still experience difficulties related to their traumatic past, suggesting that the overly optimistic views may describe defense rather than effective coping. In fact, it is within this category of postvictimization adaptational styles that relies on denial of the trauma and its effects as a primary defense that we observe the highest rates of suicide among survivors as well as their children (Danieli, 1998).

The findings that survivors have areas of vulnerability and resilience is no longer paradoxical when viewed within a multidimensional (TCMI) framework for multiple levels of posttraumatic adaptation. And tracing a history of multiple traumata along the time dimension at different stages of development reveals that, while for many people time heals ills, for traumatized people time may not heal but may magnify their response to further trauma across the full span of adult development, particularly in times of even normal transition and old age (Danieli, 1994a, 1994b) and may carry intergenerational implications.

The aging process inevitably entails losses, forcing the elderly to confront considerable stress. Recent evidence from both Holocaust survivors and combat veterans clearly support the vulnerability perspective. Schnurr (1991) reviewed and Cassiday and Lyons (1992) examined reactivation of posttraumatic reactions among American veterans. They reported that life events, such as retirement, children leaving home, death of a loved one, and other stressful events, served as triggers that accelerated and unmasked latent PTSD.

With survivors, it is especially hard to draw conclusions based on outward appearances. Survivors often display external markers of success (i.e., occupational achievement or establishing families) that in truth represent survival strategies. Clearly, these accomplishments may facilitate adaptation and produce feelings of fulfillment in many survivors. Thus, the external attainment represents significant adaptive achievement in their lives. However, there are also other facets of adaptation that are largely internal and intrapsychic. If clinicians and researchers do not look for these adaptational impairments, they can easily miss them in the presence of evidence that survivors mastered the external challenges encountered after their traumata. This may be a particular problem with aging survivors because the elderly often underreport psychic distress (Rapp et al., 1988).

Conversely, a focus on pathology can lead professionals to overlook the survivor's strengths—the clinician's major therapeutic allies. With a multidimensional framework for the multiple levels of posttraumatic adaptation, the fact that survivors have areas of vulnerability and resilience is no longer paradoxical. And tracing one's history of multiple traumata along the time dimension at different stages of development reveals that while for many people time heals ills, for traumatized people time may not heal but may magnify their response to further trauma.

It behooves us—the helpers of all professions and disciplines—to remain mindful that, even when exposed and confronted with the immediacy of an extremely overwhelming traumatic situation, this event is a segment of an individual's, family's, and community's generational and multigenerational history (and culture) that might shape, give meaning to, and intensify the immediate reactions to the present event. Indeed, this chapter has emphasized the time dimension in trauma assessment and response and presented an approach that yields the most complete assessment of an individual's, family's, and community's posttraumatic status. This status is best understood within my multidimensional, multidisciplinary framework.

In closing, it is essential for various actors to further define and develop complementary roles in their responses to disasters. Complementarity involves the tolerance of, respect for, and capitalizing on the differing strengths of all the partners: governments, professionals, and the communities they serve. For example, while people working *in* the community (very often, clergy, teachers, etc.) might be in a better position than outsiders to assess the disaster in its historic perspective, they might also be bounded by assumptions they take for granted that outsiders won't be constrained by. As well, coordinated teams should be organized such that they are not confused themselves or become victims like the ones they are there to care for. And everyone might want to prevent the possible emergence of the conspiracy of silence by participating in a concerted action to prevent further and retraumatization by it and related further traumas of the survivors, their families, and communities (see also Ahern et al., 2002; Danieli & Dingman, 2005; Krug, Nixon, &Vincent, 1996; Silver et al., 2005).

References

Ahern, J., Galea, S., Resnick, H., Kilpatrick, D., Bucouvalas, M., Gold, J., & Vlahov, D. (2002). Television images and psychological symptoms after the September 11 terrorist attacks. *Psychiatry, 65*(4), 289–300.
Breslau, N., & Anthony, J. C. (2007). Gender differences in the sensitivity to posttraumatic stress disorder: An epidemiological study of urban young adults. *Journal of Abnormal Psychology, 116*(3), 607–611.

Cassiday, K. L. and Lyons, J. A. (1992) Recall of traumatic memories following cerebral vascular accident. *Journal of Traumatic Stress, 5*(4), 627–631.

Catani, C., Jacob, N., Schauer, E., Kohila, M., & Neuner, F. (2008). Family violence, war, and natural disasters: A study of the effect of extreme stress on children's mental health in Sri Lanka. *BMC Psychiatry, 8,* 2.

Chen, A. C., Keith, V. M., Leong, K. J., Airriess, C., Li, W., Chung, K. Y., et al. (2007). Hurricane Katrina: Prior trauma, poverty and health among Vietnamese-American survivors. *International Nursing Review, 54*(4), 324–331.

Cloitre, M., Cohen, L. R., Edelman, R. E., & Han, H. (2001). Posttraumatic stress disorder and extent of trauma exposure as correlates of medical problems and perceived health among women with childhood abuse. *Women and Health, 34*(3), 1–17.

Danieli, Y., (1982). Therapists' difficulties in treating survivors of the Nazi Holocaust and their children. *Dissertation Abstracts International, 42*(12-B, Pt 1), 4927. UMI No. 949-904).

Danieli, Y. (1985). The treatment and prevention of long-term effects and intergenerational transmission of victimization: A lesson from Holocaust survivors and their children. In C. R. Figley (Ed.), *Trauma and its wake* (pp. 295–313). New York: Brunner/Mazel.

Danieli, Y. (1988). Confronting the unimaginable: Psychotherapists' reactions to victims of the Nazi Holocaust. In J. P. Wilson, Z. Harel, & B. Kahana (Eds.), *Human adaptation to extreme stress* (pp. 219–238). New York: Plenum Publishing.

Danieli, Y. (1994a). As survivors age—Part I. *National Center for Post Traumatic Stress Disorder Clinical Quarterly, 4*(1), 1–7.

Danieli, Y. (1994b). As survivors age—Part II. *National Center for Post Traumatic Stress Disorder Clinical Quarterly, 4*(2), 20-24.

Danieli, Y. (1997). As survivors age: An overview. *Journal of Geriatric Psychiatry, 30*(1), (9-26).

Danieli, Y. (Ed.). (1998). *International handbook of multigenerational legacies of trauma.* New York: Kluwer Academic/Plenum Publishing.

Danieli, Y. (2001). ISTSS members participate in recovery efforts in New York and Washington, DC. *Traumatic Stress Points, 15*(4), 4.

Danieli, Y. (Ed.). (2002). *Sharing the front line and the back hills: International protectors and providers, peacekeepers, humanitarian aid workers and the media in the midst of crisis.* Amityville, NY: Baywood Publishing Company.

Danieli, Y., Brom, D., & Sills, J. B. (Eds.). (2005). *The trauma of terrorism: Sharing knowledge and shared care, An international handbook.* Binghamton, NY: The Haworth Press.

Danieli, Y., & Dingman, R. (Eds.). (2005). *On the ground after September 11: Mental health responses and practical knowledge gained.* Binghamton, NY: The Haworth Press.

Danieli, Y., Engdahl, B., & Schlenger, W. E. (2003). The psychological aftermath of terrorism. In F. M. Moghaddam & Marsella, A. J. (Eds.), *Understanding terrorism: Psychological roots, consequences, and interventions* (pp. 223-246). Washington, DC: American Psychological Association.

Danieli, Y., Rodley, N. S., & Weisaeth, L. (Eds.)(1996). *International responses to traumatic stress: Humanitarian, human rights, justice, peace and development contributions, collaborative actions and future initiatives.* Published for and on behalf of the United Nations by Baywood Publishing Company, Inc., Amityville, New York.

Deters, P. B., Novins, D. K., Fickenscher, A., & Beals, J. (2006). Trauma and post-traumatic stress disorder symptomatology: Patterns among American Indian adolescents in substance abuse treatment. *American Journal of Orthopsychiatry, 76*(3), 335-345.

Eberly, R. E., Harkness, A. R., & Engdahl, B. E. (1991). An adaptational view of trauma response as illustrated by the prisoner of war experience. *Journal of Traumatic Stress* (4), 363-380.

Engdahl, B. E., Harkness, A. R., Eberly, R. E., Page, W. E., & Bielinski, J. (1993). Structural models of captivity trauma, resilience, and trauma response among former prisoners of war 20 to 40 years after release. *Social psychiatry and psychiatric epidemiology, 28,* 109-115.

Esposito, N. (2006). Women with a history of sexual assault: Health care visits can be reminders of a sexual assault. *American Journal of Nursing, 106*(3), 69-71, 73.

Figley, C. R. (Ed.). (1995). *Compassion fatigue: Coping with secondary traumatic stress disorder in those who treat the traumatized.* New York: Brunner/Mazel.

Galea, S., Vlahov, D., Tracy, M., Hoover, D. R., Resnick, H., & Kilpatrick, D. (2004). Hispanic ethnicity and post-traumatic stress disorder after a disaster: Evidence from a general population survey after September 11, 2001. *Annals of Epidemiology, 14,* 520-531.

Harel, Z., Kahana, B., & Kahana, E. (1993). Social resources and the mental health of aging Nazi Holocaust survivors and immigrants. In J. P. Wilson and B. Raphael (Eds.) *International handbook of traumatic stress syndromes.* (pp. 241-252). New York: Plenum Publishing.

Hudnall Stamm, B. (Ed.). (1995). *Secondary traumatic stress: Self-care issues for clinicians, researchers, & educators.* Lutherville, MD: Sidran Press.

Johnsen, B. H., Eid, J., Laberg, J. C., & Thayer, J. F. (2002). The effect of sensitization and coping style on post-traumatic stress symptoms and quality of life: Two longitudinal studies. *Scandinavian Journal of Psychology, 43*(2), 181-188.

Kaminer, H., & Lavie, P. (1991) Sleep and dreaming in Holocaust survivors: Dramatic decrease in dream recall in well-adjusted survivors. *Journal of Nervous and Mental Disease, 179*(11), 664-669.

Keppel-Benson, J. M., Ollendick, T. H, & Benson, M. J. (2002). Post-traumatic stress in children following motor vehicle accidents. *Journal of Child Psychology and Psychiatry and Allied Disciplines, 43*(2), 203–212.

Kinzie, J. D., Boehnlein, J., Riley, C., & Sparr, L. (2002). The effects of September 11 on traumatized refugees: Reactivation of posttraumatic stress disorder. *Journal of Nervous and Mental Disease, 190*(7), 437–441.

Krug, R. S., Nixon, S. J., & Vincent, R. (1996). Psychological response to the Oklahoma City bombing [Editorial]. *Journal of Clinical Psychology, 52*(1), 103–105.

Leon, G., Butcher, J. M., Kleinman, M., Goldberg, A., & Almagor, M. (1981). Survivors of the Holocaust and their children. *Journal of Personality and Social Psychology, 41,* 303–316.

Maslach, C. (1982). *Burnout: The cost of caring.* Englewood Cliffs, NJ: Prentice Hall.

Mezey, G. C., Bacchus, L., Bewley, S., & White, S. (2005). Domestic violence, lifetime trauma and psychological health of childbearing women. *BJOG: An International Journal of Obstetrics and Gynaecology, 112*(2), 197–204.

Moinzadeh, M. (1998). *Trauma symptoms and retraumatization in adult survivors of child abuse following a natural disaste.* Retrieved July 25, 2008, from http://wwwlib.umi.com/dissertations/fullcit/9904184

Mollica, R. F., McInnes, K., Poole, C., & Tor, S. (1998). Dose-effect relationships of trauma to symptoms of depression and post-traumatic stress disorder among Cambodian survivors of mass violence. *British Journal of Psychiatry, 173,* 482–488.

Nader, K. O. (1998). Violence: Effects of parents' previous trauma on currently traumatized children. In Y. Danieli (Ed.). *International Handbook of Multigenerational Legacies of Trauma* (pp. 571–586). New York: Kluwer Academic/Plenum Publishing.

Neuner, F., Schauer, E., Catani, C., Ruf, M., & Elbert, T. (2006). Post-tsunami stress: A study of posttraumatic stress disorder in children living in three severely affected regions in Sri Lanka. *Journal of Traumatic Stress, 19*(3), 339–347.

Pantin, H. M., Schwartz, S. J., Prado, G., Feaster, D. J., & Szapocznik, J. (2003). Posttraumatic stress disorder symptoms in Hispanic immigrants after the September 11th attacks: Severity and relationship to previous traumatic exposure. *Hispanic Journal of Behavioral Sciences, 25*(1), 56–72.

Pearlman, L. A., & Saakvitne, K. W. (1995). *Trauma and the therapist: Countertransference and vicarious traumatization and psychotherapy with incest survivors.* New York: W. W. Norton & Company.

Pfefferbaum, B. C., North, C. S., Doughty, D. E., Gurwitch, R. H., Fullerton, C. S., & Kyula, J. (2003). Posttraumatic stress and functional impairment in Kenyan children following the 1998 American Embassy bombing. *American Journal of Orthopsychiatry, 73*(2), 133–140.

Rapp, S. R., Parisi, S. A., & Walsh, D. A. (1988). Psychological dysfunction and physical health among elderly medical inpatients. *Journal of Consulting and Clinical Psychology, 56,* 851–855.

Rodman, J., & Engdahl, B. (2002, August). Posttraumatic growth and PTSD in WWII and Korean War veterans. In R. G. Tedeschi (Chair), *Posttraumatic growth in the aftermath of terrorism.* Symposium conducted at the meeting of the American Psychological Association, Chicago, IL.

Rosenheck, R., & Fontana, A. (1998). Warrior Fathers and Warrior Sons. In Y. Danieli (Ed.). *International Handbook of Multigenerational Legacies of Trauma* (pp. 225–242). New York: Kluwer Academic/Plenum Publishing.

Rothe, E. M., Lewis, J. E., Castillo-Matos, H., Martinez, O., Busquets, R., & Martinez, I. (2002). Posttraumatic stress disorder among Cuban children and adolescents after release from a refugee camp. *Psychiatric Services, 53*(8), 970–976.

Schnurr, P. P. (1991). PTSD and combat-related psychiatric symptoms in older veterans. *The National Center for Post-Traumatic Stress Disorder PTSD Research Quarterly, 2*(1), 1–6.

Shanan, J. (1989). Surviving the survivors: Late personality development of Jewish Holocaust survivors. *International Journal of Mental Health, 17*(4), 42–71.

Silver, R. C., Poulin, M., Holman, E. A., McIntosh, D. N., Gil-Rivas, V., & Pizarro, J. (2005). Exploring the myths of coping with a national trauma: A longitudinal study of responses to the September 11th terrorist attacks. In Y. Danieli, D. Brom, & J. Sills (Eds.), *The trauma of terrorism: Sharing knowledge and shared care, An international handbook* (pp. 129–141). Binghamton, NY: Haworth Press.

Solomon, Z., Kotler, M., & Milkulincer, M. (1988). Combat-related post-traumatic stress disorders among second generation Holocaust survivors: Preliminary findings. *American Journal of Psychiatry, 145,* 865–868.

Solomon, Z., Prager, E. (1992). Elderly Israeli Holocaust survivors during the Persian Gulf war: A study of psychological distress. *American Journal of Psychiatry, 149*(12), 1707–1710.

Sutker, P. B., Corrigan, S. A., Sundgaard-Riise, K., Uddo, M. M., & Allain, A. N. (2002). Exposure to war trauma, war-related PTSD, and psychological impact of subsequent hurricane. *Journal of Psychopathology and Behavioral Assessment, 24*(1), 25–37.

Symonds, M. (1980). The "second injury" to victims. *Evaluation and Change* (special issue), 36–38.

Trautman, R. P. et al. (2002). Effect of prior trauma and age on posttraumatic stress symptoms in Asian and Middle Eastern immigrants after terrorism in the community. *Community Mental Health Journal, 38*(6), 459–474.

Ursano, R. J. (1990). The prisoner of war. *Military Medicine, (155),* 176–180.

van Kammen, W. B., Christiansen, C., van Kammen, D. P., & Reynolds, C. F. III. (1990). Sleep and the prisoner-of-war experience—40 years later. In E. L. Giller, Jr., *Biological assessment and treatment of posttraumatic stress disorder.* (pp. 161–172). Washington, DC.: American Psychiatric Press, Inc.

Whiteman, D. B. (1993). Holocaust survivors and escapees—their strengths. *Psychotherapy, 30*(3), 443–451.

Yehuda, R., Engel, S. M., Brand, S. R., Seckl, J., Marcus, S. M., & Berkowitz, G. S. (2005). Transgenerational effects of posttraumatic stress disorder in babies of mothers exposed to the World Trade Center attacks during pregnancy. *The Journal of Clinical Endocrinology & Metabolism, 90*(7), 4115–4118.

Yehuda, R., Morris, A., Labinsky, E., Zamelman, S., & Schmeidler, J. (2007). Ten-year follow-up study of cortisol levels in aging Holocaust survivors with and without PTSD. *Journal of Traumatic Stress, 20*(5), 757–761.

Yehuda, R., Schmeidler, J., Elkin, A., Wilson, S., Siever, L., Binder-Brynes, K., et al. (1998). Phenomenology and psychobiology of the intergenerational response to trauma. In Y. Danieli (Ed.). *International Handbook of Multigenerational Legacies of Trauma* (pp. 639–656). New York: Kluwer Academic/Plenum Publishing Corporation.

Yehuda, R., Southwick, S. M., Nussbaum, G., Wahby, V., Giller, E. I., Jr., & Mason, J. W. (1990). Low urinary cortisol excretion in patients with PTSD. *Journal of Nervous and Mental Disease, 178*, 366–369.

15

Reaching Out to Create Moments of Communal Healing
Personal Reflections From the Edge of the 9/11 Abyss

Rev. Alfonso Wyatt

Tragedy in Microcosm

A man from my church took a job at the World Trade Center a few weeks before the tragedy. We found out several days after 9/11 that he died. He was a young leader in the church's Rites of Passage Program for young boys. He was dedicated to helping young people navigate the dangerous streets of the "da hood"—and he died at work. His family came to the pastor's office after church service seeking solace and sanctuary. We stood in a circle and sobbed as the pastor prayed. When he finished, I recall a long and sorrowful silence speaking loudly to the fact that sometimes there just are no words.

There were people all over this city flocking to churches, mosques, synagogues, and other houses of worship in unprecedented numbers. In many instances, members of the clergy were not able to meet the overwhelming needs of the people crying out in a loud and unmistakable voice for help. They (as well as clergy) needed assistance to cope with the cataclysmic social, economic, political, and religious upheaval that a city and world experienced. There were no footprints or blueprints to follow or read. Houses of worship were snatched into unfamiliar territory (more people in mental crisis than spiritual hunger) and trying their best to keep up.

The pain of 9/11 churned the inner dark place where fear and doubt lurked. People needed answers to questions not yet fully formed. Every day, the news would report yet another funeral or speculate about found remains. Paranoia was as thick as the debris cloud shown over and over as if it were a monster that could not be killed. This great opportunity to minister, like the random acts of love and kindness around the city, all began to slowly fade, only to be replaced by recrimination, growing jingoism, and lawsuits. The same people seeking answers, reassurance, and sanctuary soon left houses of worship in droves after the immediate trauma of the moment passed.

But, there were other victims of the tragedy who could not shake off their pain or lose their fear. A friend of mine was separated from her child (her child ended up in New Jersey while she searched frantically for her) and did not know where to start looking. Her story and reunion was captured on PBS. I heard a mother talk about how her grown daughter refuses to travel to Manhattan. I hosted a meeting focused on first responders of color. A young policewoman and experienced fireman both broke down when recalling the horrific day. I still remember weeks after 9/11 walking my dog and ducking as an airplane would fly by overhead (my neighborhood is on the LaGuardia Airport landing path). There are individuals who will never be the same. Their issues outstripped the faith community's ability to respond.

> He gives strength to the weary and increases the power of the weak. Even youths grow tired and weary and young men stumble and fall, but those who hope in the LORD will renew their strength. They will soar on wings like eagles, they will run and not get weary, they will walk and not be faint. (Isaiah 40: 29-31)

Oppressed Oppressors

On October 8, 2001, I held a citywide Celebration of Peace at my church (The Greater Allen Cathedral of New York). The Lord dropped this idea in my spirit—to bring young people and their family members from various communities and faith traditions (a first) together to celebrate peace and learn more about each other. This meeting was called against a backdrop of growing violence reported in many newspapers after 9/11 directed toward young people perceived to hail from Muslim countries located mainly in South Asia (many young Sikhs were beaten) and the Middle East. Anyone wearing a head covering, male or female, was thought to be Muslim and deserved to be hurt.

There were over 500 young people and adults in attendance. We had singers, steppers, rappers, dancers, and a choir made up of elementary school–age children from Sunset Park, Brooklyn (they sang "The Impossible Dream" and I cried), offering their talent in pursuit of love, peace, and understanding (the 60s trinity). A woman who serves as the executive director of South Asian Youth Action program was invited to speak to the group of mostly African Americans and Latinos. She gave a warm greeting, spoke elegantly about the significance of this peace vigil and then closed with a Hindu prayer for peace.

While we did not know what she said, we (I) felt like she ministered to us all. I told the young people in the audience, in as direct a manner possible, that children of oppressed people cannot become the oppressor of other people's children. This statement was picked up by a reporter from *The New York Times* in the audience and was written for the world to see and ponder:

> O my people, hear my teaching, listen to the words of my mouth. I will open my mouth in parables. I will utter hidden meanings, things from old—what we have heard and known, what our fathers have told us. We will not hide them from their children; and will tell the next generation the praiseworthy deeds of the Lord, his power, and the wonders he has done ... he commanded our forefathers to teach their children so the next generation would know them even the children yet to be born ... Then they will put their trust in God and would not forget his deeds and would keep his commandments. They would not be like their forefathers—a stubborn and rebellious generation whose hearts were not loyal to God, whose spirits were not faithful to him. (Psalms 78:1-4, 5a-8 NIV)

My Brother and Sister's Keeper

I was invited to speak at the New York Academy of Medicine several weeks after the tragedy. The focus of the meeting was to bring members of the nonprofit community together to discuss strategies to help people cope with the aftermath of 9/11. Given the fact that it now took hours for people to make trips around the city that once took 20 minutes, there was plenty of down time while waiting for people to arrive. Most of the conversation was about the new normal: machine gun–toting soldiers in the street, street closures, and what would happen next. It was during this waiting period (which no one seemed to mind at all) that I spoke to Dr. Mindy Fullilove at length about her plan to launch a citywide, civic-led movement to help people address and recover from trauma, stress, anxiety, and fear. Her theory, drawn from her earlier studies on the impact of crack cocaine on communities of color, was that it was crucial to involve people in their healing.

This made so much sense to me, I agreed to become a founding member and key partner of New York City Recovers, a group of people versed in mental health, community, and social organizing who were pooling their time, talent, and treasure to help people recover from posttraumatic stress disorder. NYC Recovers, a subsidiary of Columbia University Mailmen School of Public Health, served as the organizing arm for this effort. Dr. Fullilove and an army of volunteers launched a flurry of civic activities to encourage citizens to find innovative ways to participate in communal healing activities, such as telling stories (where were you when the towers fell, what did you do, how do you feel?). Some other activities included singing (a citywide choir sang in community centers); family cook-ins; and a rally was held at Washington Square Park for all to bear witness and to heal (I was the master of ceremonies). This and other efforts were a small part of the tremendous outpouring of love in action and participatory healing that popped up over this city and around the world.

I took a storytelling class at New York Theological Seminary; I learned the power firsthand of people being free to tell their story. It gave new meaning to standing (or sitting) on sacred ground. A friend talking to a group I organized told one story I remember. She recounted her story through her tears and sobs about how a young man of African descent (she is Latina) found her blocks from Ground Zero, stricken by fear and unable to move. He grabbed her hand and told her that he would not leave her. As the great cloud of debris swept upon them, he pounded on a glass door of an office building wedged closed by people afraid of the cloud and managed to push her inside. As the cloud of death swept by, she looked around the lobby and her angel was gone.

NYC Recovers allowed me to do something proactive instead of spending days looking at the Towers fall carried by a seemingly endless news loop—all seemed lost or so I thought. The power of involving people in activities that call for cooperation, teamwork, giving, serving, and dispensing love in large, midsize, and small doses eventually turned sorrow into joy—the very essence of true transformation.

It should be mentioned that there were faith-led efforts around the city to help locate lost love ones, feed the workers toiling day and night on the mountain of rubble, and provide chaplain services to the growing number of the bereaved gathering in the shadow of World Trade Financial Center. I met members from 40 Brooklyn churches made up of congregants from the Caribbean community incorporated to deal with the needs of their members (many of whom worked in various capacities in the World Trade Center). A dear friend who is a Christian psychiatrist was contracted to work with hundreds of government employees working blocks from the fallen Twin Towers. His blending of the psychospiritual with aroma therapy and cognitive group and individual counseling helped people recover. With this said, it became clear that the broader religious community was not equipped to launch a citywide effort like NYC Recovers. The sad reality for many leaders of houses of worship was the fact that they too needed to recover.

I am much wiser and more determined as a result of 9/11 to live a meaningful life in service to others and not allow fear to reign over hope. While I miss the random acts of love and kindness extended to strangers, I will covenant with myself and other love warriors to do what has been placed in our hearts by a loving and good God.

> The Spirit of the Lord is on me because he has anointed me to preach good news to the poor. He has sent me to proclaim freedom for the prisoners and recovery of sight for the blind, to release the oppressed, to proclaim the year of the Lord's favor. (Luke 4:18-19 NIV)

Hope Is Not Fundable

I remember a conversation with a foundation executive concerning my work with individuals and organizations (mostly secular) impacted by the World Trade Center tragedy. I was telling the program officer how important it was that I present hope to individuals. The person responded matter-of-factly, "HOPE IS NOT FUNDABLE." I was crushed inside, but I willed my outside not to betray me. Surely this person who asked me to bring a word of hope to members of her grant-funded agencies could not be saying this to me. I believe that the separation of church and state has caused a great misunderstanding about the role of the faith community in nonreligious matters. It is lost on many people that the nonprofit community in this country was largely a direct outgrowth of the faith community at the time. It was clear that the attacks on buildings also did damage to the mind, body, and spirit of people. It was also clear that people needed hope to rise up like the proverbial Phoenix from the ashes of despair. This is not religion—far from it. This is the essence of being creatures having the ability to hope even when all seems hopeless. Hope may not be fundable or quantifiable, but it is absolute. Our mind may want facts yet our soul craves hope and therein lays the separation between one's state and hope.

I began petitioning (inquisition is more like it) God as to how I was supposed to do this job He assigned to me without the proper resources.

I felt set-up and put down at the same time by this experience. A week before 9/11, a car involved in an accident jumped the curb and tore down a long section of my fence (I live on a corner). Up to 9/11, my consuming thought was "look how bad my fence looked" and "when would the insurance company honor their word and pay up." If this was not enough, my wife started to experience several concurrent serious medical challenges that drained already waning strength and resolve in me. I thought I was about to lose my mind, not to mention my tenuous hold on faith.

> ... But hope that is seen is no hope at all. Who hopes for what he already has? But if we hope for what we do not have, we wait for it patiently ... And we know that in all things God works for the good of those who love him, who have been called according to his purpose. (Romans 8: 24c-25, 28 NIV)

Face on the Lamppost

I recall leaving my job late one evening (I work less than a mile from what is now called Ground Zero) shortly after the tragedy. The acrid smell of smoke and death would cover parts of lower Manhattan (and the city) anytime the wind decided to change direction. While covering my mouth and squinting my eyes, I saw a woman putting up a poster on a nearby lamppost. I figured she was posting a picture of a missing loved one that now hang all over the city. I made it a practice to look at the faces captured in happier times of those who were missing. It was my way of sharing the pain of families, coworkers, and friends and also allowing me to pray for those brothers, sisters, husbands and wives, sons and daughters.

When I looked at the picture in the woman's hand, I was astonished to see that she was taping an 8 1/2 × 11 color picture of Jesus ostensibly praying in Gethsemane. After talking for a while, I found out that this mystery lady lived in rural Pennsylvania. She told me that she sold most of her possessions to raise enough money to have reams of her favorite childhood picture of Jesus replicated and for her room and board. She said that her family was dead set against her coming to New York by herself for all the obvious reasons. She told me that she had to come because she felt led by the Lord. We both started to cry ... for everything.

I held her hand and prayed for all of the faces of the missing on lampposts here and around the city. I prayed for her safety, for her family, and I prayed for myself. It was only after she walked away that I thought about the significance of what occurred. Here were two strangers, one Black (me) and one White, one male and one female, holding hands as brother and sister, on a dark and deserted corner in New York. It was not the least bit important to me that the picture of Jesus joining the missing was not fashioned in my image (historical/cultural/experiential) of Him. What I can surely say is that I felt the Lord standing (crying) with us …

> A thousand may fall at your side, ten thousand at your right hand, but it will not come near you … For he will command his angels concerning you to guard you in all of your ways. On their hands, they will bear you up, so that you will not dash your foot against a stone. (Psalms 91: 7, 11-12 NRSV)

Is God Dead?

Where are you, God? How could you let so many people die? Where are you, God? My grief, anger, and fear had burst through my illusions, rationalizations, and sense of safety. Where are you, God? This is supposed to be sweet land of liberty, land of the pilgrim's pride, land where forefathers died; the land proud of the fact that it was founded on the principles of religious freedom and expression. Where are you, God? We have solemnly and sincerely printed "In God We Trust" on our money in tribute to you. Where are you, God? A child has lost a mother, another child has lost a father, and the nation and the world is mourning. Where are you, God? The acrid smell of death hangs over the city casting a shawl of fear and anxiety. Where are you, God?

> And God said here I am standing in the midst of the turmoil and utter destruction inside of the towers. I am directing, encouraging and whispering to those who will never hear another loving voice. I am kneeling beside the chaplain from the fire department as he administers last rites to fallen comrades and strangers alike. I have told him that this day he will also die. I am on the stairs holding my children in my arms. Some of my children have jumped out of windows convinced that this desperate act is their only alternative. Look my child, can you see me standing near the man who refuses to leave his wheelchair-bound coworker and friend … I still say no greater love than a man who lays down his life for another …

> Then you will call and the Lord will answer; you will cry for help and he will say: Here am I. If you do away with the yoke of oppression, with the pointing finger and malicious talk and if you spend yourselves in behalf of the hungry and satisfy the needs of the oppressed, then your light will rise in the darkness and your night will become like the noonday … Your people will rebuild the ancient ruins and will raise up the age old foundations; you will be called Repairer of Broken Walls, restorer of Streets with Dwellings. (Isaiah 58: 9-10, 12)

ENLIGHTENMENT

BY REVEREND ALFONSO WYATT

children of the light
heed this urgent call
use thine power o'er darkness
stumble never fall
illum dark corners
in all hearts and minds
share this precious flame
the tie that binds
hatred is thine enemy
ignorance another foe
so band together small flames
wherever ye may go
there is strength in numbers
remember ye are light
and every flicker
a wound to darkness
this our
eternal
fight.

16

Normative and Diagnostic Reactions to Disaster

Clergy and Clinician Collaboration to Facilitate a Continuum of Care

Glen Milstein and Amy Manierre

Introduction

In the days after September 11, 2001, St. Paul's Chapel, an Episcopal church in lower Manhattan, was a main place of refuge for relief workers near the World Trade Center site. In the church, a handwritten sign near the entrance said, "Counselor available. Please ask." In the dust and smoldering destruction, the fear and anger, the exhaustion and sadness, there was offered a continuum of care, which recognized that body, spirit and mind were all being battered. Too often, as the previous chapters of this book make clear, disaster care is provided through compartmentalized responses. We use our resources to meet immediate physical needs and then move on, and when we recognize that disasters have traumatic sequelae, we tend to spend our resources bringing in expert healthcare providers to treat symptoms of immediate mental dysfunction, and then leave. Without an understanding of the individual's community context, such clinical treatment may be misdirected at persons whose response is normative and who could be helped through existing relationships within their community.

Disaster recovery requires a flow of responses in order to provide people with a continuum of care. The best responses will come from integrated community networks that have formed and been enacted before a disaster strikes. This chapter will describe a model of coprofessional collaboration between clergy and clinicians that facilitates expert dialogue, which then helps persons to recover from trauma and ease community restoration.

Background

For the past 16 years, we have examined the roles of clergy as de facto mental health care providers, and the interactions between clergy and mental health professionals, in providing care for persons with emotional needs. One of our surprising findings was that while a majority of clergy was willing to work with clinicians to help with mental health problems, fewer clinicians recognized a role for collaboration with clergy. Rather, clinicians saw clergy as one-way referral sources. In the context of disaster, clergy tend to be viewed as leaders of commemorative rituals, as well as assets to provide infrastructure for distributing basic needs (e.g., food, clean water, and information dissemination). These actions are seen as distinct from clinical care. This is an illogical stance as treatment must follow diagnosis. Diagnosis begins with the recognition that a person demonstrates change from some baseline behavior. We do not grow up under clinical care. We grow up in communities. We raise ourselves and our children in communities. This community context is our baseline. It is to this context that we wish to be restored. When community clergy are full members of the disaster response team from its inception, they can provide information to help determine if individuals' emotional well-being has changed from their normative baseline. This information will be both biographical and cultural.

Therefore, we emphasize both the complementarity, as well as the continuity, of the distinct functions of clinicians and clergy in response to disaster. Clinicians provide professional treatment to relieve individuals of their pain and suffering and move them from dysfunction to their highest level of functioning. In most cases, assuming resources are available, the less clinicians are seeing those under their care, the more successful the clinicians are. With some serious cases of posttraumatic stress disorder (PTSD), clinical relationships—although they will wax and wane—can last for many years.

Unlike clinicians, clergy expect and hope to see their congregants as often as possible through the course of their lives. Through their relationships with congregants, clergy acquire comprehensive information, which (with consent) they could share with clinicians. The clergy's personal familiarity and experience can be invaluable to facilitating appropriate and continuous mental health care for their parishioners through "contextualizing" an individual's response to disaster by sharing salient aspects of the person's life history and cultural worldview with the treating clinician.

Therefore, rather than think of clergy-led commemorative events as a part of the clinical response, we need to organize clinical treatments as part of the community response. The goal of disaster mental health care is community restoration. With restoration as our goal, it is necessary for emergency responders to seek guidance from coprofessional community clergy. What follows (see Figure 16.1) is a description of a model of Clergy Outreach and Professional Engagement (COPE) that provides guidance to clinicians and clergy on how to optimize their collaboration before, during and after disasters.

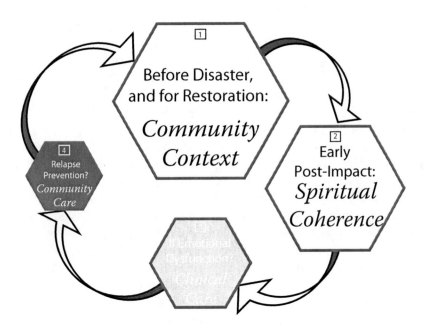

© 2009 Glen Milstein, Ph.D.

Figure 16.1 A continuum of care in response to disaster through Clergy Outreach and Professional Engagement (COPE).

Data

Religious congregations provide sacred space where daily lives are celebrated and mourned through familiar liturgy, ritual, and sacred stories. Whether it is daily prayer, weekly worship, or holiday attendance, whether a bris or baptism, the joining of individuals in marriage, the welcoming of new congregants into the fold, or the celebration of a life now past, religious institutions provide familiar frame and structure to recognize life's transitions and facilitate transformation.

This is precisely why, in response to trauma, religious attendance increases dramatically and the walls of religious institutions nearly burst with attendees seeking succor and orientation in times of fear, suffering, and disorientation. Much like the grounding effect of a lightning rod to a lightning strike, religious institutions offer a "grounding effect" in the midst of trauma. The theologian Paul Tillich refers to the ground of being as that which wards off nonbeing. And, it is the fear of the undoing of "being" that is challenged during trauma. It is no wonder that political figures promptly call on clergy when disaster occurs. When there is an "offense" on community whether a natural disasters, riot, terrorist, or domestic attack, clergy are among the first to be mobilized by politicians.

In order to assure that the salient roles of clergy and clinicians are optimally used to assist in disaster care, we have developed the COPE model, which provides guidance to clinicians and clergy on how to optimize their collaboration before, during, and after disasters (see Figure 16.1). Two central ideas guide the COPE program. The first is that clergy (with their discrete expert knowledge about religion as well as their community) and clinicians (with their discrete expert knowledge about mental health care) can better help a broader array of persons with emotional difficulties and disorders through professional collaboration than they can by working alone. The second idea, which we emphasize in all programming, is that to perpetuate collaboration, clergy, and clinicians must find their work eased by COPE One must design programs so that they result in burden reduction for each group. The objective of COPE is to improve the care of individuals by reducing the care-giving burdens of clergy and clinicians through consultation and collaboration.

For clinicians, COPE elucidates the significant roles of clergy and religious communities in the day-to-day efforts by humans to find meaning and purpose. COPE advises clinicians on how to encourage clergy to refer congregants in clinical distress for professional treatment and then advises clinicians on how (with congregants' consent) to maintain communication with clergy during treatment. Finally, COPE advises clinicians on how to return patients to their communities to receive the social support that could ameliorate, resolve, or at least delay the relapse of traumatic symptoms or posttraumatic stress disorder.

For clergy, COPE recognizes the clinical utility of their normative functions and guides them on when and how to make a referral to clinicians, as well as how to protectively welcome back congregants who have suffered from trauma and have received necessary clinical care. This continuum of collaboration will encourage vigilance in religious communities in the care of persons traumatized by disaster and to allow for early intervention in the case of relapse.

With Figure 16.1, you see the schematic design of the COPE model. This single sheet allows us to visually and conceptually describe a hierarchy of mental health needs of persons in their own communities.

The diagram begins with a large unshaded hexagon, which recognizes the mental health support provided by the clergy and their congregations before disaster. These normative relationships do not require the presence of clinicians. It is this *Community Context* that we seek to restore after disaster. This stage recognizes that healthy adults may further their psychological well-being by taking part in what Erik Erikson called activities of generativity. Generativity is the work we do in our homes, our communities, and our religious congregations to improve the well-being of future generations.

The increased shading of the hexagons represents increasing severity of psychological distress. During the Early Postimpact stage of disaster, all persons may question the meaning of what has occurred and why it occurred to them. Clergy are frequently called on to answer such vexing questions and strive to provide people with *Spiritual Coherence* and to restore a sense of meaning sufficient to move forward. In this second stage, when there are emotional difficulties (e.g., a person bereaved by the sudden loss of a spouse in a disaster), the clergy and religious community provide social support that can help the individual to cope. Depending on the wisdom traditions and theological orientation of an individual's religion, at this stage the congregation may provide faith-based rituals of support. These first two stages describe normative parts of the multifaceted duties of clergy, which would not require professional clinical consultation or care.

The switch from statements to questions, as well as the switch from black to white lettering in the third hexagon, represents situations that would involve contact with mental health clinicians by the clergy. Clergy, as persons who regularly comfort grieving families, could be the first to recognize signs of disordered responses to disaster. At the third stage, the clergy could be instructed to call on the clinician's expertise to determine whether the congregant has clinical needs. Now the parishioner may need to receive professional *Clinical Care* to reduce disorder and to regain function. The COPE model is designed to provide burden reduction to clergy at this stage by facilitating referrals to clinicians.

In the fourth stage, patients' symptoms subside and function increases, but they may remain at risk for relapse. As clinical care is reduced, the normative social support offered by their religious congregations can help to sustain the individuals' mental health. This fourth stage is an opportunity for a return to the first stage through role restoration. Restoration, facilitated by Community Care provides burden reduction for clinicians, as they plan for a patient's transition out of acute clinical care and toward relapse prevention.

Synthesis

When we systematize our field such that we assess and respond only to the deficits brought on after a disaster, we miss the rest of life as lived by people. Imagine if botanists organized their work as the study of how to keep leaves from turning yellow. As we know, botanists first study the natural course of how plants grow green and then investigate those variables that help plants thrive in the face of environmental challenges. So too, before a disaster, we must catalog our communities' natural contexts of social support. The goal of a community is to thrive. The goal of emergency responders is to leave. Therefore, it is the responsibility of responders to develop collaboration plans before a disaster, so that community leaders, such as the clergy, are recognized for the leaders of continuity and generativity that they are. Therefore: Think *Continuity*, Prepare for *Continuity*, Build *Continuity*, Enact *Continuity*.

Conclusion

How do we enact continuity? First, we recognize the continuum of mind, body, and spirit within community that was embraced at St. Paul's Chapel in the days after September 11, 2001. The chapters of this book note the structural and cultural challenges to providing a complementary continuum of care. These chapters also provide examples of how to achieve continuity through collaboration. This chapter provides you with a model of how to create a continuum of care in response to disaster through Clergy Outreach and Professional Engagement (COPE). The context of persons' meaning making is established before a disaster and for most persons is connected to a religious community. After a disaster, most persons seek sufficient and appropriate support directly from their communities without need for clinical intervention.

The goal of disaster relief is community restoration. Emergency responders will be most effective if they collaborate with clergy to learn the community context to which persons can be restored. Clergy can be the clinicians' guides to the cultures of the communities that these responders seek to assist. With collaboration, COPE can offer seamless and sensitive service delivery for disaster relief mental health care. COPE's organic design encourages early identification of clinical need, smoothes the clinical referral process, and acknowledges the importance of relapse prevention. COPE supports clergy when congregants need clinical care, and encourages clinicians to seek clergy expertise when theological and existential questions are asked by patients in clinical care. Successful collaboration will culminate in community restoration and a return to generativity.

Further Readings

American Public Health Association. (1946). Can the clergy aid the health officer in the upbuilding of mental health? *American Journal of Public Health, 36*(11), 1313–1314.

Budd, F. C. (1999). An Air Force model of psychologist-chaplain collaboration. *Professional Psychology: Research & Practice, 30*(6), 552–556.

Corrigan, P. W. (2005). *On the stigma of mental illness: Practical strategies for research and social change* (p. 343). Washington, DC: American Psychological Association.

Department of Defense Task Force on Mental Health. (2007). *An achievable vision: Report of the Department of Defense Task Force on Mental Health.* Falls Church, VA: Defense Health Board.

Erikson, E. H., & Erikson, J. M. (1997). *The life cycle completed* (Extended / ed.). New York: W.W. Norton.

Gordon, R., Steinberg, J. A., & Silverman, M. M. (1987). An operational classification of disease prevention. In *Preventing mental disorders: A research perspective* (pp. 20–26). Rockville, MD: National Institute of Mental Health.

Hinshaw, S. P. (2007). *The mark of shame: Stigma of mental illness and an agenda for change.* New York: Oxford University Press.

Maslow, A. (1962). *Toward a psychology of being*. Princeton, NJ: D. Van Norstrand.

McAdams, D. P., Logan, R. L., de St. Aubin, E., McAdams, D. P., & Kim, T.-C. (2004). What Is Generativity? In *The generative society: Caring for future generations*. (pp. 15-31). Washington, DC: American Psychological Association.

Milstein, G. (2003). Clergy and psychiatrists: Opportunities for expert dialogue. *Psychiatric Times, 20*(3), 36–39.

Milstein, G., Kennedy, G. J., Bruce, M. L., Flannelly, K., Chelchowski, N., & Bone, L. (2005). The Clergy's Role in Reducing Stigma: Elder Patients' Views. *World Psychiatry*, 4(S1), 26-32.

Milstein, G., Manierre, A., Susman, V., & Bruce, M. L. (2008). Implementation of a program to improve the continuity of mental health care through clergy outreach and professional engagement (COPE). *Professional Psychology: Research and Practice, 39*(2), 218–228.

National Advisory Mental Health Council Workgroup on Mental Disorders Prevention Research. (1998). *Priorities for prevention research at NIMH* (NIH Publication No. 98-4321). Rockville, MD: National Institute of Mental Health.

New Freedom Commission on Mental Health. (2003). *Achieving the promise: Transforming mental health care in America*. Final Report (No. SMA-03-3832). Rockville, MD: Department of Health and Human Services.

Rosen, A. (2006). Destigmatizing day-to-day practices: What developed countries can learn from developing countries. *World Psychiatry, 5*(1), 21–24.

U.S. Department of Health and Human Services. (2001). *Mental health: Culture, race, and ethnicity—A supplement to mental health: A report of the Surgeon General*. Rockville, MD: Author, Substance Abuse and Mental Health Services Administration, Center for Mental Health Services.

U.S. Public Health Service. Office of the Surgeon General. (1999). *Mental health: A report of the Surgeon General*. Rockville, MD: Department of Health and Human Services, Author.

Wakin, D. J. (2001, September 30). Terror attacks could change paths of faith. *The New York Times*.

Ware, N. C., Tugenberg, T., Dickey, B., & McHorney, C. A. (1999). An ethnographic study of the meaning of continuity of care in mental health services. *Psychiatric Services, 50*(3), 395-400.

World Health Organization. (2001). *The World Health Report 2001, mental health: New understanding, new hope*. Geneva: Author.

World Health Organization World Mental Health Survey Consortium. (2004). Prevalence, severity, and unmet need for treatment of mental disorders in the World Health Organization world mental health surveys. *JAMA, 291*(21), 2581–2590.

Young, B. H., Ford, J. D., Ruzek, J. I., Friedman, M. J., & Gusman, F. D. (1998). *Disaster mental health services: A guidebook for clinicians and administrators*. Retrieved June 22, 2008, from http://www.ncptsd.va.gov/ncmain/ncdocs/manuals/nc_manual_dmhm.html.

Index

Collaboration, xi. *See also* Hurricane Katrina,
    collaboration following; Hurricane
    Katrina, models for collaborations
    following
  -in-action, xvii
  major themes, xii–xiv
    anthropological perspective, xii
    goals, xiii
    intimate experiences, xiii
    opportunities for growth, xiii
    prevention of adverse events, xiv
    self-reflective processes, xiii
  participant energy and engagement, 103
  resilience and trauma, xvii
  school-based initiatives, 137–140
  tone, xii
Collaboration, fundamentals of, 3–18
  approach, 16
  associational processes, disruption of, 7
  dissociation, 7
  effects of variable groups, 10–11
  fliessgleichgewicht, 9
  framework, 7–9
  Incident Command System, 6
  leader responsibility, 16
  levels of complexity, 9–10
  mutual negotiation, 17
  mutual respect, 17
  National Incident Management System, 6
  overview, 4–7
  phase of disaster, 10–11
  pragmatic approaches, 11–16
    assessment and referral of individuals, 14
    decisions and work flow, 15–16
    identification of strategies, 15
    recording of lessons learned, 15
    regular meetings, 13
    staying in contact, 13–14
    training exercises, 14–15
  spin-off crises, 3
  tipping point, 7
  us–them attitude, 7
Colors, seeing red, 32
Communal healing, partnerships in, xi
Communication. *See* Risk communication
Community college, relationship with. *See*
    Hurricane Katrina, collaboration
    following
Compassion fatigue, 202
Complementarity, 205
Confirmatory bias, 43
Conspiracy of silence, 200
Contemplative prayer practices, stress
    reduction through, 88

COPE. *See* Clergy Outreach and Professional
    Engagement
COPE model, 222, 225
Critical incident stress management (CISM)
    teams, 153
Cumulative trauma, 195

D

Datamart, 111
Death notifications, 151
Defensive patterns, 33
Depression, paralyzing, 36
Diagnostic reactions to disaster, 219–225
  activities of generativity, 223
  background, 220–221
  COPE model, 222, 225
  data, 222–224
  recovery responses, 219
  religious institutions, grounding effect of,
    222
  synthesis, 224
Diagnostic and Statistical Manual, 125, 188
Disaster(s). *See also* Psychospiritual impact of
    disaster
  airline, 147
  diagnostic reactions to, 219–225
    background, 220–221
    data, 222–224
    recovery responses, 219
    synthesis, 224
  effect of on communities, 84
  frequently asked questions, 65–66
  obstacle to response, 76
  recovery financial assistance, 106, 110
  response, volunteers, 147
  spiritual care providers, preference for, 151
  spiritual meaning in, 89
  work, emotional theory in, xvi
Disaster Mitigation Act of 2000, 117
Disaster Psychiatry Outreach (DPO), xiv, 75, 186
Disaster relief, 25–38
  adaptive emotions, 30
  cognition, 29
  depression, 36
  emotional identity, 34
  empathy, 36
  implication, 26
  interpersonal emotional experience, 29
  mantras, 27
  mourning, 35–36
  myself angry, 32
  pathological mourners, 26
  primary motivational system, 28